Textual Criticism since Greg
A Chronicle, 1950-1985

TEXTUAL CRITICISM SINCE GREG

A Chronicle
1950-1985

G. THOMAS TANSELLE

Published for
THE BIBLIOGRAPHICAL SOCIETY OF THE UNIVERSITY OF VIRGINIA
by the UNIVERSITY PRESS OF VIRGINIA, CHARLOTTESVILLE

THE UNIVERSITY PRESS OF VIRGINIA
Copyright © 1987 by the Rector and Visitors
of the University of Virginia
First published 1987

Library of Congress Cataloging-in-Publication Data
Tanselle, G. Thomas (George Thomas), 1934–
    Textual criticism since Greg : a chronicle, 1950–1985 / G. Thomas
Tanselle.
    p.   cm.
    Reprinted from Studies in Bibliography, 1975–1986.
    Contents: Greg's theory of copy-text and the editing of American
literature, 1950–74—Recent editorial discussion and the central
questions of editing, 1974–79—Historicism and critical editing,
1979–85.
    ISBN 0-8139-1166-4 (pbk.)
    1. English literature—History and criticism—Theory, etc.
2. English literature—Criticism, Textual.   3. American literature—
History and criticism—Theory, etc.   4. American literature—
Criticism, Textual.   5. Criticism, Textual—History—20th century.
6. Editing—History—20th century.   7. Greg. W. W. (Walter Wilson),
1875–1959.   I. Title.
PR77.T36 1987
801'.959—dc19

87-23758
CIP

Printed in the United States of America

Contents

Preface vii

Greg's Theory of Copy-Text and the Editing of
 American Literature: 1950–74 1

Recent Editorial Discussion and the Central
 Questions of Editing: 1974–79 65

Historicism and Critical Editing: 1979–85 109

Preface

THE three essays in this volume are reprinted here directly from the pages of *Studies in Bibliography*, where they appeared in 1975 (28: 167–229), 1981 (34: 23–65), and 1986 (39: 1–46). I am grateful to the editor of *Studies*, Fredson Bowers, and to the Council of the Bibliographical Society of the University of Virginia for making this reprinting possible. These essays attempt to survey the theoretical writings in English since 1950 dealing with the textual criticism and the scholarly editing of post-medieval literature—each one taking up the years immediately preceding its own original publication (the first covering 1950–74, the second 1974–79, and the third 1979–85). Together they form a chronicle of one of the most active and provocative periods in the long history of textual criticism.

W. W. Greg's 1949 paper "The Rationale of Copy-Text" has proved to be a watershed. It is the culmination of the editorial thinking that emerged from the work during the first half of the twentieth century of a small group of scholars—principally British, and most notably A. W. Pollard, R. B. McKerrow, and Greg himself—who focused on the textual problems posed by the early printed editions of English Renaissance drama. Their central contribution was the recognition that the texts of printed books, like those of manuscripts, are affected by the physical processes of their production; the search through books for evidence of the details of their own manufacture (an activity now called "analytical bibliography") thus became a prerequisite for the textual criticism of this important body of dramatic literature. Greg's editorial rationale, developing out of these investigations, emphasized the usual deterioration of texts from one edition to the next and consequently recommended the earliest edition of a work as generally the most reliable, at least for its punctuation and spelling if not for all its words, some of which may have been revised by the author for a later edition.

In the years following the appearance of Greg's essay, his approach was adapted and extended, under the leadership of Fredson Bowers, to the literature of the three and a half centuries from the Restoration to the present. Bowers's own great series of editions, ranging from Marlowe to Nabokov, became a dominant influence, supplemented by his theoretical essays. These publications coincided with, and indeed further stimulated, a growing interest in the production of reliable scholarly editions of the major post-Renaissance writers. This movement had its center during the 1960s in the United States, where a massive series of editions of American authors was inaugurated, based in general on Greg's rationale and Bowers's adaptation of it. Since then several editions of British authors, undertaken by scholars on both sides of the Atlantic, have reflected the Greg-Bowers position. The dominance of this approach has not, however, been uncontested. The appropriateness of extending Greg's ideas to later periods, particularly to authors whose own manuscripts still exist, has been repeatedly challenged; and some scholars, disagreeing with the view of literature and drama that they felt was implicit in his rationale, have questioned its applicability to the writings of any period. As a result, the last three decades have been a time of controversy, in which the central issues of textual study have been vigorously debated.

My account of this debate, having been produced seriatim while the debate was still in progress, is also a part of it, and I have throughout these essays assessed the strengths and weaknesses of the various arguments as I saw them. Not everyone will agree with my judgments, of course, but I hope that readers will find my summaries of particular positions, along with the accompanying references to most of the related writings, a convenient starting point for studying a body of work that has now attained formidable proportions. This account can also, I believe, serve as a commentary on the basic questions that all scholarly editors must face. Although the discussions described here were occasioned by the editing of writers from the last five or six centuries, the issues are fundamentally the same as those struggled with for a longer time by editors of ancient writings. (I have tried to make this connection in a 1983 piece for *Studies in Bibliography* called "Classical, Biblical, and Medieval Textual Criticism and Modern Editing" [36: 21–68].) What I have attempted to do in these essays, therefore, is not only to present the story of a significant episode in the history of scholarship but also to offer—perforce indirectly, in reaction to the arguments of others— my own rationale of textual criticism (which is set forth more directly in my 1987 Rosenbach Lectures).

The process of following the details of a controversy, if it deals with basic concerns, is always a good introduction to a field. In textual criticism, as in other fields, truths are created by coherent arguments that accommodate what seem to be the facts. Often more than one coherent argument will fit those facts, validating more than one approach to textual matters. We should not expect to find that there is only a single truth or imagine that we can edit a work so that it will not have to be reedited by someone with a different point of view. But we can learn to recognize incoherences of thought and to demand that our editions, varied as they may be, all stand on solid foundations. The excitement of textual criticism in recent years, despite a number of flawed arguments, comes from its engagement with essential issues. Textual criticism and literary criticism are, more than ever, seen to be inseparable, as are the concerns of scholarly editors and those of everyone else who reads.

G.T.T.

Textual Criticism since Greg
A Chronicle, 1950-1985

Greg's Theory of Copy-Text
and the Editing of American Literature
1950-74

ALTHOUGH THE EDITING OF LITERARY TEXTS HAS LONG BEEN regarded as one of the basic tasks of literary scholars, I think it can be said that in the last fifteen years an unusual amount of scholarly attention has been directed toward editing and editorial theory. The situation is particularly striking in the field of American literature, for these years have witnessed the development of a coordinated effort—on a scale rare in scholarly endeavor generally and unparalleled in the editing of literature in English—to produce full-scale editions of most of the major (and several other important) nineteenth-century American writers. The need for reliable editions of the principal American figures had been given official recognition much earlier, when the American Literature Group of the Modern Language Association of America established—in 1947-48—a Committee on Definitive Editions, with Willard Thorp as chairman. Although that committee was unsuccessful in securing financial support for such editions, it laid the groundwork for continued discussion, which, after two conferences in 1962, resulted in the establishment in 1963 of the Center for Editions of American Authors. Since that time the Center has coordinated the work on fourteen editions[1] and since 1966 has allocated funds amounting to more than one and a half million dollars, provided by the National Endowment for the Humanities of the National Foundation on the Arts and Humanities. (In addition, many universities and university presses, as well as the Office of Education of the Department of Health, Education, and Welfare, have helped with individual editions.) As a result, more than one

---

1. Presenting the work of twelve authors: Cooper, Stephen Crane, John Dewey, Emerson, Hawthorne, Howells, Irving, Melville, Simms, Thoreau, Mark Twain, and Whitman.

hundred volumes have now been completed, and others are in various stages of preparation.[2]

The fact that an accomplishment of such magnitude, involving the cooperation of more than two hundred scholars, could be produced in little more than a decade of concentrated work—to say nothing of the existence of the Center as an official committee of the MLA or of its support by public funds—suggests a widespread recognition of the importance of the whole undertaking. This is not to say, however, that there is any unanimity of opinion as to the precise editorial principles which ought to be followed, and the CEAA editions have been the subject of a considerable number of critical attacks, directed both to particular editions and to general matters of policy. Now one of the unusual features of the CEAA as a scholarly coordinating committee is that it has insisted, from the beginning, that certain editorial principles be followed in any edition that is to be associated with it and receive its approval. To this end, it has established a seal to be printed in every volume which meets the requirements, certifying that the text is "An Approved Text" of the CEAA. The administration of this plan obviously involves the pre-publication inspection of each text by an examiner appointed by the Center, and the result is that any reader who sees the CEAA seal on a volume knows that its text has been prepared in conformity with a set of carefully defined guidelines, relating not only to editorial theory but to the practicalities of setting forth evidence and of proofreading as well. In essence, the editorial principles of the CEAA—set forth in its *Statement of Editorial Principles and Procedures* (originally published in 1967 and revised in 1972) —are those enunciated by W. W. Greg in his famous paper for the 1949 English Institute, "The Rationale of Copy-Text." Although he was talking specifically about English dramatic literature of the Renaissance, his discussion raised basic questions applicable to editorial theory in general, and his "rationale" has since been adopted by

---

2. A more detailed account of the history of the CEAA can be found in William M. Gibson's "The Center for Editions of American Authors" and in John H. Fisher's "The MLA Editions of Major American Authors" (and the chronology which follows it) in *Professional Standards and American Editions: A Response to Edmund Wilson* (Modern Language Association, 1969), pp. 1-6, 20-28. A survey of editions in progress and proposed editions at the time of the inception of the CEAA (and based on the 1962 discussions) is provided by William M. Gibson and Edwin H. Cady in "Editions of American Writers, 1963: A Preliminary Survey," *PMLA*, 78 (September 1963, part 2), 1-8 (reprinted in an MLA pamphlet, *The Situation of English, 1963*); another essay useful for background relating to the inception of the CEAA is Willard Thorp's "Exodus: Four Decades of American Literary Scholarship," *MLQ*, 26 (1965), 40-61.

various editors working in later periods of English literature as well as in American literature. But some scholars have questioned the applicability of Greg's principles to later literature and have thus questioned the wisdom of the CEAA requirements descended from Greg.

The time now seems appropriate—since both the CEAA and its critics have a substantial amount of material in print—to review the phenomenon of this debate.[3] Certainly the existence and the accomplishment of the CEAA as an institution constitute a phenomenon unique in the history of literary scholarship in English; but the response to the CEAA also is phenomenal in the amount of critical notice which it has bestowed on editorial and textual concerns. The controversy has doubtless caused people who normally pay little attention to editing to focus on some of the problems involved in editorial work, and as a result editing may have moved somewhat nearer to being a matter of vital concern to the scholarly literary world at large. Even if the tone of some of the discussion has served as a poor introduction to scholarly debate in this area, the fact remains that a number of respected figures have raised objections on matters of principle, and their criticisms deserve to be given serious attention. Sometimes, as it happens, their comments prove to be beside the point because of a misconception as to the nature of Greg's rationale or of its use by the CEAA; but some legitimate issues, worthy of continuing scrutiny, are raised in the process. An analysis of these discussions, it seems to me, must begin with a re-examination of Greg's seminal essay. By this time, that essay has reached the status of a classic; and, like any classic statement, it has so frequently been adduced to support or refute particular arguments that renewed exegesis of the document itself seems called for periodically. An understanding of exactly what Greg said is a prerequisite for examining, first, what application of his principles the CEAA stands for and, second, what criticisms of his and the CEAA's position have been put forth. In such an examination, it is important always to distinguish between theoretical and practical concerns. Criticisms on either level demand careful attention, but it is no aid to orderly thinking to treat purely practical questions as if they involved theoretical issues. I hope that these notes can begin to clarify the context within which each of the arguments must be judged and can thus help to provide a perspective from which the whole controversy can profitably be viewed.

3. A convenient record of the books and articles related to CEAA editorial theory and practice is provided as an appendix (entitled "Relevant Textual Scholarship") to the CEAA *Statement* (2nd ed., 1972), pp. 17-25.

I

Greg's contribution to the 1949 session of the English Institute, "The Rationale of Copy-Text"—read for Greg by J. M. Osborn on 8 September 1949—was first published in the third (1950-51) volume of *Studies in Bibliography* (pp. 19-36). (There is a certain appropriateness, therefore, in re-examining the essay, on the twenty-fifth anniversary of its original appearance, in the pages of the same journal.) Since that time it has been republished in the posthumous volume of Greg's *Collected Papers* (1966), edited by J. C. Maxwell, who incorporated into its text a few minor revisions and a new footnote, as indicated by Greg in his working papers.[4] The essay is not long or complicated and is expressed with Greg's usual clarity. That such an essay should have given rise to so much discussion, and even controversy, is not surprising, however, for it has the kind of simplicity frequently characteristic of great concepts—a sweeping simplicity that results from having penetrated beyond peripheral complexities and arrived at the heart of a problem. Just as it is not easy to achieve such simplicity, neither is it always easy for others to follow or accept it.

Greg begins by referring to the first use of the term "copy-text"— by R. B. McKerrow in 1904 in his edition of Nashe—and sketches the history of the idea of "the most authoritative text"; it is evident, from this kind of beginning and from later references to McKerrow's and his own changes of position, that he is presenting his ideas on copy-text as the outgrowth of an evolving train of thought extending back over many years. Indeed, his opening paragraph says nothing about putting forth a new theory but only that he wishes to consider the "conception" and "implications" of a change in McKerrow's position. Although he soon admits (p. 377) that he is drawing a distinction which "has not been generally recognized," his emphasis is not on the

---

4. The added footnote, enclosed in brackets on p. 382 of *The Collected Papers*, is the one which attributes the phrase "the tyranny of the copy-text" to Paul Maas. (He used it in his review of Greg's *The Editorial Problem in Shakespeare*, *RES*, 20 [1944], 76; Greg's reaction appears on pp. 159-160 of the same volume.) The 1966 text also adds the second "are" to "what readings are possible and what are not" at 381.31; it inserts the comma in "In the folio, revision and reproduction are so blended" at 390.32; and it adds the clause set off by commas in the statement that "the quartos contain, it is generally assumed, only reported texts" at 391.19. Another difference in the 1966 text is an error: in the quotation from McKerrow's *Prolegomena* at 380.32, "what we call inner harmony" ought to read "what we may call inner harmony," as it did in the original *SB* printing. As one would expect, the essay has been included in anthologies: *Bibliography and Textual Criticism*, ed. O M Brack, Jr., and Warner Barnes (1969), pp. 41-58; *Art and Error*, ed. Ronald Gottesman and Scott Bennett (1970), pp. 17-36. Both of these anthologies reprint the *SB* text rather than the text from *The Collected Papers*.

novelty of his contribution but rather on the way in which it seems but a natural step in the line of thinking already pursued both by him and by McKerrow. In effect he is saying that he has finally come to recognize something which he had overlooked earlier and something toward which McKerrow had gradually been moving.

It is important to notice the historical framework of Greg's essay: for Greg, stepping into the discussion at a particular point in its development, accepts without further analysis certain ideas about scholarly editing—two in particular—which he feels have already been adequately established. First, he makes clear that he rejects "purely eclectic methods," in which an editor has no restraints placed on his freedom to choose among variant readings on the basis of his subjective judgments of their aesthetic appropriateness; the "genealogical method," developed by Lachmann and his successors in the nineteenth century, was, he says, "the greatest advance ever made in this field," because it provided a more objective basis for preferring one text over another. McKerrow's concept of "copy-text"—taking the term to mean, in Greg's words, "that early text of a work which an editor selected as the basis of his own"—is clearly placed in the context of the genealogical method, for it implies that an editor has determined, through genealogical analysis, the "most authoritative text" and therefore the one to which his own text should adhere. By introducing Housman's criticism of the mechanical application of this procedure (the fallacy of believing that the readings of the "authoritative text" which are not manifestly impossible are in fact correct), Greg suggests the direction in which his argument is to move. But he sees no necessity to argue the general superiority of genealogical methods over eclectic ones; at mid-twentieth century this superiority can simply be asserted. A second assumption is that one can reject without discussion the notion of choosing the last edition published during the author's lifetime as the most authoritative. Placing his comment in a footnote—and in the past tense—to suggest how little attention the idea deserves, Greg says, "I have above ignored the practice of some eccentric editors who took as copy-text for a work the latest edition printed in the author's lifetime, on the assumption, presumably, that he revised each edition as it appeared. The textual results were naturally deplorable" (p. 378). Obviously Greg is not saying that one should ignore late revisions which one has reason to think are authorial; but, he is implying, it is no longer necessary to bother refuting the assumption that the last edition in the author's lifetime is automatically the most authoritative.

Without going over ground which he regards as already established, then, Greg begins to reflect on current editorial practice and observes that the situation facing editors of English texts is different from that facing editors of classical texts, since the preference for "old-spelling" editions is now "prevalent among English scholars," whereas editors of classical texts normalize the spelling. Greg explicitly says that he does not wish to argue the virtues of old-spelling editions but accepts this "prevalent" view—that is to say, he accepts the view that editions of English works for scholars' use should not involve normalized or modernized spelling and punctuation. It should be clear, therefore, that his essay deals with one particular, if basic, kind of edition and implies nothing about the relative merits of modernized editions for other purposes—a point sometimes overlooked. If the editor of English texts properly follows the general tradition of the genealogical method inaugurated by classical editors, and if he must be concerned with the spelling and punctuation of his text in a way different from classical editors, it follows that his conception of copy-text must contain an additional element. In fact, viewed in this way, as Greg says, "the classical theory of the 'best' or 'most authoritative' manuscript . . . has really nothing to do with the English theory of 'copy-text' at all" (p. 375)—because, under the classical theory, the spelling and punctuation are not involved in selecting the copy-text.

By the beginning of the fourth paragraph of his essay, Greg has led the reader, with astonishing ease, to see the current situation in English editing against the background of its development and to anticipate the distinction he is about to set forth between, on the one hand, spelling and punctuation, and, on the other, the words themselves. The rhetorical strategy of the essay demands proceeding explicitly to make this distinction before returning to an examination of McKerrow's changing position (which thereby takes on a new dimension), and this remarkable fourth paragraph (pp. 375-377) contains the essence of what is now referred to as "Greg's theory of copy-text." First of all, it makes the point that an old-spelling edition must rely on some contemporary document, for the "philological difficulties" of attempting to recreate or establish spellings for a particular author at a particular time and place are overwhelming. Second, in view of this practical necessity, it says, one must distinguish between the actual words of a text and their spelling and punctuation:

. . . we need to draw a distinction between the significant, or as I shall call them "substantive", readings of the text, those namely that affect the author's meaning or the essence of his expression, and others, such in general as spelling, punctuation, word-division, and the like, affecting mainly its formal presentation, which may be regarded as the accidents, or as I shall call them "accidentals", of the text. (p. 376)

The explicit separation of these classes for separate editorial treatment is one of Greg's key contributions; the third major point of the paragraph is what that separate treatment amounts to. Separate treatment is justified, the argument goes, because copyists and compositors are known to treat the two categories differently; since they generally attempt to reproduce accurately the substantives of their copy but frequently are guided by their own preferences in matters of accidentals, it follows that later transcripts of a work may depart considerably from earlier ones in accidentals and at the same time be very close to them in substantives. What an editor should do, therefore, as a practical routine, is first to determine the early text which is to be his copy-text; then, Greg says,

I suggest that it is only in the matter of accidentals that we are bound (within reason) to follow it, and that in respect of substantive readings we have exactly the same liberty (and obligation) of choice as has a classical editor, or as we should have were it a modernized text that we were preparing. (p. 377)

In other words, because a copyist or a compositor reproduces substantives more faithfully than accidentals, substantive variants in later transcripts or editions are more likely to be worth editorial consideration as possible authorial revisions than are variants in accidentals.

Now a few observations are worth making in regard to what Greg does and does not say in this statement of his "theory"—particularly as an anticipation of some of the points which, as we shall see, have been raised in recent years. To begin with, while the terms "substantive" and "accidental" are not very happy choices,[5] what is crucial to

5. Greg himself calls attention in a footnote (p. 378) to the fact that McKerrow used the word "substantive" to refer to "an edition that is not a reprint of any other," and he adds, "I do not think that there should be any danger of confusion between 'substantive editions' and 'substantive readings.'" Nevertheless, it is unfortunate that the word should be given two special meanings in editorial discourse. The awkwardness of "accidental" (when it is not used as a plural noun, "accidentals") is obvious and is in fact demonstrated by Greg's own prose a few lines after his introduction of the term: "As regards substantive readings . . . they will doubtless sometimes depart from them accidentally and may even . . . do so intentionally: as regards accidentals, they will normally follow their own habits . . ." (pp. 376-377). Furthermore, since both terms are used by grammarians, one might at first suppose that editors, also concerned with language, might use them in the same way; but "substantive" in grammar means "noun" (which is a less inclusive concept than Greg's "substantive"), while "accident" (or "accidence") refers to inflection for case, number, tense, and so on (which is not "accidental" alteration in Greg's sense but

the theory is the distinction itself, and one should not be distracted from it by other associations which these words have. The terms have by now become so well established in editorial commentary that it would be foolish to attempt to change them, even though their use tends unfortunately to give the impression to the general reader that editing involves an arcane vocabulary and mysterious concepts. The situation is ironic because Greg did not pretend to be dealing with any abstruse concepts: he merely hoped that these two words could serve as a shorthand means for making a distinction between what are popularly regarded as content and form in verbal expression, a distinction with which everyone, in one way or another, has come in contact. Indeed, he goes out of his way to emphasize the fact that he is not setting forth a philosophical theory about the nature of language but is only drawing a practical distinction for use in the business of editing.[6] Naturally he is aware that content and form are never completely separable and that the line separating meaning and formal presentation in written language is not distinct (and philosophically raises complex issues); but for his purposes it is enough to append a footnote (p. 376) acknowledging "an intermediate class of word-forms about the assignment of which opinions may differ and which may have to be treated differently in dealing with the work of different scribes." Since the purpose of the substantive-accidental division is to assist the editor in deciding what variants in a text can reasonably be attributed to the copyist or compositor rather than the author, the focus is pragmatic—on the habits of individuals—and Greg is therefore more concerned with providing a suggestive approach, which can be used with flexibility to meet various situations, than in defining as philosophic concepts two mutually exclusive terms. The procedural recommendation which concludes Greg's paragraph is similarly couched in practical, and flexible, terms: the reason for selecting a copy-text in the first place is the limited nature of historical knowledge about accidentals (the copy-text is selected "on grounds of expediency, and in con-

---

rather falls within the scope of "substantive" changes). Perhaps the closest parallel is the use of "substance" and "accident" in philosophy to signify the essential and the nonessential; yet Greg insists, rightly, that his concern is not with a philosophical distinction. (Greg had used the word "accidents" in 1942 in *The Editorial Problem in Shakespeare*, where one section is entitled, "Note on Accidental Characteristics of the Text," pp. l-lv; but instead of "sub-stantives" the term "essentials of reading" is employed.)

6. After defining the two terms (p. 376), he says in the body of his text, "The distinction is not arbitrary or theoretical, but has an immediate bearing on textual criticism"; and in a footnote to the definitions he emphasizes, "The distinction I am trying to draw is practical, not philosophic." See also footnote 12 below.

sequence either of philological ignorance or of linguistic circumstances"), and therefore one should follow the copy-text in regard to
accidentals—but "within reason." This last phrase underscores Greg's
approach: one follows the "theory" when there is no persuasive reason for doing otherwise, but when one has reason to depart from it, a
rigid application of it would be foolish. Because the editor generally
has fewer means for rationally determining authorial readings in accidentals than in substantives, he generally follows the copy-text in
accidentals; but Greg is not asking him to fly in the face of reason by
adhering to this procedure in situations which are exceptions to the
generalization. Nowhere does Greg claim that following his rationale
will invariably produce "correct" readings; what he suggests is that it
offers the safest approach when one has otherwise no particular reason
for choosing one reading over another as authorial. The theory clearly
is one of expediency.

The skillful organization of Greg's essay is nowhere better exempli-
fied than in his return to the subject of McKerrow in the pages following this basic exposition of his theory. The rigidity of McKerrow's
approach is the more evident in contrast, and the reader is now in a
position to see its limitations; at the same time he recognizes how
Greg's ideas developed from McKerrow's and how McKerrow was on
the verge of the same insight as Greg. In the 1904 Nashe (which Greg
quotes), McKerrow had held firmly to the view that an editor should
take as his copy-text the latest edition which could convincingly be
shown to contain authorial revisions; so long as some of the variants
in that edition were authorial, all its readings should be accepted
(since conceivably they could all be authorial), except when they were
obviously impossible. McKerrow allowed for some editorial discretion
in the determination of what was obviously impossible, but in general
he was determined to preserve the "integrity" of individual texts. But
by 1939, when he published his *Prolegomena for the Oxford Shakespeare*, he had come to believe that a later edition, even one with
authorial revisions, should not serve as copy-text, for—with the exception of those revisions—it would be less likely to reflect the author's
manuscript than an earlier edition, which stood that much closer to
the manuscript. He thus understood, without explicitly stating, something very close to the distinction between substantives and accidentals,
since he now believed that the edition closest to the manuscript preserved the general texture of the work better than later editions and
that authorial revisions should be incorporated into the text of that
edition. Although this position represented a considerable move away

from his earlier fear of eclecticism,[7] he was still not ready to allow an editor to combine readings from more than two editions. When the editor believed a particular edition to contain authorial revisions, he said, all the variants in that edition "which could not reasonably be attributed to an ordinary press-corrector" (that is, in general, all the substantive variants) must be accepted into the copy-text. By the time of his death, therefore, McKerrow was well on his way to the position finally advanced by Greg,[8] the essential difference between the two being in the amount of responsibility given to editorial judgment. For McKerrow, the editor uses his judgment in determining what edition should be copy-text, what edition, if any, contains authorial revisions, and what readings are impossible, but he cannot go further and reject some of the variants in that authorially revised edition as not authorial.[9] For Greg, the editor who has already made certain basic decisions should be allowed to go on and choose among the possibly authorial variants. The effort to eliminate as much editorial decision as possible, he believes, is misguided:

7. Although Greg does not say so here, McKerrow's attitude doubtless sprang from his overreacting against the abuses of some nineteenth-century editors, who felt free to choose among variant readings without adequate study of the nature and origin of the editions in which those variants appeared. Later Greg does make a similar point in general terms: "The attitude may be explained historically as a natural and largely salutary reaction against the methods of earlier editors. Dissatisfied with the results of eclectic freedom and reliance on personal taste, critics sought to establish some sort of mechanical apparatus for dealing with textual problems . . ." (p. 383). For a development of this point, see Fredson Bowers, "McKerrow's Editorial Principles for Shakespeare Reconsidered," *SQ*, 6 (1955), 309-324; and "Multiple Authority: New Problems and Concepts of Copy-Text," *Library*, 5th ser., 27 (1972), esp. 90-91.

8. Greg did not move all at once to his final position. In "McKerrow's Prolegomena Reconsidered," *RES*, 17 (1941), 139-149, and, more fully, in the Prolegomena to *The Editorial Problem in Shakespeare* (1942), he recognized the unnecessary rigidity of McKerrow's insistence on adopting all the substantive variants from an edition which contains some authorial revisions, but he followed McKerrow's inclusion of "wording" as one of the criteria for choosing a copy-text. By the end of the decade, however, in this "Rationale," he had developed his distinction between substantives and accidentals and therefore admitted in a footnote, "There is a good deal in my Prolegomena that I should now express differently, and on this particular point I have definitely changed my opinion. I should now say that the choice of the copy-text depends solely on its formal features (accidentals)" (p. 386). In making revisions in 1950 of *The Editorial Problem*, he added a new preface repeating this point and referring to the "Rationale" essay.

9. More than once Greg calls attention to McKerrow's use of the word "reprint" for "critical edition" (e.g., pp. 379, 380). "Reprint," of course, implies complete absence of editorial interference; but while McKerrow expects an editor to use critical judgment in correcting obviously impossible readings he does not conceive of the result as a "critical edition." Greg calls this confusion "symptomatic"—that is, of McKerrow's pervasive reluctance to give rein to individual judgment.

Uniformity of result at the hands of different editors is worth little if it means only uniformity in error; and it may not be too optimistic a belief that the judgement of an editor, fallible as it must necessarily be, is likely to bring us closer to what the author wrote than the enforcement of an arbitrary rule.   (p. 381)

Again Greg's emphasis is on the use of reason and discretion, as it is in the brief summary which follows immediately: "the copy-text should govern (generally) in the matter of accidentals, but . . . the choice between substantive readings belongs to the general theory of textual criticism and lies altogether beyond the narrow principle of the copy-text" (pp. 381-382). Greg is careful here to insert a qualifying adverb even in the first part of his statement, which deals with accidentals and thus the more mechanical part of his theory; but in the second part he makes clear that the handling of substantive variants is a matter of critical judgment and cannot be regarded as mechanical in any sense. Not to recognize that substantives and accidentals must be treated in different ways, he points out, has led in the past to a "tyranny of the copy-text"—a tyranny because its readings were thrust on the editor, without the benefit of his critical thinking about their merits.

The remainder of Greg's essay, amounting to about half of it, consists of illustrative examples and discussions of particular problems in the application of the theory but does not add any essential point to the basic idea set forth economically in the first half. After citing examples from F. S. Boas's edition (1932) of Marlowe's *Doctor Faustus* and Percy Simpson's edition (1941) of Jonson's *The Gipsies Metamorphosed* to show the operation of the "tyranny of the copy-text,"[10] Greg provides a second brief recapitulation of his rationale (pp. 384-385), reiterating the limitations of mechanical rules and concentrating on the nature of the editorial judgment required for dealing with substantive variants. That judgment depends partly on an evaluation of the circumstances of the production of the editions in which those variants appear and partly on the relative reliability of those editions

10. The examples are effective in demonstrating not only undue reliance on the copy-text but also the self-confidence required to alter the copy-text, and in both instances Greg perhaps overstates the obviousness of the emendations he proposes. His arguments for emending the copy-text in each case are persuasive; but the larger argument of his essay does not require him to assert that these emendations are in fact correct but only to show that an editor ought not to be prevented from seriously considering them by too rigid an adherence to the copy-text. It is one thing to say that Boas and Simpson might have adopted his emendations if they had not been under the tyranny of the copy-text, but quite another to imply that they certainly would have done so.

as suggested by the number of "manifest errors" in them; but the heart of the matter is the editor's evaluation of particular variants in terms of "the likelihood of their being what the author wrote rather than their appeal to the individual taste of the editor" (p. 385). Then, to provide more practical help, Greg expands on three points already introduced. First, he suggests that an editor may legitimately decide to alter some of the accidentals of the copy-text and thus provides a gloss on the expressions "within reason" and "generally" which he had inserted parenthetically in his earlier statements about following the accidentals of the copy-text. Spelling or punctuation known to be at variance with the author's can be altered, for instance, and, when substantive emendations are made on the basis of later texts, the spelling of such words can be made to conform with the habitual spelling (if there is one) of the copy-text. Second, he restates in somewhat more detail his belief that an editor should not accept from an authorially revised edition any substantive variant that seems obviously incorrect, that seems not to be a reading which the author would have inserted, or that seems completely indifferent. The latter point illustrates once again the expedient nature of what Greg is proposing: if a variant appears so indifferent to the editor that he has no basis for arguing either for or against its adoption, then he simply follows the copy-text reading as a practical means for deciding what to do. "In such a case," Greg points out, "while there can be no logical reason for giving preference to the copy-text, in practice, if there is no reason for altering its reading, the obvious thing seems to be to let it stand" (p. 386). Third, he makes explicit (pp. 389-390) what was only implied before, that the choice of copy-text itself varies with circumstances and that situations arise in which one must choose a revised edition as copy-text, as when an author is thought to have overseen a revised edition so carefully that its accidentals as well as its substantives must be taken to carry his approval, or when revision is so complex or pervasive that it is not meaningful to think in terms of emending the unrevised text with later readings (*Every Man in His Humour*, *Richard III*, and *King Lear* are cited).

In connection with all three of these points Greg again defends the use of editorial judgment. When discussing the first he says, "These [decisions to alter accidentals], however, are all matters within the discretion of an editor: I am only concerned to uphold his liberty of judgement" (p. 386). In his discussion of substantives he repeats the view emphatically:

I do not, of course, pretend that my procedure will lead to consistently correct results, but I think that the results, if less uniform, will be on the whole preferable to those achieved through following any mechanical rule. I am, no doubt, presupposing an editor of reasonable competence; but if an editor is really incompetent, I doubt whether it much matters what procedure he adopts: he may indeed do less harm with some than with others, he will do little good with any. And in any case, I consider that it would be disastrous to curb the liberty of competent editors in the hope of preventing fools from behaving after their kind.   (p. 388)

And in the third instance, dealing with the choice of copy-text, he states that no "hard and fast rule" can be laid down but that, whatever text is chosen, the editor "cannot escape the responsibility of distinguishing to the best of his ability" between authorial revision and "unauthorized variation":   "No juggling with copy-text will relieve him of the duty and necessity of exercising his own judgement" (p. 390). This sentiment is clearly the dominant motif of the essay; if McKerrow had been reacting against nineteenth-century eclecticism in restricting the role of editorial judgment, Greg is here turning toward more reliance on judgment, but within a framework that does not encourage undisciplined eclecticism. It is in keeping with his approach throughout that Greg ends by saying, "My desire is rather to provoke discussion than to lay down the law."

I hope that my account of Greg's essay, by its very repetitiousness, has shown that the essay itself consists of repeated statements of a simple idea. Three times he presents a concise summary of his theory followed by a discussion of particular points implied by it, as if he were turning over an object in his hand, focusing his attention alternately on the piece as a whole and on certain of its details. The simplicity of his proposal is certainly one of its most remarkable features and is a natural result of the emphasis on individual judgment, for a methodology inevitably becomes more complicated the more one tries to substitute rules for judgment in the handling of the various situations that may arise. In somewhat blunt language, Greg's theory amounts to this: it tells the editor what to do when he otherwise does not know what to do. If he does know otherwise—that is, if his analysis of all available external and internal evidence (including, of course, his own intimate knowledge of the author and the period) convinces him that a particular text comes closest in all respects to the author's wishes or that a particular variant is the author's revision—then he does not need further guidance. But when there remains a doubt in his mind, after thorough analysis, about whether, for example, the author gave close attention to the punctuation of a revised edition or whether a particular altered wording, in a text which contains many clearly authorial revisions, was the author's, the editor does need further help, since he has gone as far as reasoning can take him and the results are inconclusive. All that Greg suggests, in effect, is that the editor can most sensibly extricate himself from this situation by keeping two points in mind:　(1) successive editions based on earlier editions become increasingly divergent from the earliest edition in the sequence, particularly in such matters as punctuation and spelling, not merely through carelessness but through the natural tendency of compositors to utilize their own habitual forms; (2) when an author makes revisions in a later edition, he may be likely to give considerably less attention to spelling and punctuation than to the words themselves, and even some of the differences in wording in a revised edition may in fact result from the process of resetting rather than from the author's revision. It follows that the editor who chooses the edition closest to the author's manuscript as his copy-text when he does not have strong reason for choosing a later one, and who follows the readings of that copy-text when he does not have strong reason to believe them erroneous or to believe that a later variant in wording (or, more rarely, in punctuation or spelling) is the author's—that such an editor is maximizing his chances of incorporating the author's intended readings in his text. No one would claim—and Greg specifically does not—that this procedure always results in the correct choices, but it tells an editor how to proceed when he most needs such advice (when he has exhausted the available evidence without reaching a decision) and it is more satisfying than tossing a coin (since there is at least a rationale involved, based on a generalization about the incidence of human error and the behavior of human beings in dealing with written language). The fundamental common sense of this approach can be seen foreshadowed in Samuel Johnson's comments on the editing of Shakespeare, when he says that "though much credit is not due to the fidelity, nor any to the judgement of the first publishers, yet they who had the copy before their eyes were more likely to read it right, than we who read it only by imagination."[11] The probabilities favor the correctness of the first edition, and it makes sense to rely on that edition except when there is compelling evidence for not doing so.

Expressed in this way—which emphasizes the flexibility and lack of dogmatism basic to Greg's position—this "rationale of copy-text" would seem to apply to all situations. But it is important to raise the

11. *Johnson on Shakespeare*, ed. Arthur Sherbo (1968), I, 106.

question of its universality, for Greg's primary interest, after all, was in the printed drama of the English Renaissance, and all his illustrations are taken from that literature. Did he believe that his rationale was more widely applicable? He was dealing with a period from which relatively few manuscripts have survived, but can the same procedure be applied to texts for which manuscripts do survive? He was working with a period in which greater variations in spelling were tolerable than in later times and in which any editorial supervision of a printed text normally occurred in the printing shop rather than, as later, in the publisher's office with its more highly developed editorial routine; but can Greg's rationale be applied to the products which emerged from the very different publishing circumstances of later periods? Greg's own answer to these questions, I think it can be plainly inferred from his essay, would be Yes. It is true that he limits himself in his illustrations to the field he knows best and limits his more abstract discussion for the most part to printed books, but there are indications that he is thinking in broader terms. For example, in that crucial fourth paragraph, distinguishing substantives and accidentals, he twice refers to "scribes" and "compositors" simultaneously, suggesting that the way human beings react to the two categories is the same regardless of whether they are copying by hand or setting type. He goes on, in the paragraph which follows, to restrict himself to printed books for the historical reason that "the idea of copy-text originated and has generally been applied in connexion with the editing of printed books" (p. 378). The focus of the essay, it must be remembered, is historical: a new approach to editing is set forth as a corrective to what had been developing over the previous century. Since the principal developments in editorial theory had taken place in connection with the editing of Elizabethan and Jacobean drama, it was natural that he should set forth his criticisms of current procedure with reference to the same field—and convenient, also, since that was his own area of competence. But he clearly implies that he is dealing with a larger principle that could be illustrated in other ways than the one he has chosen. Indeed, he suggests that the editors he is criticizing might have taken a different approach if they had been more familiar with the problems of variation in works transmitted in manuscript. And then he adds:

For although the underlying principles of textual criticism are, of course, the same in the case of works transmitted in manuscripts and in print, particular circumstances differ, and certain aspects of the common principles may emerge more clearly in the one case than in the other.   (p. 378)

The implication certainly is that he is concerned with a basic concept[12] which might not be clear to one who has dealt only with a particular class of problems. And while his illustrations come from Renaissance drama, some of them do involve authorial proof-correction (*Every Man in His Humour*) and revised editions incorporating corrections derived from authorial manuscript (*Richard III* and *King Lear*). In any event, his whole approach, stressing expediency and judgment, suggests that he thinks of his procedure as one capable of fitting widely varied situations. When an editor judges that he has sufficient evidence for proceeding in a particular way, he has no need for a plan of expediency; but a lack of sufficient evidence is a common occurrence in dealing with works of every period, and Greg's rationale commands respect in such situations because it is based on what observation shows to be characteristic human behavior. If I have set forth accurately here what Greg says, then it would appear to be a self-evident proposition that his recommended procedure would serve in handling editorial problems involving manuscripts as well as printed books, arising in twentieth-century literature as well as sixteenth.

There is one kind of editorial problem, however, which clearly lies outside the scope of Greg's essay. To place presumptive authority for accidentals, as a general rule, in the edition closest to the author's manuscript presupposes an ancestral series, in which the line of editions—with each edition based (for the most part, at least) on preceding ones—leads back to the manuscript. Although some of Greg's examples involve complicated variations (such as the revisions incorporated in the folio text of *Every Man in His Humour*), in which a later edition is chosen as copy-text because of the extent and nature of fresh authority (authorial revision or recourse to authorial manuscripts), those examples do not include situations in which two or more texts stand in exactly the same genealogical relationship to a lost ancestor, with no earlier texts surviving. In such a case, Greg's approach offers no help in selecting a copy-text, for no one of these texts is nearer the manuscript (or the antecedent text) than any other. The inapplicability of Greg's rationale to this kind of situation is obvious,

---

12. It should be clear that there is no contradiction involved between the assertion that Greg is dealing with a concept and his own repeated emphasis on the practical rather than the theoretical. Obviously, as the word "rationale" in his title suggests, his argument is conceptual and theoretical, since it attempts to formulate a general statement which can be illustrated by reference to specific situations. But the theory itself is proposed as a matter of expediency, as a workable practical solution to a problem, rather than as a philosophic truth. One can say that it is a theory suggesting how best to accommodate one's ignorance but not that it is a theory leading to a reduction of that ignorance.

once it is pointed out, but it has only recently been examined in detail. Fredson Bowers was confronted with the problem in editing Stephen Crane's syndicated newspaper pieces: the variant texts of a given piece, as they appeared in various newspapers, are all equidistant from the syndicate's proofs which had been sent to those newspapers; in the absence of the proofs, the editor is faced with several texts, any one of which could be chosen as copy-text under Greg's rationale. The solution, as Bowers sets it forth in "Multiple Authority: New Problems and Concepts of Copy-Text,"[13] is to combine the features of these "radiating texts," as he calls them, through a statistical and critical analysis of the variants. In effect, one has to construct a copy-text, and the more surviving texts there are the more accurately can the common ancestor (the lost syndicate proof) be reconstructed. From that point on, naturally, Greg's rationale takes over, and the text thus constructed may be emended with variants from later printings, as may happen with an ordinary copy-text. The essential difference is that, in the case of radiating texts, no one document can serve as copy-text, for no one of the radiating texts can be presumed to have reproduced the accidentals of the syndicate proof more accurately than another. Bowers's detailed exposition of his solution therefore becomes a major supplement to Greg; his essay—which incidentally offers an extremely useful statement of Greg's position—deserves to be taken as a companion piece to Greg's "Rationale," and the two essays together provide a comprehensive editorial theory.

Bowers's discussion of radiating texts, in other words, does not invalidate Greg's theory in any sense, but it does show one respect in which that theory is not all-encompassing. No comparable supplement to Greg's theory has been made in the twenty-five years since its first

---

13. *Library*, 5th ser., 27 (1972), 81-115. His later article, "Remarks on Eclectic Texts," in *Proof*, 4 (1974), furthers the discussion by elaborating upon and providing numerous examples to illustrate the distinction between single-authority and multiple-authority situations. There are, of course, many instances of multiple authority in which the earliest surviving texts (earliest in each line) are not equidistant from the lost common ancestor. But Greg's theory operates in such cases, because—in the absence of contrary evidence—one can presume the text nearest the lost ancestor to be the most reliable in accidentals. At times, as in any other copy-text situation, an editor may have reason to believe that some text other than the nearest one is the most reliable, and he would then select it as copy-text; otherwise he would select the nearest one. Unlike a situation of equidistant radiating texts, the editor in these instances has a presumptive authority to fall back on when there is no other means for reaching a decision. In other words, it is the existence of authoritative texts that are equidistant from a lost ancestor, not simply the existence of texts representing independent lines of descent from that ancestor, which poses a problem for the application of Greg's approach.

appearance, though many questions have been raised. But these questions (such as the extent to which the idiosyncrasies of nineteenth- or twentieth-century authors' manuscripts should be preserved in print), often interesting in themselves, involve matters of editorial judgment, not the basic theory. It is unfortunately true that such questions have frequently been posed as an attack on the theory; and the failure to distinguish between the theory itself and the individual decisions of editors who are following the theory has rendered much of the discussion less useful than it might have been, if not wholly beside the point. My own summary of Greg in these pages has tried to emphasize those elements of his essay which anticipate the later criticisms. Seemingly it takes many words to explain something which is simple and many assertions to proclaim lack of dogmatism; but the simplicity and lack of dogmatism of Greg's rationale have apparently not been perceived by a number of people, for many of their criticisms are undercut by a recognition of those qualities. A renewed close examination of Greg's essay does not suggest to me any reason to question Bowers's description of its thesis as "the great contribution of this century to textual criticism."[14]

II

In the years since Greg's "Rationale" appeared, the person who has done most to make Greg's theory widely known and to demonstrate its broad applicability is Fredson Bowers. His contributions have been of two kinds: (1) general discussions of editing, which call attention to and recapitulate Greg's ideas and which sometimes specifically take up the question of applying his rationale to areas other than Renaissance drama; (2) actual editions based on Greg's rationale, not only showing its workability on a large scale but also developing an appropriate apparatus to accompany texts edited in that way.

Bowers began his commentary on Greg's essay, even before it appeared in print, in his 1950 article on "Current Theories of Copy-Text, with an Illustration from Dryden."[15] To use several examples from *The Indian Emperour* to support the rightness of Greg's approach obviously suggests its usefulness for Restoration, as well as Renaissance, drama; but, more important, Bowers anticipates three objections which he thinks may be raised. One is that editors, afraid of the greater role given to editorial judgment, will complain that too much weight has been given to it; but the reply is that, if an editor is preparing a *critical* text, "editorial responsibility cannot be disengaged

14. "Multiple Authority," p. 91.   15. *MP*, 48 (1950-51), 12-20.

from the duty to judge the validity of altered readings in a revised edition" (p. 13). A second objection is that the result will be a conflated or eclectic text; but, again, a *critical* text, as opposed to a reprint, is by definition eclectic, and there is no reason to fear eclecticism for its own sake but only irresponsible eclecticism. It is in connection with the third objection, however, that Bowers most usefully expands on Greg's remarks—the objection that even an editor who accepts the responsibility of judging between authorial and nonauthorial substantive readings may hesitate to judge the authority of accidentals and may feel that the accidentals of a revised edition at least possibly preserve some authorial alterations. Bowers's reply calls attention to a point which Greg had not perhaps sufficiently made clear: it is precisely because an editor has less evidence for judging accidentals that he should normally fall back on the first-edition copy-text for them, since one of the few generalizations that can be made about accidentals is their gradual corruption from edition to edition and the unlikelihood of close authorial attention to accidentals in revised editions. If an editor chooses a revised edition for copy-text, as Bowers succinctly puts the matter, "in order to preserve a single accidentals variant which *may* have been the author's, he is introducing a very considerable number of other alterations which under no circumstances could possibly have been authorial" (p. 16). Bowers preserves Greg's emphasis on the expedient by repeatedly using an expression which helpfully captures the spirit of the procedure: he speaks of the "odds" favoring the readings of the first edition and of the editor "playing the correct odds" in retaining those readings.[16]

This first apologia for Greg's theory was promptly buttressed when, only three years later, the first volume of Bowers's edition of Dekker appeared, inaugurating the first full-scale edition to be produced according to Greg's rationale. Besides making that rationale more widely known and demonstrating its use in handling the problems of an actual edition (as opposed to isolated examples of textual problems), the Dekker introduced a form of apparatus which broke with tradition and which was particularly appropriate for reflecting the central ideas of Greg's approach. The traditional apparatus, which

16. Bowers calls it "one of Greg's three criteria for determining the authority of variants that when a choice seems indifferent, the odds are in favor of the specific authority of the original reading" (p. 15). Actually Greg does not make this one of the three criteria (as stated on p. 385 of *Collected Papers* and summarized above, p. 177, in the sentence beginning "That judgment depends partly") but rather a procedure to follow when use of these criteria proves inconclusive (for if they were not inconclusive, the choice would not be indifferent).

McKerrow still supported in his 1939 *Prolegomena,* was to have two sets of notes, one for recording variant readings and one for making more discursive comment on any matter which the editor wished to address; and the first of these kinds of notes, though not always the second, was placed at the foot of each page of text. The departure of the Dekker edition from this plan is two-fold: it divides the record of variants into several categories (editorial alterations of substantives in the copy-text, editorial alterations of accidentals in the copy-text, press-variants, and substantive variants in pre-1700 editions) and it relegates part of that record to an appendix (all but the first category). The result is to dramatize the differing status of the copy-text from that of later texts by segregating the record of its readings and by specifying every change—in accidentals as well as in substantives—which the editor has made in it. Given Greg's reasoning about the accidentals of the copy-text, it is important for the reader to know where the editor has altered them, so a full record is provided; but it is of no importance, in most cases, for the reader to know the thousands of variants in accidentals which entered the text in later editions, so only the substantive variants in those editions are listed. There is a clear distinction between the record of editorial decisions to emend the copy-text and the historical record of substantive variants in later editions. This apparatus, while it does not clutter the reading page with any but the most significant category of editorial decisions,[17] does enable the reader easily to focus on all the editor's decisions—which is especially important in view of the prominence given to editorial judgment in Greg's rationale.

Bowers continued through the 1950s to keep Greg's theory before the scholarly public, in the successive volumes of the Dekker and in various theoretical discussions.[18] But as his work on Dekker neared completion and he turned his attention to the editing of Hawthorne, he produced the first detailed illustration of the application of the theory to the period of machine printing and highly developed publishing firms. His 1962 paper, "Some Principles for Scholarly Editions of Nineteenth-Century American Authors,"[19] is the principal docu-

17. This streamlining of the apparatus extends also to the simplification of the symbols employed, utilizing considerably fewer than were envisaged by McKerrow in his *Prolegomena.*

18. Such as that in *On Editing Shakespeare and the Elizabethan Dramatists* (1955), pp. 71-83; "Old-Spelling Editions of Dramatic Texts," in *Studies in Honor of T. W. Baldwin,* ed. D. C. Allen (1958), pp. 11-12; and *Textual and Literary Criticism* (1959), pp. 141-142.

19. Read before the American Literature section of the South Atlantic Modern Language Association on 22 November 1962 and published in *SB,* 17 (1964), 223-228.

ment which stands between Greg's "Rationale" and the large series of CEAA editions currently in progress. This paper begins by establishing two crucial points which underlie all the others: that a scholarly text must be unmodernized[20] (recognizing this as an issue even for nineteenth-century works) [21] and that it must be critical[22] (recognizing that probably "no nineteenth-century text of any length exists that is not in need of some correction").[23] Bowers, like Greg, and like the CEAA editors to follow, is concerned with *unmodernized critical texts*, presenting "classic texts in as close a form as possible to the authors' intentions"; the fact cannot be overemphasized, in the light of later events, that these editors are not attempting to lay down rules for all kinds of editions for all purposes but are concerned with one particular kind of edition.[24] After summarizing Greg's rationale for an audi-

20. The term often used in connection with Renaissance texts is "old-spelling"; but "unmodernized" is probably better, since it more clearly suggests that the modernizing of accidentals in general, not just spelling, is the point at issue.

21. The fact that nineteenth-century accidentals are nearer our own than those of the sixteenth century means that the general reader or the classroom student has less difficulty in using an unmodernized text for this period; but it has nothing to do with the fact that a scholar requires a text representing as accurately as possible the author's own accidentals, regardless of the ease or difficulty with which that text can now be read. There are, in fact, a considerable number of differences between nineteenth- and twentieth-century accidentals, particularly punctuation; but, as Bowers says, "one may flatly assert that any text that is modernized can never pretend to be scholarly, no matter at what audience it is aimed" (p. 223). Obviously, if accidentals form part of an author's expression of meaning, one cannot modernize and still have what the author wrote and meant. One can always argue that the authors themselves would not want their punctuation and spelling to be preserved at the cost of not being read; but such an argument has no bearing on the needs of scholars to have before them, insofar as it is possible, exactly what the author wrote. Modernized editions can then follow, when

they seem necessary, though they must inevitably be a compromise. Some of the issues involved in the question of modernizing are discussed in John Russell Brown, "The Rationale of Old-Spelling Editions of the Plays of Shakespeare and His Contemporaries," *SB*, 13 (1960), 49-67; Arthur Brown, "The Rationale of Old-Spelling Editions . . . A Rejoinder," *SB*, 13 (1960), 69-76; and Jürgen Schäfer, "The Orthography of Proper Names in Modern-Spelling Editions of Shakespeare," *SB*, 23 (1970), 1-19. See also footnotes 93, 98, and 99 below.

22. That is, it must result from editorial decisions and not be simply a reprint of one particular text. It could, of course, in rare instances be such a reprint—but only because the editor judged no emendations to be necessary, not because he was committed to reproducing a single document without alteration.

23. He continued to demonstrate the bibliographical and textual problems raised by nineteenth-century works in "Old Wine in New Bottles: Problems of Machine Printing," in *Editing Nineteenth-Century Texts*, ed. John M. Robson (1967), pp. 9-36.

24. But one which, it seems reasonable to assume, is basic, since it can provide the details necessary for use in preparing other kinds of editions.

ence which at that time was not likely to have been particularly familiar with it, Bowers proceeds to show how Greg's approach accommodates the two principal differences in the kinds of materials with which the editor of a nineteenth-century work is likely to deal: (1) the fact that nineteenth-century American books were normally plated does not mean that alterations do not appear in later printings, and examples from Hawthorne illustrate the necessity for making machine collations[25] of copies of the first printing from a set of plates against copies of the last printing; (2) the fact that authors' fair-copy manuscripts frequently survive from this period means that in such cases the editor will generally find himself employing a manuscript, rather than a first printing, as copy-text, for what Greg said about the usual degeneration of the accidentals from edition to edition applies also to the initial step from manuscript to print. In making the latter point, Bowers clearly restates the view of accidentals which is basic to Greg's whole theory: "if an author's habits of expression go beyond words and into the forms that these take, together with the punctuation that helps to shape the relationships of these words, then one is foolish to prefer a printing-house style to the author's style" (p. 226).[26] The other concern of Bowers's paper is an appropriate apparatus for the kind of edition he is describing, and he lists five classes of material which scholars should expect to find recorded: (1) variants among copies of a single edition, revealed by machine collation of multiple copies; (2) emendations made by the editor in the copy-text (along with discussions of any problematical readings); (3) substantive differences in editions published during the author's lifetime[27] and in

---

25. The use of the Hinman Collator, developed by Charlton Hinman for the detection of variant formes in the Shakespeare first folio, to make collations of copies of machine-printed books from the same typesetting or plates is another instance of the application to later books of methods conceived in connection with earlier ones. For a list of articles dealing with mechanized collation, see the CEAA *Statement* (2nd ed., 1972), pp. 19-20.

26. He also emphasizes, like Greg, the practical side of the point: "This distinction," he says, "is not theory, but fact." Obviously the "fact" is not that the editor can always distinguish correctly between the author's and others' changes but that Hawthorne's manuscripts do exhibit many

differences from their first printings and that unauthorized changes are likely to enter a text every time it is set in type.

27. Bowers, using the example of Hawthorne, speaks of reporting all the editions during the author's lifetime. But since the reason for choosing that period is to cover any editions which might incorporate authorial changes, one can infer that any pirated edition—which can be established as pirated and thus as having no connection with the author—can be excluded from the listing. A collation of such an edition, however, is naturally still called for, so that the editor can be sure that the variant readings in it do not suggest authorial revision in spite of the external evidence.

any posthumous editions that the editor judges to be of sufficient interest; (4) "all the rejected readings and revisions during the process of inscription" of the manuscript, when a manuscript exists—in other words, the pre-copy-text variants; (5) compound words hyphenated at the ends of lines in the copy-text (and thus requiring editorial judgment to determine how they should be printed in the critical text),[28] along with the copy-text forms of words which are divided at line-end in the critical text. This list is obviously an adaptation of the Dekker apparatus to a situation in which a manuscript may be available, and it also recognizes for the first time the editorial problems which line-end hyphens produce. Acknowledging the amount of effort involved in preparing such an edition, Bowers ends with an explicit reference to the continuity of editorial problems by calling on scholars of American literature to "bring to their task the careful effort that has been established as necessary for English Renaissance texts."

In the same year the first volume of the Ohio State ("Centenary") edition of Hawthorne (*The Scarlet Letter*, 1962) was illustrating in detail the points made in this paper and was exhibiting the kind of apparatus advocated there. By providing a comprehensive essay analyzing the textual history of the work and the editorial procedures employed and by keeping the pages of the text entirely free of apparatus (unlike the Dekker, all emendations were listed at the end), the Hawthorne edition was to furnish a practical model for the later CEAA editions. Influential as Bowers's work on this edition was, his exposition of Greg which was perhaps of the greatest potential influence came the next year. In 1963 the MLA published a pamphlet, edited by James Thorpe, on *The Aims and Methods of Scholarship in Modern Languages and Literatures*;[29] consisting of four essays, on linguistics, textual criticism, literary history, and literary criticism, it was intended, according to Thorpe's introduction, to offer a "review

28. This point again reflects Greg's rationale in its focus on the accidentals of the copy-text. Once the importance of preserving the accidentals of the copy-text is established, the importance of deciding when to retain, and when to omit, copy-text line-end hyphens becomes evident—as well as the importance of informing the reader in this respect, as in others, of exactly what occurs in the copy-text.

29. The history of the pamphlet is sketched by Thorpe in his introduction.

The MLA's Committee on Research Activities had earlier presented a report (edited by Helmut Rehder) entitled "The Aims, Methods, and Materials of Research in the Modern Languages and Literatures," published in *PMLA* (67, no. 6 [October 1952], 3-37) and as a pamphlet. The section of that report on "Editing and Textual Criticism" (pp. 15-19), written by Lawton P. G. Peckham, does not mention Greg's rationale and sets forth the idea that "the last edition revised by an author, or published in his lifetime with his consent, is most likely to satisfy literary needs" (p. 16).

of some current ideas" for "any members of the scholarly community," particularly those "into whose hands the future of American scholarship will in due course fall." Such a pamphlet, circulated by the MLA—even though it was not claimed to be "an official statement" of the organization—was bound to be widely read and referred to, and Bowers's essay on "Textual Criticism,"[30] being concise, up-to-date, and readily accessible, became the most convenient source of information on editing literary texts. In his essay Bowers not only suggests[31] the wide applicability of Greg's rationale, by citing illustrations from Shakespeare, Dekker, Dryden, Fielding, Sheridan, Shelley, Hawthorne, Whitman, F. Scott Fitzgerald, and Sinclair Lewis, among others, but also sets forth a practical routine to be followed in the process of collating and emending and some considerations to keep in mind in constructing an apparatus and a textual introduction. Because the only editions at that time which illustrated the use of Greg's rationale —and of apparatus which separates the listing of emendations from the historical record of variants—were those with which Bowers himself was associated, he cites the Dekker and the Hawthorne (along with the forthcoming Beaumont-Fletcher and Fielding), thus bringing to those editions the attention of a wider audience than might otherwise have been expected to examine them.

When, that same year, the Center for Editions of American Authors was established as an official committee of the MLA, it had available, in Bowers's work, the reasoned and detailed application of Greg's theory to nineteenth-century American literature. And when its *Statement of Editorial Principles* emerged in 1967, several drafts having been previously circulated for criticism among interested scholars, the principles were those of Greg and the categories of apparatus were those of Bowers's 1962 paper and thus of the Hawthorne edition. It was necessary, of course, for the CEAA to have a public statement outlining its standards, if it was to award a seal (and dispense funds) to individual editions on the basis of adherence to those standards. But the pamphlet has served a larger function, for its practical recommendations of procedure are more detailed than any available in the earlier discussions of editing in the light of Greg's "Rationale." As

---

30. The essay appears on pp. 23-42 of the original edition. In 1970 a revised edition was published; Bowers's essay, on pp. 29-54, was enlarged chiefly by the insertion of illustrations from the writings of Stephen Crane (the longest such insertion occurs on pp. 51-52).

31. In addition to covering, as one would expect, such matters as whether a text is to be critical, whether it is to be modernized, and what role analytical bibliography plays in editing.

indicated by its subtitle, "A Working Manual for Editing Nineteenth Century American Texts," the pamphlet concentrates on a step-by-step explanation of the processes of bringing together the "authentic forms" of a text, selecting the copy-text, performing collations (by machine and by "sight"—that is, without a machine), presenting the evidence, writings notes and introductions, and proofreading. It thus attempts to set forth the principles behind this kind of editing as well as to offer practical advice on how to proceed; while addressed specifically to editors who seek CEAA support and approval, it functions also as a way of informing a larger audience, wishing to keep abreast of developments in the scholarship of American literature, of what is involved in these editions. Two features of the *Statement* deserve particular notice. One is its emphatic recognition of the importance of proofreading in the production of a reliable edition; it sets a minimum of five proofreadings against copy as a requirement for any edition applying for the CEAA seal (p. 11). Second is its provision for the dissemination of these editions by attaching certain conditions to the seal: the editors of editions which received public funds are to forgo royalties, and the publishers of those editions are to make the texts (not necessarily the apparatuses) "available to reprinting publishers no longer than two years after the date of original publication for reasonable royalties or fees" (p. 14). These provisions remain as important parts of the CEAA requirements in the revised edition of the *Statement* published in 1972,[32] although the new edition makes clearer the fact that the seal is available to any edition which meets the standards, whether or not it has been funded through the Center, and that in such cases no stipulations can be made about royalties or the availability of a text for reprinting. The CEAA, as its *Statement* indicates, is concerned not only with the production of sound texts and informative apparatuses but also with the practical problems of fostering a general demand for reliable editions and of encouraging their widespread distribution.[33]

---

32. Under the revised title *Statement of Editorial Principles and Procedures*. The revised discussion of proofreading adds a further requirement, based on the experience of several editions: that a final check be made to determine whether printers' errors have entered after the final proofs, by performing a machine collation of the unbound printed gatherings against the last set of proofs.

33. The seal itself was of course devised as a shorthand way of informing the reader or buyer that certain standards had been met and of promoting a broader general awareness of the need for reliable texts— with the potential result that readers would begin to demand, and publishers to seek, texts which qualified for the seal.

It should be clear that the CEAA's endorsement of Greg's theory and its requirement of a particular kind of apparatus are separate matters. Greg says nothing about apparatus in his "Rationale,"[34] and his approach entails no specific form of apparatus; obviously one can edit a text according to Greg's principles without supplying the reader any apparatus at all. The position of the CEAA on the two must be examined separately. As to its choice of Greg's theory, it could not responsibly have chosen any other. Greg was building on the experience of McKerrow and thus represented the main line of bibliographical development of this century; his theory not only emerged from long experience but had a compelling internal logic of its own. Since, by 1963, Bowers had amply demonstrated—what Greg himself had implied—that this approach was not limited to Renaissance literature, the CEAA was fortunate, at the time of its organization, in having readily available a theoretical position that it could scarcely ignore if it was to promote unmodernized critical texts. Clearly, one might wish to argue that it ought to have decided to promote some other kind of text in the first place; but, aside from the fact that the MLA, as a learned society, has a responsibility to support scholarly work, any text which is modernized or in some other way prepared for the "general reader" must, if it is to be reliable, first entail the research involved in producing a scholarly (that is, unmodernized and critical) text. The CEAA decision, therefore, makes practical sense, particularly if the results of that research are made available, so that editors who wish to produce different kinds of editions can take the evidence already amassed and reinterpret it according to different principles. Here is where the CEAA requirements for apparatus come in. The Center was again fortunate, at its inception, in having previous work to turn to, for the Hawthorne edition provided the obvious example—the work of a nineteenth-century American figure, edited according to

34. Except for one footnote, which suggests that the "graphic peculiarities of particular texts" should probably not be recorded in the "general apparatus" but "may appropriately form the subject of an appendix" (p. 386). Apparently the "general apparatus" Greg has in mind consists of footnotes; and, since he believes that "in this respect the copy-text is only one among others," he is expressing the view that emendations of accidentals in the copy-text should "probably" not be listed at the foot of the page but rather at the end of the volume—the practice which Bowers adopts in the Dekker. As early as 1760 Edward Capell, in his *Prolusions*, employed a similar system, in which one category of readings is listed at the foot of the page, and at the end come "all the other rejected readings of the editions made use of" (p. iii). Capell saw the value of making a specific text the "ground-work" of his own and of recording all departures from it as well as variant readings from other editions, so that the reader would have "all the materials that can be procur'd for him," in order to re-examine the editor's decisions.

Greg, and supplied with an appendix containing a list of editorial decisions as well as a historical record of substantive variants. Recognizing that the precise form in which this material is to be laid out need not follow that of the Hawthorne, the CEAA has never prescribed the physical arrangement of the data; but it has always insisted on the presence of the same categories of information as are found there, because those categories are essential for any reader who wishes to reconstruct the copy-text with which the editor worked and to examine the evidence on which the editor's decisions were based.[35] Inevitably the Hawthorne has served as an influential model in formal matters,[36] but there is no uniformity among CEAA editions in the exact forms employed—only in the kinds of material included.[37] The practice of the Hawthorne in presenting so-called "clear text"—pages of text entirely free of editorial apparatus—has been of particular importance. While the CEAA *Statement* does not insist on clear text, it strongly urges the use of clear text whenever feasible (there are some kinds of material—especially those not intended for publication, such as letters or journals—for which clear text may be impractical or even misleading);[38] and most of the CEAA volumes have in fact presented clear text. The decisions of the CEAA, in regard to editorial theory

35. The only way in which adherence to Greg's theory affects the content of the usual CEAA apparatus is that the historical record of variants normally lists only substantives, not accidentals. There would obviously be no objection to the inclusion of the accidentals as well, but in most cases the number involved would be so great that the effort and expense of listing them would not seem to be justified, in view of the lack of importance attaching to accidentals in later editions under Greg's theory. If someone disagrees with the editor's choice of copy-text, therefore, and wishes to re-edit the work using a different copy-text, he cannot reconstruct the accidentals of that text from the usual CEAA historical collation. Nevertheless, the editor of a CEAA edition explains his choice of copy-text in his textual essay, citing not only external evidence but illustrative readings from the texts; he generally provides enough evidence so that a reader will have an adequate basis for agreeing or disagreeing with his choice. Naturally a person who decides to re-edit the text employing a different copy-text will have to turn to a copy of the edition containing that copy-text; but he should be able to rethink the question of copy-text in the first place on the basis of what is included within the CEAA volume.

36. Obviously it makes sense to follow established forms whenever there is no particular reason for not following them, so that readers will have fewer adjustments to make as they turn from one edition to another.

37. For an examination of the variations in apparatus among CEAA volumes and of certain considerations to keep in mind in choosing among them, see G. T. Tanselle, "Some Principles for Editorial Apparatus," *SB*, 25 (1972), 41-88; and "Editorial Apparatus for Radiating Texts," forthcoming in the *Library*.

38. For some discussion, see William H. Gilman, "How Should Journals Be Edited?", *Early American Literature*, 6 (1971), 73-83.

and to apparatus, were prudent ones, both in the historical sense that they took advantage of the most advanced current thinking and in the more practical sense that they allowed for maximum future use of the material—since they resulted in basic scholar's editions, which at the same time contained easily readable texts that could be reproduced photographically in paperback and other editions and which offered the evidence that could be utilized by other editors in re-editing the text along different lines.

What emerges from all this is the fact that the CEAA does not regard the editions it approves as the only respectable or desirable editions of those works that are possible. After all, its seal reads "An Approved Text," not "The Approved Text"—which can be taken as implying two possibilities: first, since emendations are based on the editor's judgment, another editor, still aiming at an unmodernized critical text and following Greg's theory, may arrive at different judgments and may therefore conceivably produce another "approved text," even under the same general guidelines; second, since a CEAA text is one particular kind of text, the existence of a CEAA text of a work does not preclude the possibility that another kind of text might be worthy of approval for other purposes.[39] What is now referred to as a "CEAA edition," then, is the specific combination of two elements—a text edited according to Greg's theory, combined with an apparatus providing the essential evidence for examining the editor's decisions.[40] In a paper presented in 1968 on the occasion of

39. The CEAA has recently begun to offer a seal for "An Approved Facsimile." The first facsimile to be published under this plan is that of the manuscript of *The Red Badge of Courage*, edited by Fredson Bowers with extensive introductory material and appendixes and published in two volumes in 1973 by Microcard Editions Books. The next two such facsimiles are to be those of F. Scott Fitzgerald's *Ledger* and of the manuscript of *The Great Gatsby*, edited by Matthew J. Bruccoli.

40. The CEAA seal, reading "An Approved Text," is awarded only to editions which contain these two elements. However, when a CEAA text is leased by a reprinting publisher, the "An Approved Text" seal remains on the new volume, so long as the text is faithfully reproduced, even if the apparatus is not also reprinted. Perhaps logically the original CEAA edi-

tion should contain a seal for "An Approved Apparatus" as well as for "An Approved Text," since the "Text" seal, when it appears in the originating edition, covers more than the text. Such a seal—reading "An Approved Apparatus"—already exists for a different purpose: it is available to editors who have gone through precisely the same CEAA editorial process but find that publication of the actual text is not feasible (because of copyright restrictions, for example, or lack of interest on the part of a publisher). In these cases the apparatus is keyed by page-line references to the copy-text edition, and a reader, entering the listed emendations on a copy of that edition, can bring its text into conformity with the critical text established (but not published) by the editor. The first apparatus of the CEAA pattern to be published separately from a text was Matthew J. Bruccoli's "Material for a Cen-

the publication of *The Marble Faun* in the Hawthorne edition, Bowers undertook to define the relationship between a "CEAA edition" and the kinds of editions commonly encountered in classroom use.[41] The first he called a "definitive edition," which "establishes with absolute accuracy the exact documentary forms of all authoritative early texts of the work being edited" (p. 52), presents in lists "the concrete evidence on which the establishment of the text has rested" (p. 54), and offers a text reflecting "the author's final intentions insofar as these can be recovered by systematic, principled selection from among the variants of different authoritative forms of the text, supplemented by editorial emendation" (p. 54). The research required for this kind of edition is time-consuming and is carried through without regard for financial return, whereas the editions usually circulated among students and the general public are commercial products, in the preparation of which the factor of expense has to be taken into account. The latter are "practical editions," which "present to a broad audience as sound a text (usually modernized and at a minimum price) as is consistent with information that may be procurable through normal scholarly channels and thus without more special

---

tenary Edition of *Tender is the Night*," *SB*, 17 (1964), 177-193; the advantages of and appropriate occasions for such an approach are discussed in James B. Meriwether's "A Proposal for a CEAA Edition of William Faulkner," in *Editing Twentieth-Century Texts*, ed. Francess G. Halpenny (1972), pp. 12-27. Bruccoli has recently prepared the first separate apparatus to receive the CEAA seal and to be issued as an independent publication (*The Great Gatsby*, University of South Carolina Press); see his discussion of it and the proposed series of which it is to be a part, in "The SCADE Series: Apparatus for Definitive Editions," *PBSA*, 67 (1973), 431-435.

41. "Practical Texts and Definitive Editions," delivered on 16 February 1968 and published, along with a paper by Charlton Hinman, in *Two Lectures on Editing: Shakespeare and Hawthorne* (1969), pp. 21-70. Bowers's essay includes (footnotes 8, 9, 11, 16, 17, on pp. 36-39, 42, 46-48) some comments on Richard H. Fogle's unfavorable review of the Hawthorne edition in

American Literary Scholarship: An Annual, 1965, ed. James Woodress (1967), pp. 21-27; Fogle's comparison of the Ohio State edition of *The House of the Seven Gables* with a classroom edition (Riverside) prompted Bowers's decision to elaborate on the differences between the two kinds of editions: "without the stimulation of his confusion of the true issues it is unlikely that this paper would ever have been written" (p. 38). Bowers has continued to discuss the differences in later articles, such as "The New Look in Editing," *South Atlantic Bulletin*, 35 (1970), 3-10 (which also comments on Jesse H. Shera's review of the Hawthorne edition in *American Notes & Queries*, 1 [1962-63], 159-260); and "The Ecology of American Literary Texts," *Scholarly Publishing*, 4 (1972-73), 133-140. Joseph Katz discusses the shortcomings of certain practical editions in "Practical Editions: A Bad Resource for American Literary Study," *Resources for American Literary Study*, 3 (1973), 221-229 (which includes references to the *Proof* articles surveying the practical editions of individual works).

research than is economically feasible" (p. 26). Practical editions, while useful in the absence of more scholarly editions, clearly represent a compromise, and better practical editions can come only as more "definitive editions" are produced to serve as the source of information for them. The CEAA, it is true, is supporting work principally on only one carefully defined kind of edition—but one that provides the materials basic to other kinds of editions, if they are to be reliable. By focusing on these basic editions and at the same time encouraging the use of clear text and the photographic reproduction of these texts by other publishers, the CEAA is accommodating both the needs of scholars and the long-range interests of the general reading public.

Of course, some people may feel that it is proper for the CEAA to support basic scholarly editions without believing that Greg's theory (or, perhaps, any other single theory) ought to be the required approach, and they may be inclined to think that such a requirement contradicts the freedom from dogmatism which Greg himself emphasized. This position, however, involves several confusions. To begin with, any standard against which performance is measured must inevitably be dogmatic to the extent that it asserts a particular position, and the CEAA cannot avoid taking a position if it is to attempt to control the quality of work performed under its auspices or published with its endorsement. But that kind of dogmatism, if it can be called such, is an entirely different matter from the dogmatism, or lack of dogmatism, of the position actually taken. Since Greg's approach allows for the operation of individual judgment (providing a dogmatic, or arbitrary, rule only when there is no basis for rational judgment) and since the CEAA has adopted Greg's approach, it follows that the CEAA's dogmatism amounts only to insisting on an approach which in itself minimizes the role of mechanical rules and maximizes that of critical judgment.

Furthermore, whatever rigidity there is in the adoption of a single approach is reduced by the inclusion, in CEAA editions, of the materials out of which texts based on other approaches can be prepared. To call these editions "definitive" may sound dogmatic, but Bowers's definition makes clear that "definitive edition" has come to be a technical term, referring to an edition which includes a text prepared in a particular way along with an apparatus containing certain information. The word "definitive" has undoubtedly been used too freely and unthinkingly and may even at times have been applied loosely, though still incorrectly, to a *critical text* rather than an *edition*. If a critical text depends on editorial judgment and critical perception, it cannot be definitive in itself, for judgments and perceptions are always, at least to some extent, arguable. But such a text can be based on a definitive assemblage of relevant material, on painstaking research which, if done properly, does not have to be repeated.[42] No serious student of literature would wish to put a stop to the endless process of rethinking the nuances of a text; but none would desire to repeat the process of accumulating the factual evidence necessary as background for informed judgment if that process had already been satisfactorily completed. A so-called "definitive edition" thus achieves its status through the inclusion of a definitive apparatus; the text presented in such an edition commands respect, because of the thoroughness of the research involved, but it cannot be regarded as the element of the edition which justifies the appellation "definitive." Confusion has arisen because the word "edition" sometimes is used to mean simply "a text" and sometimes refers to a text and its appurtenances. The CEAA, with its dual focus on a rationale for editing and a rationale for presenting evidence, has clearly been aware of these problems and has obviously recognized in its requirements the desirability of encouraging critical thinking about a text by providing the reader with the basic factual information necessary for such thinking. The CEAA's use of Greg's theory, therefore, has perpetuated Greg's recognition of editing as an activity of informed criticism.

III

When one understands Greg's theory and the CEAA's implementation of it, one cannot help regarding many of the recent discussions (both favorable and unfavorable) of this joint subject as naïve and parochial, and frequently as uninformed or misinformed.[43] A few,

42. This point has been well put by Leon Howard in his review of the Hawthorne edition in *NCF*, 22 (1967-68), 191-195, when he remarks that, "even though textual theory might change, the work has been done and the information made available for every serious student of American literature" (p. 193). Of course, new information can turn up later, as Bowers recognizes when he says that "definitive" is "only a comparative term, since we must always believe that from time to time the accumulation of scholarship will enable an editor to improve on the work of his predecessors" ("Old-Spelling Editions of Dramatic Texts" [cited in footnote 18

above], p. 13). Similarly, he begins his discussion of "Established Texts and Definitive Editions," *PQ*, 41 (1962), 1-17, by noting, "Nothing but confusion can result from the popular assumption that only one form of an established text can ever exist, and hence that a definitive edition of a single form of a literary work is invariably possible."

43. Although I shall be commenting here principally on essays which take an adverse view of Greg's theory and the CEAA (since they naturally bring into sharpest focus the issues involved), it is clear that some of the reviewers who have written favor-

however, do raise important issues, and it is regrettable that a survey of these discussions must begin with one of so little substance as that of Edmund Wilson. In a two-part article entitled "The Fruits of the MLA," published in the *New York Review of Books* on 26 September and 10 October 1968, Wilson offered what can only be called an ill-tempered and incoherent attack on the CEAA editions, making references to six volumes ostensibly under review;[44] in December of that year the article, with a postscript commenting on some of the correspondence provoked by it,[45] was published in pamphlet form as "A New York Review Book," and in 1973 it was collected into the posthumous volume *The Devils and Canon Barham* (pp. 154-202), edited by Leon Edel.[46] Because of Wilson's stature, this article has received

---

able, but often perfunctory, notices of CEAA volumes have no real conception of the aims of those editions. References to some of the more significant reviews are made in the CEAA *Statement* (2nd ed., 1972), p. 23; a number of other reviews, principally from 1969, are listed (along with other CEAA publicity) in *CEAA Newsletter*, No. 3 (June 1970), pp. 36-38. Although a few of these reviews, and some others, are referred to in these pages, I do not take up individual reviews in any detail, since the questions they raise usually involve judgment of particular cases rather than general principles and procedures.

44. In the 26 September installment (pp. 7-10), headed "Their Wedding Journey," he comments not only on this volume of the Indiana Howells edition but also on *Typee* in the Northwestern-Newberry Melville and *The Marble Faun* in the Ohio State Hawthorne; on 10 October (pp. 6, 8, 10, 12, 14) he limits himself to "Mark Twain," taking up three volumes of the California edition of Mark Twain papers—*Satires and Burlesques, Letters to His Publishers,* and *Which Was the Dream?*

45. The *New York Review of Books* for 19 December 1968, pp. 36-38, contained letters from William H. Y. Hackett, Jr., and Theodore Besterman, which Wilson prints in his postscript; letters from George B. Alexander, Ronald Gottesman, and Paul Baender, which Wilson refers to; and letters from Frederick Buechner and Frank J. Donner, which Wilson does not mention

(but whose correction of "Albert Payson Terhune's" to "Albert Bigelow Paine's" is incorporated in the text at 189.6).

46. As Wilson notes in the 1968 pamphlet, the article had originally appeared "in a slightly different form." For pamphlet publication a number of stylistic revisions were made (e.g., "persistent" for "acute" at 179.21 [all page references are to the 1973 volume, as the most accessible text]), some errors were corrected (e.g., the comments on the Constable Melville and the Russell & Russell reprint at 191.6-9), some additions were incorporated (e.g., the parenthetical sentence at 172.8-11), and five footnotes were added (those on pp. 164, 166, 182, and 186, and one not retained in the 1973 book: attached to the sentence ending at 156.4, it read, "These volumes now range in price here from $10 to $14"). Three of those footnotes cite information supplied by correspondents (those on pp. 164 and 166 based on Gottesman's published letter, and that on p. 186 credited to Alexander's published letter). As Wilson points out in his postscript, other revisions were based on comments in letters, particularly Gottesman's (though in describing one of the corrections—"Reedy" to "Rudy" at 164.5—he reverses the two words); but some corrections available to him in letters were not in fact utilized (see footnote 49 below). The 1973 volume incorporates a few more corrections (e.g., "Newberry" for "Newbury" at 163.22) and omits one footnote (as noted above).

a considerable amount of attention and will continue to have an audience in the future as part of his collected essays; if it had been written by a lesser figure, however, its obvious motivation and manifest confusion would have prevented its being taken seriously. Wilson makes transparent his motive for discrediting the CEAA editions by quoting, at the start, a letter he had written to Jason Epstein in 1962 setting forth the idea of "bringing out in a complete and compact form the principal American classics," based on "the example of the Editions de la Pléiade" (pp. 155-156); this undertaking he had hoped would be supported by the National Endowment for the Humanities, but the MLA, he says, "had a project of its own for reprinting the American classics and had apparently had ours suppressed" (p. 159).[47] Thus determined to find fault with the results of the MLA project, Wilson never addresses himself to the basic editorial rationale (that is, to Greg's theory) but instead is content to ridicule such matters as the laboriousness of the research involved, the extent of the apparatus, and the physical size of the volumes. The article is, uncharacteristically, full of confusions, if not inconsistencies,[48] the most egregious perhaps being his professed admiration for a "sound and full text" (p. 157) combined with his view that collation is unrewarding if it does not uncover "serious suppressions and distortions" (p. 161) or

47. Epstein and John Thompson submitted a proposal—for a series of editions of the kind Wilson desired—to various foundations and eventually to the National Endowment; in 1966, at the time of the initial award of $300,000 to the MLA, $50,000 was to be made available for the Wilson plan whenever facilities for administering it were developed (they never were). The *New York Review of Books*, edited by Epstein's wife, had included, eight months before Wilson's article, another review critical of a CEAA edition—Lewis Mumford's "Emerson Behind Barbed Wire" (18 January 1968, pp. 3-5). Mumford objected to the Harvard edition of *The Journals and Miscellaneous Notebooks of Ralph Waldo Emerson* because of its inclusion of material discarded by Emerson and its use of editorial symbols within the text to record Emerson's revisions. The Mumford piece provoked considerable correspondence, including a letter from Wilson criticizing the MLA "stupid academic editions" and describing his Pléiade idea.

The issue of 14 March 1968 (pp. 35-36) contained letters from (besides Wilson) Lewis Leary, William M. Gibson, and G. S. Rousseau, and a reply from Mumford; another letter, from M. H. Abrams and Morton W. Bloomfield, along with another reply from Mumford, appeared in the issue of 23 May (p. 43). Mumford's review, of course, does not touch on the subject of Greg's rationale, since the choice of copy-text is not an issue in connection with Emerson's manuscript journals.

48. For example, he approves the inclusion in the Pléiade Proust of "an omitted episode" and the restoration in the Soviet editions of Pushkin and Tolstoy of "cut or altered passages," and he looks forward to a complete edition of Mark Twain's *Autobiography*, since "we have never had the whole of this work"; yet he believes that one of the pieces included in *Which Was the Dream?* ("Three Thousand Years among the Microbes") "might well be omitted from the canon" because "it turns out to be disappointing" (p. 178).

interesting variants ("the scrutinizing of variants may, in some cases, be of interest," p. 172). What Wilson is unwilling to acknowledge is that the CEAA's concern extends beyond a scholarly audience to the general public: the CEAA, he says, is "directing a republication of our classics which is not only, for the most part, ill-judged and quite sterile in itself but even obstructive to their republication in any other form" (p. 190). He fails to note that the pages of text, unencumbered in most cases by editorial intrusions, are suitable for photographic reproduction in volumes more convenient to hold and that the apparatus (which, admittedly, helps to make some of the volumes cumbersome), rather than being "sterile," may serve to generate other editions, based on differing evaluations of the evidence—or at least to encourage analysis of the editor's judgments. Wilson's piece scarcely demands any reply, but the celebrity it achieved caused the MLA to feel that some sort of official notice was appropriate, and in March of 1969 the MLA published a pamphlet entitled *Professional Standards and American Editions: A Response to Edmund Wilson*, containing two accounts of the history and aims of the CEAA, by William M. Gibson and John H. Fisher, along with letters from five scholars enumerating errors or confusions in Wilson's remarks.[49] Actually, all that was necessary, if a reply was to be made, was Gordon Ray's brief comment which stands as the epigraph to the pamphlet. Recognizing that "this attack derives in part from the alarm of amateurs at seeing rigorous professional standards applied to a subject in which they have a vested interest" (and thus recognizing the attraction which Wilson's position had for a number of people one might have expected to see through it),[50] Ray observes, "As the American learned world has come

49. Gibson's essay, "The Center for Editions of American Authors" (pp. 1-6), was reprinted from *Scholarly Books in America*, 10 (January 1969), 7-11. Two of the letters (pp. 7-12), by Ronald Gottesman and Paul Baender, had previously been published in the *New York Review of Books* (19 December 1968); two others (pp. 13, 17-19), by Frederick Anderson and Oscar Cargill, also addressed to the *New York Review*, had not been published before; and a fifth (pp. 14-16), by John C. Gerber, had been sent directly to Wilson and had not been published. (A footnote to Gerber's letter points out that Wilson did not correct in the pamphlet his misstatements about the Mark Twain *Papers* and *Works* noted here.) Fisher's essay,

"The MLA Editions of Major American Authors" (pp. 20-26), besides providing a historical account which includes information about Wilson's "Pléiade" plan, makes some response to Wilson's articles. The pamphlet ends with "A Calendar" (pp. 27-28), listing relevant events back to 1947. Bowers's comments on Wilson's articles appear in *Two Lectures on Editing*, pp. 23-25 (footnote 2) and p. 70 (footnote 30). Benjamin DeMott's "The Battle of the Books," in the *New York Times Book Review*, 17 October 1971, pp. 70-72, offers a journalistic account of the controversy.

50. It is symptomatic that Wilson, and Mumford before him, both try to divorce these editions from humanistic learning.

to full maturity since the second World War, a similar animus has shown itself and been discredited in field after field from botany to folklore. In the long run professional standards always prevail."

In contrast to Wilson's article, which makes no reference to Greg's theory, two brief essays which appeared soon after it—the work of Paul Baender and Donald Pizer—do raise questions directly about the applicability and usefulness of Greg's "Rationale." Although each of these essays is weakened by a partial misunderstanding of Greg, they at least raise issues the discussion of which may serve to clarify certain points in some people's minds. Baender, an editor associated with a CEAA edition, published in 1969 a note entitled "The Meaning of Copy-Text,"[51] which asserts that the term has become "ambiguous and misleading," principally for two reasons: first, that it is a "banner word" which "tends toward the superlative" and which thus implies "authority beyond its denotation, as though the term itself ratified an editor's choice of text"; second, that it is "not suited to the full range and complexity of editorial problems" (p. 312). The first point has nothing to do with the word "copy-text" or the concept but only with unscholarly reactions to it—unscholarly because they depend on the "prestige" (as Baender calls it) of the term rather than the arguments lying behind it. The second is of more consequence but is based on an oversimplification and distortion of Greg's position. If it were accurate to say flatly that Greg's theory is eclectic with respect to substantives but maintains "a single-text criterion" with respect to accidentals (p. 314), or if it were fair to suggest that its application to situations involving prepublication texts results in "another stage for a retrogressive pursuit of copy-text" (p. 316), then one would have grounds for claiming that it is "not suited to the full range and complexity of editorial problems." But nothing in Greg's theory, as we have seen, prohibits the emendation of accidentals in the copy-text when one has grounds for doing so; nor is it consistent with his theory to assume that a surviving manuscript must necessarily—regardless of its nature— become copy-text, since he allowed for the possibility that in some

Mumford says ·that the culprit behind the Emerson edition is the "Academic Establishment," fostering "the preconceptions and the mock-scientific assumptions governing the pursuit of the humanities today" (p. 4). Wilson makes disparaging remarks about editors who are not interested in literature (p. 170), exaggerates the technical language employed (p. 169), and prints with obvious delight a letter from

W. H. Y. Hackett, Jr., ridiculing, among other things, the Hinman Collator (pp. 198-99). Ray's comment, though printed without a citation of source, is taken from his "Foreword" to *The American Writer in England: An Exhibition Arranged in Honor of the Sesquicentennial of the University of Virginia* (1969), p. viii.

51. *SB*, 22 (1969), 311-318.

cases a later, rather than an earlier, text is the appropriate choice. One of Baender's illustrations[52] rests on a basic confusion (of which Baender is not alone guilty) between "copy-text" and "printer's copy." Baender cites a situation in which the number of authorial alterations in a later printing makes it more convenient for the editor to use a reproduction of that later printing as the basis for his text, entering onto it the readings of the first printing wherever the later readings are not judged to be authorial. Such a procedure, of course, does not violate Greg's theory (however risky it may be in practical terms, since one is increasing the probability that nonauthorial readings may inadvertently be allowed to remain in the text); but Baender's feeling that one follows the procedure "despite this convention of copy-text" makes clear that he is not focusing on the distinction between "text," meaning a particular arrangement and formal presentation of a group of words, and "printer's copy," meaning a specific physical copy of a text furnished to the printer. Greg's "copy-text" is a "text"—which can exist in more than one physical embodiment (for example, the individual copies of an edition)—and Greg did not comment on the manner in which that text should be reproduced for the use of the compositor who is setting type for the editor's new edition. The CEAA *Statement* does go on to recommend, for obvious practical reasons, the use of a photographic reproduction of the copy-text as printer's copy; but not to follow this course, whether for convincing or questionable reasons, does not in itself contradict Greg's theory, since no theoretical matter is at issue.[53]

Two years later Donald Pizer raised again,[54] but in broader terms, the question of the applicability of Greg's theory to recent literature

---

52. The other of his principal illustrations deals with collateral texts, deriving independently from a lost common ancestor; in these situations he believes that it would be "misleading" to denominate one of the collateral texts a "copy-text." An editor's statement, however, ought to make clear the reasons for selecting a particular text as the basic one, so that the reader will not find the label "misleading." If the collateral texts are equidistant in descent from the lost common ancestor, of course, it is true that there may be no basis for selecting one over another, and the editor must then construct a copy-text on the basis of all these texts, as Bowers has explained in his discussion of "radiating texts," referred to above (footnote

13); but from that point on Greg's theory of copy-text applies as usual. And if the collateral texts are not equidistant from the lost common ancestor, the editor is able to follow Greg's rationale directly, by selecting the one nearest the ancestor unless he has strong evidence pointing toward another choice.

53. My views on Baender's argument are set forth in greater detail in "The Meaning of Copy-Text: A Further Note," *SB*, 23 (1970), 191-196. See also Bowers's comment in "Multiple Authority" (cited in footnote 13 above), p. 82 (footnote 1).

54. "On the Editing of Modern American Texts," *BNYPL*, 75 (1971), 147-153.

by enumerating five ways "in which copy-text theory is unresponsive to the distinctive qualities of [that is, the historical circumstances lying behind] modern American texts" (p. 148).[55] Although Pizer calls attention to some issues that deserve careful consideration, his article is ineffective as an argument against the general usefulness of Greg's rationale because it fails to distinguish between theoretical and practical concerns and to recognize fully the lack of dogmatism in Greg's approach. The last three of his points are irrelevant to an analysis of Greg's theory—what they are relevant to is a consideration of the particular kind of edition (in the sense of text plus apparatus or other commentary) appropriate for modern (nineteenth- and twentieth-century) American literature. While this subject is of course a legitimate matter for debate, the issue is only confused by the implication that the adoption of Greg's theory determines the nature of the apparatus (or whatever accompanies the text) as well as of the text itself. Thus his third point—that the multiplicity of manuscripts, typescripts, and proofs which survive for some modern works makes the task of recording all variant readings excessively onerous[56]—presupposes that something in that theory of copy-text necessitates a complete record of variants, for he concludes: "the theory of copy-text either hinders the preparation of critical editions or encourages the production, at immense expense, of unusable editions" (p. 151). But whether or not one wishes to follow the practice of CEAA editions in recording variants (and the CEAA does not require as an absolute rule that all pre-copy-text variants be noted in print) has nothing to do with whether or not one edits a text in accordance with Greg's theory; and naturally the job of editing a reliable text is complicated by the survival of numerous documents, for the variants in them must be examined carefully regardless of whether a listing is to be published. Pizer's fifth point is a related one, dealing also with apparatus: he objects to clear text in a "critical edition" because turning to the back of a book to consult the apparatus is more difficult than looking at the foot of a page, and he disapproves specifically of the sections of apparatus which the reader of a CEAA edition must "juggle" (p. 152). The

55. Although Pizer continually refers to "the" theory of copy-text, it is obviously Greg's theory which he is discussing. One should understand, however, that an editor necessarily has a "copy-text," whatever he may call it, and that Greg's is only one among many conceivable rationales for selecting a copy-text.

56. That the result might be "complex and bulky" is undeniable; that it is therefore "all but unusable" does not follow. Anyone who wishes to comprehend a complex textual history would presumably not expect to find the evidence as easy to follow as it might be in less complicated situations.

possibility that a more efficient apparatus can be devised is always open; but the plan of the apparatus does not alter the editorial procedure, and a dislike of "the tendency toward clear-text publication" cannot through any argument become an "objection to copy-text theory."[57] The fourth of Pizer's observations amounts to nothing more than the recognition that some editors may choose to edit works which some readers deem unworthy of the effort expended. He speaks of "the absolutism of copy-text procedures"—meaning the uniform treatment of major and minor works—without acknowledging that the decision to edit is a critical evaluation in itself. Not all the CEAA editions are "complete" editions, and those that are reflect—rather than any requirement of Greg's theory—the critical belief that the stature of the authors involved demands full-scale investigation of even their lesser pieces.[58] Very few people (and certainly not the CEAA) would dissent from the view that—since time and money are not unlimited— "practical editions" must suffice for many literary works; but there will never be complete agreement on exactly what works those are.

Pizer's first two objections, in contrast, do raise questions about theory, but not, as he implies, solely about Greg's theory; they are serious questions which any editor must face, whether in the context of Greg's rationale or not. It is Pizer's contention that Greg's theory, by leading an editor normally to adopt the accidentals of a manuscript in preference to those of a first printing, ignores the fact that modern authors sometimes "rely on the taste" of particular publishing-house

---

57. Pizer is particularly worried about the future republication of CEAA clear texts without accompanying apparatus: "It is a nice point," he believes, "whether a clear-text critical edition sans apparatus is any different from an unedited text"— because "in either case the reader must go to considerable effort to check the evidence" (p. 152). A critical text exists to present an informed reconstruction of an author's intended text, based on an examination of all known evidence and on critical insight into the author's aims and methods; a text which is "unedited" (presumably edited only by the original publisher's editor or reproduced from a contemporary printing by a later editor) does not purport to serve this purpose. There is nothing similar about the two except that they are texts of the same piece of writing and that they are texts as opposed to apparatuses. If a reader wishes to consult the documentation which an apparatus provides and finds no apparatus accompanying his text, he may be somewhat inconvenienced by having to go to a library to examine a CEAA edition (text plus apparatus), but surely less so than if he had to collect the evidence himself with which to judge an "unedited" text.

58. If Pizer is concerned (as he seems to be in his proposal of "textual organicism," pp. 152-153) to preserve as a respectable possibility the idea of a collected set which includes some "definitive editions" along with some "practical editions" (to use Bowers's terms), all one can say is that there is no theoretical objection to it, so long as each text is clearly labeled for what it is.

editors, who thus "have increasingly participated in the creative process of their authors." He argues, in other words, that an author who expects or encourages certain kinds of alterations to be made in the publisher's offices must be said to prefer or "intend" the resulting text. "If an author," as Pizer concisely puts it, "within such a relationship and for whatever motives, accepts an editorial change or suggestion, his acceptance is the equivalent of a creative act, even though the act is the initial responsibility of an editor" (p. 148). The aim of Greg's theory, with which no scholarly editor would quarrel, is to establish the text which the author intended; and by concentrating on unmodernized texts it aims to establish the author's intended text in respect to accidentals as well as substantives. What constitutes the author's "intention" is of course the crucial question, and in answering it the editor must always depend, to a greater or lesser degree, on his critical insight. It is axiomatic that an author's own statements of his intention, when they exist, do not, for a variety of reasons, necessarily coincide with his actual intention—the only guide to which is the work itself. An author may acquiesce in his publisher's decisions and then rationalize his behavior; or he may genuinely be grateful for changes which make his work, in one way or another, more acceptable (and salable) to the public; or he may approve of alterations in many other kinds of situations—without truly believing that the result quite represents his own style or approach. What appears in a prepublication form of a text is normally a better representation of the author's habits than what appears in a first printing, and the text of a fair-copy manuscript or typescript reflects the author's intention, whether or not it turns out to be his final intention in every respect. It is true, as Pizer says, that choosing "an early copy-text encourages a frame of mind which requires later variants to 'prove themselves' as authorial rather than as editorial or printer's variants" (p. 149); but such would seem to be the safest course in most instances, since the author's responsibility for a later reading—especially in accidentals—is normally less certain than his responsibility for an early one.[59] Of course, such editorial caution may occasionally produce a text reflecting "an author's dis-

---

59. Pizer, in his footnote 5 (p. 148), gives the impression that he has not fully grasped Greg's central insight: that there is no reason to expect authority in substantives and authority in accidentals to reside in the same text. What Pizer says is that the "suspicion of later texts . . . affects the entire matter of the choice of copy-text while receiving explicit expression primarily in relation to accidentals." That is of course just the point: the potential authority of a later text in respect to substantives is in no way affected by the choice of an early text as the authority in accidentals.

carded rather than final intentions," but at least it reflects his, rather than someone else's, intentions. The editor's critical judgment—his literary taste exercised in the light of his intimate knowledge of the author and all known relevant external evidence—must finally determine the case; and there is nothing in Greg's theory to prevent him, on this basis, from deciding that the later variants have indeed "proved themselves." If, however, he starts from the assumption that the author and the publisher's editor are creative collaborators, he will, to be sure, produce an unmodernized text—in the sense that it reflects the author's period—but it may be far from the text which the author wished (finally, or at any other time).[60]

This question leads to a consideration of eclecticism, and Pizer's second point is that an eclectic text, incorporating later substantive readings into an earlier copy-text, violates the integrity (or "imaginative 'feel,' " as he calls it) of individual stages of an author's work. The result, which "may incorporate changes made by the author over many years," is, he says, "a text which never existed and which has little or no critical interest" (p. 150). Certainly it never existed, for a critical text by definition differs from any single extant documentary form of the text; but whether it is of critical interest depends on how well the editor has performed his task, for his aim is to produce a text which accords with the author's intention more fully than that of any given extant document or printing. The fact that an author may make alterations in a work over a long period of years does not necessarily mean that they reflect different conceptions of that work; when they do, then of course each version should be edited separately as a work in its own right (following the theory of copy-text with regard to each). But surely it blurs a critical distinction to insist that every revision "constitutes a distinctive work with its own aesthetic individuality and character" (p. 149).[61] What this argument leads toward, obviously, is the abandonment of the editor's critical function and the restriction of editing to the production of accurate facsimiles. It is somewhat puzzling that Pizer is reluctant to allow the scholarly editor to attempt

60. Pizer's sixth footnote (p. 148) recognizes this fact and is a more trenchant discussion of the issue than what appears in the body of his article: "I should note my awareness of the great range of variation possible within the publisher-author relationship and of the consequent need for editorial knowledge and discretion in determining the degree of authorial acceptance of a publisher's changes."

61. While it is possible to argue that the change of even a single word in a text produces a new work, critical discrimination has not advanced very far which makes no attempt to locate that point along the spectrum of revision where alterations to improve the expression of one conception give way to alterations that shift the conception itself.

a historical reconstruction of the author's intended text, when he is quite ready to believe that contributions of the original publisher's editor were accepted by the author as furthering his intentions. And it is paradoxical that a person who objects to the uniform editing of major and minor works for its failure to make "critical distinctions" ("which is what the study of literature is all about for most scholars and students") should disapprove of texts that involve an editor's critical judgment and should hesitate to offer to the public clear-text editions without apparatus, since they constitute "only the editor's beliefs about the author's final intentions" (p. 152). If, as he recognizes, editing is "in varying degrees an aesthetic enterprise," the "editor's beliefs" command respect to the extent that the editor is at once a careful historian and a sensitive critic; and the existence of insensitive editors casts no more doubt on the undertaking as a whole than the existence of obtuse literary critics does on the activity of literary analysis. When Pizer calls Greg's theory of copy-text " 'scientific' in its central impulse" because it "establishes a principle (albeit a flexible one) that is supposed to work in every instance" (p. 153), he disregards the fact that the principle is "flexible" for the very reason that it places no restriction on the operation of informed judgment.

In the months following the appearance of Pizer's article, several communications stimulated by it were published in the pages of the same journal. Norman Grabo, in April 1971, and Hershel Parker, at greater length in October, criticized Pizer's position.[62] Then in November John Freehafer, applauding Pizer, set forth what he considered to be three additional "major deficiencies of the CEAA editions."[63] It is significant that the deficiencies are said to be "of the CEAA editions" and not of Greg's theory, for what Freehafer objects to is not Greg's approach but the way it has been put into practice in CEAA editions, along with the decisions reflected in those editions about the kinds of material to be presented. His first two points are patently argumentative: the CEAA editions, he believes, exhibit "a failure to learn from the best editorial practice of the past," because the history of Shakespearean scholarship has shown that the "empty boasts" of an editor like Theobald prove in the long run to be of little substance

---

62. Grabo, "Pizer vs Copy-Text," *BNYPL*, 75 (1971), 171-173; Parker, "In Defense of 'Copy-Text Editing,' " 337-344. Bowers makes a few remarks on Pizer's article in "Multiple Authority" (cited in footnote 13 above), pp. 86-87 (footnote 11).

63. "How Not to Edit American Authors: Some Shortcomings of the CEAA Editions," *BNYPL*, 75 (1971), 419-423.

(whereas critical discussions, like Johnson's, are often of lasting value); and they demonstrate "a failure to present literary works as such" by not providing critical analyses[64] and explanatory notes, by being "almost totally concerned with bibliographical questions." The first point springs from the CEAA use of the word "definitive." As I have said before, this word was an ill-advised choice and has been too freely used; nevertheless, it should be clear to any reader of a CEAA apparatus, from its discussion of various problematical points, that CEAA editors are not claiming (nor did Greg expect editors following his rationale to be able to claim) that they have made all the right decisions and thus produced a "definitive" text; all they can aim for as a goal is to provide a definitive apparatus, recognizing that it is at least possible sometimes to establish facts. The decision to emphasize the history of the text (including the history of critical reaction to it) in CEAA introductions and afterwords is obviously related to this point, for those essays constitute another part of the apparatus, directed toward laying out what historical facts can be established.[65] That these editions are historically oriented, however, does not mean that they fail "to present literary works as such" but simply that they do not present literary works accompanied by any one critical interpretation.[66]

Freehafer's third point, however, raises an issue which deserves to be commented upon, even though what must be said is implicit in Greg's theory and will therefore seem redundant to some readers. He

64. Because Freehafer cites Hershel Parker's reply to Pizer in connection with this discussion, Parker makes a further brief comment in "Historical Introductions vs Personal Interpretations," *BNYPL*, 76 (1972), 19. Freehafer's statement that "those who cannot successfully criticize an author ought not to edit him" (p. 420) seems not to recognize editing as a critical activity itself; what constitutes "successful" criticism is of course an open question.

65. As for explanatory notes, the CEAA editions have not by any means uniformly excluded them, and the CEAA *Statement* encourages them for certain kinds of works. In any case, Freehafer's belief that an editor who does not provide explanatory notes will be less likely to detect, for example, errors in the spelling of proper names is merely questioning editorial competence in general; any responsible editor investigates the spelling of names of per-

sons and places as a routine part of his job, and, if he makes a mistake in a given instance, the fault surely cannot be traced to the fact that he was not obliged to write explanatory notes.

66. The view that the CEAA editions "will probably be looked upon in the future as a monument to a temporary overemphasis on an imperfectly borrowed and excessively bibliographical style of editing" (p. 421) is puzzling. The "bibliographical" emphasis is an emphasis on establishing the history of each text, and the CEAA editors could be charged with "excess" in this regard if they claimed that all future editions of these works should have the same emphasis; but it is odd to regard as "temporary overemphasis" the effort to put on record information which will be useful in the future for producing different kinds of editions with texts based on other principles.

complains that the CEAA editions have failed "to use Greg's theory of copy-text with sufficient boldness and imagination to reconstruct ideal authorial texts of many of the works being edited" (p. 419). In support of this proposition he cites the differences in the texture of accidentals between *The Scarlet Letter* and *The House of the Seven Gables* in the Ohio State edition, resulting from the fact that copy-text for the former is a first printing (the manuscript not having survived) and for the latter is a manuscript; these differences, he says, can be regarded as "valid reconstructions of the author's intentions . . . only on the incredible supposition that within a year Hawthorne turned from a passionate devotion to house-styling to a passionate rejection of it" (p. 422). What this argument fails to notice is that Greg's theory, as a scholarly procedure, must operate on the basis of the available materials for a given text and aims at reconstructing the author's intention insofar as surviving evidence permits. One can well believe, with Freehafer, that Hawthorne's preferences did not shift so drastically within a year. But can one therefore say that the features of one known manuscript would also have been those of another, now missing, manuscript from approximately the same time, and that an editor would on that basis know how to set about inserting those features into the text for which no manuscript survives? Answering No could perhaps be called unimaginative, but one should then add that to be more "imaginative" would be inconsistent with the scholarly goal of exercising critical judgment within the bounds set by ascertainable fact and documentary evidence. The belief that the accidentals in one CEAA text should be identical to those in another contemporary text by the same author stems from an assumption that the CEAA goal is to reconstruct the author's "intention" in an absolute sense, rather than in the more realistic sense of that intention for which there is documentary evidence for a particular work. Naturally the editor's knowledge of the author's practice in other works, for which a different range of documents exists, ought to play a role in any decision he makes; but it would be a rare instance indeed in which such knowledge was so certain and comprehensive that the editor could feel confident in his ability to repunctuate or respell for the author without introducing far more readings that never existed than those that did. Anyone who wishes to take a more "imaginative" approach and to interpolate the habits of one manuscript or a group of manuscripts into the texts of other works would of course be able to examine and utilize the evidence present in the texts and apparatuses of the relevant CEAA volumes. A second illustration of Freehafer's is again indicative of a fundamental misunderstanding of what kind of text the CEAA is attempting to provide. Turning to a different period, he cites two recent editions of Dryden's *The Indian Emperour* (one in the University of California Press *Works*, 1966, and the other in the University of Chicago *Four Tragedies*, 1967) and observes that, by selecting two different copy-texts, these editions present, even after editing, two very different texts. Since both attempt to reconstruct the author's intention, both should theoretically, he says, "have arrived at identical texts" which "agree word for word, letter for letter, comma for comma" (p. 422); that they do not so agree he attributes to an unimaginative use of Greg's theory, to "tyranny of the copy-text." But Greg, precisely because he recognized the role of imagination and judgment, would never have expected two editors to make all the same choices and emerge with identical texts. What the scholarly editor is striving to do is to put his critical judgment at the service of recogniz- ing what the author intended, and no one, including the CEAA editors, would claim that any one attempt at this is the final or "defini- tive" one. Freehafer's urging of a more imaginative use of Greg's rationale to produce an "author's ideal text" seems rather at odds with his criticism of the Ohio State Hawthorne, both here and in an earlier detailed discussion of *The Marble Faun*,[67] for making too many emendations; the existence of arguable emendations and variants sug- gests the impossibility of universal agreement on critical issues, and a more imaginative approach would not be likely to lessen the range of disagreement. Several times Freehafer speaks of "definitive texts"— not "definitive editions"—and in that earlier essay says that how defini- tive the Hawthorne edition is "largely depends upon how the editors

---

67. "*The Marble Faun* and the Editing of Nineteenth-Century Texts," *Studies in the Novel*, 2 (1970), 487-503. This article is a detailed review of the Ohio State edition of *The Marble Faun* and makes fewer general observations than the title might suggest. It represents the kind of close examination of a CEAA volume which has been all too infrequent, but for the most part it is concerned with the evaluation of particular emendations rather than with questions involving the use of Greg's rationale. One paragraph (pp. 498- 499), however, does say that, because Greg's theory seems to work in connection with *The Marble Faun* manuscript, it does not follow that the theory can be applied "to all fair-copy manuscripts of the nineteenth century," since certain authors (several are cited) are known not to have punc- tuated their manuscripts for publication and others (Henry James) are known to have carefully revised their punctuation for later editions. It should not be neces- sary to repeat that Greg's theory does not demand the use of manuscript as copy-text when there is convincing evidence favoring another course. Freehafer makes some of the same criticisms of the Hawthorne edi- tion, especially in regard to emendations resulting from a policy of "normalization," in his reviews of Hawthorne scholarship in *Jahrbuch für Amerikastudien*, 15 (1970), 293-294, and 16 (1971), 268-269.

have used their collations, concordances, and other data in establishing Hawthorne's texts" (p. 487); however, the distinction between a "critical" *text* and a "definitive" *edition* (which embodies such a text along with other information) cannot be overlooked if debates about these matters are to get anywhere. Pizer, too, in his response in December 1971 to Grabo and Parker,[68] reiterated the need for "flexibility" and for resistance to "the tidy and neat," apparently without recognizing that CEAA critical texts and their apparatuses reflect those qualities.

The same month saw the appearance of the first volume of *Proof*, which contained a long essay by Morse Peckham, "Reflections on the Foundations of Modern Textual Editing."[69] Peckham is the only critic of Greg's theory thus far to explain his criticisms in the context of a thoughtfully developed analysis of the nature of human communication. Most of the previous comments, as we have noticed, either arose from a misunderstanding of Greg or dealt with largely superficial matters; Peckham, on the other hand, attacks Greg's central assumptions by setting forth a view of human behavior incompatible with them. Although I shall try to show why his argument does not seem

68. " 'On the Editing of Modern American Texts': A Final Comment," *BNYPL*, 75 (1971), 504-505. Pizer has published remarks on CEAA editions or on Greg's theory in a number of other places. For example, he has commented unfavorably on the Crane edition in a review in *MP*, 68 (1970-71), 212-214, and in his survey of Crane scholarship in *Fifteen American Authors before 1900*, ed. R. A. Rees and E. N. Harbert (1971), p. 100 (the edition reflects "the present emphasis on critical texts and common sense be damned"). And his Rosenbach lecture, "Dreiser's Novels: The Editorial Problem" (published in *Theodore Dreiser Centenary*, 1971), asserts that Greg's theory, by causing editors to focus on that prepublication state which is "at once chronologically closest to the printed book and still completely sanctioned by the author" (p. 10), results in neglect of earlier prepublication states. A twentieth-century author, he says, "was more apt than his fellow novelist of a hundred years earlier to find that what appeared in a first edition was indeed what he wanted to appear in that edition" (p. 11); as a result, the real editorial problem becomes—for Dreiser, at any rate—"not

to determine his final intention but to use the material at hand to demonstrate how he reached that intention" (p. 12). Most editors, however, unless they have decided to edit a particular early version of a work, are inevitably concerned with "final intentions"; but that concern does not mean that their editions cannot include data relevant to a genetic study of the prepublication stages of the work, and indeed the CEAA *Statement* urges editors to include a record of at least the substantive pre-copy-text variants. (The principal difference between the two approaches is that Pizer prefers printing selected passages from earlier states as footnotes to the main text, whereas the CEAA *Statement* recommends a discussion, illustrated by quotations, of the nature of the various stages of prepublication revision.)

69. *Proof*, 1 (1971), 122-155. Peckham's ideas had earlier appeared, in compressed form, in the discussion of "General Textual Principles" in the first and second volumes of the Ohio University edition of Robert Browning (1969, 1970), pp. vii-ix; beginning with the third volume (1971) this section is somewhat expanded (pp. vii-xiii) and contains a reference to this *Proof* essay

to me to invalidate Greg's rationale, I hope it will be clear, at the same time, that Peckham is raising the kind of fundamental questions that have been too little discussed. His essay—aside from its examination of whether analytical bibliography can be regarded as "scientific"[70]—attacks Greg's theory in two respects: (1) it denies that substantives and accidentals can be meaningfully segregated; (2) it denies that the reconstruction of a text representing the author's intention is a meaningful (or attainable) goal. Although the argument supporting the first can be seen as consistent with and deriving from the larger propositions underlying the second, the first point can be taken up separately and is discussed first by Peckham.

The distinction between substantives and accidentals, Peckham says, was necessary to Greg because of the nature of the material he was dealing with: "the sparse and inconsistent punctuation in [Renaissance] dramatic manuscripts *that have survived*" (p. 124).[71] But, he adds, the distinction "is useless outside of his very special class of texts" (p. 125), because most later authors (and some Elizabethans as well) were aware that punctuation affects meaning and were not helpless victims of a house-style imposed by their publishers. Punctuation, he argues, does more than affect meaning, for, without punctuation, "it is frequently impossible to decide on that meaning":

Punctuation is not a form or dress of substantives, something different from words. It is part of speech. Juncture, pitch, and stress are inseparable components in the semantic continuum of the spoken language. Their signs are punctuation. (p. 124)

Thus "an educated author produces his punctuation as he produces his words; together they make up an unbroken semantic continuum." Clearly Peckham is correct in believing that no fixed line separates punctuation (or other "accidentals") from wording in the expression of meaning; and I am not aware of any editor who accepts Greg that would take issue with this point. But it does not therefore follow that

70. I have discussed this part of his essay in "Bibliography and Science," *SB*, 27 (1974), 55-89.

71. It is not clear, however, why "sparse and inconsistent" punctuation in itself justifies the separate treatment of substantives and accidentals. Similarly, Peckham states in the next paragraph, "Greg's distinction rests upon the fact . . . that nobody but Ben Jonson [among Renaissance dramatists] took writing for the public theater seriously" (p. 125). Does this imply that later writers of "serious" literature normally managed to exert careful control over the printed forms of their work? And does it imply that for works of later periods editing usually involves only the correction of obvious errors in a text which otherwise embodies the author's final wishes in every respect?

no practical distinction can be made between them. Greg, of course, insisted that he was concerned with a "practical," not a "philosophic," distinction; but Peckham finds illogical (because it does seem to claim a "philosophic" basis for the distinction) Greg's footnote in the "Rationale" which asserts that punctuation "remains properly a matter of presentation," despite the fact that it can affect meaning. Now that footnote, it must be admitted, is not written with Greg's characteristic clarity, but the point he was getting at (as the drift of his whole essay suggests) is not, in my opinion, illogical. A paraphrase might go something like this: "Although punctuation and spelling are, from a theoretical (or 'philosophic') point of view, inseparable from words in the written expression of meaning, in practice people (i.e., scribes, compositors, and even authors at times) do react to them as if they were somehow less significant." What Greg meant by a "practical" distinction is one which, however mistaken it may be, has in fact operated to govern human behavior; and, since the editor is concerned with analyzing the behavior of certain individuals, such a distinction may be useful to him. It is certainly true, as Peckham later points out (p. 145), that Elizabethan compositors felt freer to depart from the punctuation and spelling of their copy than later compositors. But does not a modern publisher's editor generally feel less compunction about inserting a comma than altering a word? Does not the author who acquiesces to a suggested change of punctuation more readily than to one of wording, or who believes that his punctuation but not his diction actually demands revision, feel that there is some sort of distinction? So long as one can say, "I think my quotation is accurate, though it may differ in a mark of punctuation here and there," and not be regarded by most people as uttering nonsense, one can believe that a "practical" distinction between the two does widely exist in people's minds. To the extent that punctuation and spelling are popularly regarded as distinct from what is being said—and it scarcely requires demonstration that they are, and have been, so regarded—the transmission of texts is correspondingly affected. However much an editor may deplore the confusion behind this attitude (analogous to the popular oversimplification of the relation between form and content), it is his business to take into account, as realistically as he can, the factors that influence textual transmission. (Of course, some accidentals do have less effect upon meaning than others: a comma marking a phrase-ending that would be recognized even without the comma serves less purpose than one which marks the beginning of a nonrestrictive clause. But no definite line separates this second type of accidental, sometimes called "semi-substantives," from the first, which also, though more subtly, may affect the sense.) What I take Greg to be saying, then, is that the editor distinguishes substantives and accidentals not because he believes that he is making a valid conceptual distinction between two elements in written language but because the distinction is one which is likely to have been made by the persons who have been involved in the transmission of any given text (and which therefore may be useful in segregating different features of that text which may have been accorded different treatment).

Obviously Greg does not expect an editor to be bound by this distinction in his own thinking, for he makes no requirement that the editor always accept the accidentals of a first edition or that he always accept all the accidentals of whatever text he selects as copy-text. He merely observes that, given the popular tendency to be less careful with accidentals than with substantives, more of the author's accidentals are likely to be present in a first edition than in later editions. And, of course, the whole point of attempting to recover the author's accidentals is that they do indeed constitute an important part of his expression. The distinction between substantives and accidentals has no influence on what an editor decides to do when he believes that he has convincing reasons for doing a particular thing,[72] but when he does not have such reasons, the distinction enables him to make a decision in accord with what common experience shows to be a widespread attitude (one which is thus likely to have been operative in any given instance).[73] Although English spelling has become more fixed over the centuries and styles of punctuation have altered, I see no evidence that the popular conception of spelling and punctuation as the accouterments of words has shifted[74]—or any reason, therefore, not to find

---

72. When Peckham says that "what to do about punctuation is an empirical matter, not a theoretical matter, not a matter of editorial principles or rules" (p. 126), he is actually agreeing with Greg's position that each situation must be examined on its own terms; Greg was providing a "rule" only for those situations in which empirical evidence does not convincingly settle the question.

73. Of course, errors are made in the transmission of substantives as well as accidentals. David J. Nordloh, in "Substantives and Accidentals vs. New Evidence: Another Strike in the Game of Distinc-

tions," *CEAA Newsletter*, No. 3 (June 1970), pp. 12-13, cites an instance in which a substantive variant between a manuscript and a magazine text can be shown to have resulted from a typist's error in the intervening typescript. It may be that without the typescript an editor would have taken the magazine reading as the one intended by the author; but the existence of such instances does not affect the general proposition that substantives as a class have normally received more careful treatment in transmission than accidentals.

74. Peckham's recollection of having heard, as a boy, stories about the serious

Greg's approach applicable to later writings. Greg's choice of the terms "substantive" and "accidental" was, as I have said before, unfortunate, and the fun which Peckham has with them, calling them "strangely medieval," is deserved; there would have been fewer misunderstandings (and certainly fewer complaints about unnecessary jargon) if, as Peckham suggests, plain terms like "words," "punctuation," and "spelling" had been employed. But surely the point Greg was getting at is not completely hidden behind the terms he chose.[75]

Peckham's principal argument, however, deals not with accidentals but with the concepts of "text" and "author." He believes that many literary scholars—including Greg and his followers, who attempt to establish the author's intended text—are guilty of literary hagiolatry, exalting the ideas of "author" and "work of art" in ways not consistent with the nature of human communication. An author, he says, is simply an organism which produces utterances, not as a result of any special inspiration but as a result of being human:

A writer produces utterances because he is a human being. It is a condition of being human. We do not know why human beings produce utterances, nor even how. It is a primitive, or surd, with which we begin and, to make matters worse, within which we must operate. To talk about self-expression, or projections, or mental ideas being expressed in language, is at worst to cover up our ignorance with pseudo-explanations, and at best to use a

---

consequences of incorrect punctuation in government documents (p. 125) does not really illustrate any common awareness "that punctuation cannot be separated from words," for the point of telling such stories is that the situations involved are exceptional and contradict everyday experience. Similarly, the "shift from rhetorical to syntactical punctuation in the first half of the nineteenth century" is not convincing evidence of such an awareness; both approaches support Peckham's view that punctuation consists of written signs for juncture, pitch, and stress and thus is part of the meaning, but he does not make clear why the *shift* from one to the other reflects a general awareness of this point.

75. One further observation of Peckham's on accidentals deserves notice. A logical consequence of his view that accidentals and substantives are inseparable is to deplore the absence of accidentals variants

in the historical collations in CEAA volumes. The CEAA *Statement* naturally does not prohibit their inclusion; but it is undeniable that their absence springs not merely from the great expense that would be incurred in most cases by listing them but also from the emphasis of Greg's theory itself on the lack of significance of post-copy-text accidentals. As Peckham points out, a record of variants in accidentals would be important for the historical study of punctuation, and in addition, of course, it would give the reader a still fuller picture of the evidence which the editor had at his disposal. My own view is that variants in accidentals ought to be included whenever feasible (and particularly when the copy-text is a manuscript); but the time and money involved may in many—perhaps most—instances seem out of proportion to the amount of use that would be made of such information. See also footnote 35 above.

verbal category to subsume the production of language and the production
of nonverbal behavior.   (p. 139)

But the author is different from other utterers in that he assembles a
series of utterances into what "he judges to be a discourse" and makes
this series available to others, proposing "that they too judge it to be
a discourse" (p. 138). The development of the discourse up to that
point has involved a combination of producing utterances and changing (or revising) them;[76] thus the author, even before his work becomes
public, has already been in the position of looking back over something previously written, reacting to it as a reader, since he is not at
that moment the producer. This process, Peckham argues, continues
indefinitely: sometimes   other   human   beings   (such   as   publishers'
editors) react to and change the discourse, and sometimes the author
continues to change it. Each is responding to a particular version, and
each "can make a change acceptable to the author or to anyone else
involved" (p. 141). The "textual editor" is but one more human
organism in this sequence, producing one more version of "a *postulated* work, that is, of a construct" (p. 128). Whether a valid distinction can be made between changes by the author and by others, therefore, turns on

the question of whether the author is an organism engaged in the production of utterances, an activity which as a human organism he cannot avoid,
even when alone and engaged in covert utterance, or whether he is an
individual. So far there have appeared no grounds, save linguistic hyposta-
tization and literary hagiolatry, for considering him an individual. The
notion to be understood here is that he is but an organism and not an
individual or monad or entity which can be differentiated from other
similar entities.   (p. 143)

As a result, one cannot speak meaningfully of a single ideal "text" of
a work; if the development of the concept of individuality ("self-
mediated divergence from a cultural norm") had not caused the editor
to confer "sainthood" on the supposed "author" and exalt certain
works as canonical (p. 149), he would realize that he is "simply continuing an activity initiated by the author" (p. 144).

Although this is a greatly simplified summary of Peckham's analysis,
I think that it does not distort the main outlines of his position. But
one does not have to disagree with this general position in order to

---

76. Peckham uses the word "change" as
more neutral than "revise," for he is under
the impression that " 'revise' now generally
means to change for the better" (pp. 138-
139).

believe that such editors as those of the CEAA volumes are pursuing a sensible, meaningful, and useful goal. The "textual editor" whom Peckham describes—he defines the term as subsuming "both analytical bibliographer and textual critic" (p. 141)—is naturally, in Peckham's general terms, just another person making changes in a text; but it would seem to be more illuminating to go on and note how he is to be distinguished from others who do that. For persons who make changes in pieces of writing—and are admittedly engaging in basically similar actions—fall into two groups, those performing scholarly editing and those performing what may be called "creative editing."[77] There is no reason why one cannot regard a piece of writing as the common product of all beings who have come in contact with it and reacted to it; when it is viewed in this way, any change, made at any time, whether by the original publisher's editor, by the author, or by a later "editor," has the same status and may be judged to have improved the work, harmed it, or left it the same. From this point of view a critic is not performing his function conscientiously if he does not alter the work to make it, according to his standards, more satisfying than it has ever been before. There is, as I say, no objection to this proce- dure—so long as one's goal is critically rather than historically oriented. But the scholar sets a goal of historical reconstruction.[78] That the "author" has some individuality is suggested, even in Peckham's approach, by the recognition that he *initiated* the discourse, which is then operated upon by himself and others. If that discourse is of sufficient interest, a historical interest may also attach to the initiator; and if the same being initiates a number of such discourses, the interest may be correspondingly greater. What the scholarly editor attempts— recognizing the difficulty of the task and even the impossibility of its absolute achievement—is to remove from the discourse those features for which the initiator was not responsible.[79] The result is not neces-

77. As I called it in "Textual Study and Literary Judgment," *PBSA*, 65 (1971), esp. 113-114. I do not mean that "scholarly" editing is not also creative in a general sense but am using "creative editing" as a shorthand way of referring to editing which has a different aim from that of his- torical reconstruction. Lewis Leary, who uses the term in "Troubles with Mark Twain," *Studies in American Fiction*, 2 (1974), does not, in my view, sufficiently distinguish between the editor who adopts a reading which seems "best" to him and the editor who selects what he thinks

would have been regarded as "best" by the author.

78. In the section of his essay on analy- tical bibliography and science (pp. 129-136), Peckham recognizes that the analytical bib- liographer is a historian; see Tanselle, "Bibliography and Science" (cited in foot- note 70 above), pp. 83-87.

79. Whether one is attempting to recon- struct his first, or last, or some other, intention is an important matter but is beside the point until one grants the goal

sarily what the editor himself prefers but what he believes to be the author's contribution to a given discourse. The scholarly editor is thus a different kind of responder from the others in the chain Peckham is talking about; it may be that the editor, if he lives in the mid-twentieth century, cannot avoid reacting in part in mid-twentieth-century terms, but his aim is to use his critical faculties[80] to place himself in the frame of reference of the author and the author's environment. That such an aim is impossible of full attainment does not invalidate it as a guideline for a direction in which to move, despite Peckham's labeling of this attitude as "pure hagiolatry" (p. 138).[81]

The difficulty with accepting Peckham's statement of the case is evident when he remarks that the concepts of "text" and "author" require the "textual editor" to "produce a definitive edition, which he cannot do, instead of producing a new version more satisfactory for some specific purpose than any existing version, which he can do" (p. 151). What Peckham says the editor can do is in fact what CEAA editors do (and realize they are doing): they produce a critical (not definitive) text which they believe to be more satisfactory for the purpose of the historical study of literature than any previous text,

---

of reconstructing authorial intention of some sort. The question of "original" versus "final" intentions is helpfully illustrated by examples from Melville in Hershel Parker's "Melville and the Concept of 'Author's Final Intentions,'" *Proof*, 1 (1971), 156-168.

80. When Peckham says that "textual editing" is "logically independent of problems of aesthetics" (p. 136), he means that the artistic status of a work (whether or not it is generally considered to be an effective work of art) has nothing to do with the process of editing the work. But that does not mean that critical or aesthetic judgment is not involved in the editor's assessment of the evidence. At another point (p. 151) Peckham states, "The notions of text and author have been responsible for the fact that a discipline which came into existence as a reaction against textual eclecticism has returned to textual eclecticism"; but the more likely explanation would seem to be simply the growing recognition that it is foolish to attempt

to eliminate critical judgment from historical research.

81. Let me repeat: I recognize that Peckham is asserting the essential identity of all "editorial" actions and that the scholarly editor I am speaking of cannot avoid, in Peckham's terms, producing his own version of a work. I am not disagreeing with Peckham on this point but am trying to show that there are valid discriminations to be made nevertheless among the versions produced and that it is not meaningless to regard some as approaching more closely than others to an "authorial" version, even if what is "authorial" must be to some extent a subjective judgment. (A "critical" edition, of course, by definition involves an editor's inferences about authorial intention, as Bowers makes clear by using the word "inferential" in his description of an editor's aim as "an attempt to approximate as nearly as possible an inferential authorial fair copy"—in "Textual Criticism" [cited in footnote 30 above], p. 33.)

and they regard the edition embodying that text as "definitive" only in its recording of certain classes of data. Part of the problem, throughout the essay, is Peckham's interchangeable use of "text" and "edition" and his belief that CEAA editors really think they are producing definitive *texts*.[82] Perhaps, indeed, this is the fundamental problem, for his concluding section (pp. 153-155), recognizing that the "textual editor" may decide to produce a text representing any given stage in the history of a work, goes on to assert, "No misplaced confidence in inadequately based theory can justify his evasion of the problems of an empirical situation." But when one observes that Greg's approach is an attempt to confront the empirical realities involved in the reconstruction of a particular stage in the history of a work and that it does not proclaim the result to be the only useful text of the work (even for historical study), the issue Peckham raises is no longer an issue. It seems to me that Peckham's final description of "the task of the textual editor" is—after one has penetrated the vocabulary—accurate:

to produce a new version from a series of a postulated text by a postulated author by making up for the policing, validating, and changing deficiencies in the long, complex, and interlocking series of behaviors the consequence of which was the production of that series.   (p. 155)

But when he proceeds to say that there is no definitive version to be arrived at and "no one set of instructions" to follow, he is responding to a nonexistent argument. Much of Peckham's essay helpfully focuses on the nature of written language, and his suggestion that editors ought to be aware of the nonliterary uses to which their apparatuses can be put (as in a study of human behavior) is worth serious consideration; but as a critique of Greg's "Rationale" and the CEAA editions, it misses the mark.

During the following year (1972) there appeared two books with general-sounding, but somewhat misleading, titles, James Thorpe's *Principles of Textual Criticism* and Philip Gaskell's *A New Introduction to Bibliography*. Each raises some questions, either explicitly or implicitly, about the validity of CEAA procedures—questions which, by this time, seem very familiar. Thorpe's most direct comment on the CEAA—a brief discussion of its *Statement*—is related to his underlying belief that textual criticism has become too bibliographical in approach and that bibliographers are trying to make textual criticism

---

82. Their whole approach shows their recognition of the impossibility of a defini-tive *text*, even though they, too, sometimes contribute to the confusion by an imprecise use of the words "text" and "edition."

a "science." Despite his assemblage of quotations intended to serve as background, these issues are in fact illusory: for the leading bibliographers over the years have recognized that textual criticism can never be mechanical and that bibliography is simply one tool among several useful in dealing with textual problems.[83] Thorpe paints a picture of bibliographers greedy to annex the whole "province of textual criticism," as he calls it; but whether the present emphasis of textual criticism is excessively bibliographical is a question that cannot be approached in general or theoretical terms but only in relation to the details of specific situations. After all, if bibliography offers one kind of evidence to the textual critic, he cannot sensibly say that he desires only so much, and no more, of that kind of evidence; but if his attention to those details causes him in a particular case to neglect his search for letters or documents or other kinds of external evidence, then obviously he can be criticized in that instance for undue concentration on one type of evidence. What Thorpe tries to argue, however, is that the CEAA *Statement*, by requiring attention to bibliographical details, implies such attention to be "the efficient cause of an ideal edition" (p. 72).[84] The *Statement*, he believes, reflects "the view of a text as a system of infinitely perfectible details, by which scrupulous attention to all details will ultimately yield ideal results" (p. 57). Although he does not wish "to suggest that meticulous care is pedantry" (p. 76), he does suggest that close analysis of what seem to be unimportant variants is a waste of time (e.g., p. 74). He does not acknowledge the fact that laborious collation of texts[85] and analysis

83. I have commented in somewhat more detail on these parts of Thorpe's argument in "Bibliography and Science" (cited in footnote 70 above), pp. 78-80. Thorpe devotes an entire chapter, "The Province of Textual Criticism" (pp. 80-104), to setting forth the view that the "bibliographical orientation" of textual criticism is excessive; and his discussion of textual criticism as a "science" occupies the second section (pp. 57-68) of his chapter on "The Ideal of Textual Criticism" (this chapter was originally read on 8 February 1969 at a Clark Library Seminar and published that same year, along with a paper by Claude M. Simpson, Jr., in a pamphlet entitled *The Task of the Editor*, pp. 1-32).

84. Thorpe believes that the title *Statement of Editorial Principles* should be "Statement of Editorial Methodology"

(p. 73), and he takes the title to be indicative of a confusion between aims and techniques. Actually the CEAA pamphlet deals with both, as the title of the 1972 revised edition (*Statement of Editorial Principles and Procedures*) attempts to indicate.

85. Thorpe is correct in saying that "actual collations never provide more than some facts on which the trained intelligence can work" (p. 73); but the point he misses in the *Statement*'s remark that relevance is decided by collation is simply the fact that external evidence (e.g., an author's statement that a particular edition is a piracy) must be tested by what appears in the text itself (e.g., the presence or absence of differences that could reasonably be regarded as authorial revisions). See footnote 27 above.

of variants accomplish just as much when they demonstrate the absence of significant variants—or the presence of variants only in "the relatively trivial matters of spelling, punctuation, and capitalization" (p. 51)[86]—as when they show the existence of dramatically different readings. And no editor that I have heard of ever claimed that "scrupulous attention" to details and "meticulous care" are "a complete substitute for intelligence and common sense" (p. 78).[87] One must agree with Thorpe's later insistence (pp. 179-183) on the importance of a thorough knowledge of the author's works and period and of a diligent search for external evidence. But there is nothing inherent in the attention to bibliographical detail which prevents an editor from giving attention to other essential matters. The CEAA *Statement* does set forth the importance of accuracy in collating and proofreading, but it also points out the necessity for knowing the author's works and for searching out all relevant documents bearing on the history of a text[88]—and the CEAA editions have repeatedly been responsible for the uncovering of new documents and the assembling of comprehensive collections of reference material. An editor who neglects any part of his duty is open to criticism, and Thorpe's conclusion that editors should exploit "every kind of relevant evidence" (p. 79) is unexceptionable; but his belief that the "strongly bibliographical cast" (p. 103) of the CEAA *Statement* leads to a "glorification of method" (p. 79) rests on the fallacious assumption that attention to one kind of detail necessarily involves the neglect of other kinds. Some editors may of course be guilty of neglecting evidence, but it seems perverse to search for the cause of their incompetence in their careful attention to one kind of relevant detail.

86. If Peckham needs evidence that people still do react differently to accidentals than to substantives, Thorpe's statement here (and elsewhere, as on p. 74) provides a good illustration. Philip Young, like Thorpe, seems to judge the worth of editorial labor by how dramatically the text is altered, when he remarks that he "cannot find a single really significant difference between the new text [Ohio State *Scarlet Letter*] and that of the Riverside Edition (1883), regularly referred to in the bibliographies as Standard" ("Hawthorne and 100 Years: A Report from the Academy," *Kenyon Review*, 27 [1965], 215-232; reprinted as "Centennial, or the Hawthorne Caper," in *Three Bags Full* [1972], pp. 79-98). Young's discussion fails to recognize that what he regards as insignificant may appear significant to another critic and that the evidence, whatever it is, should be available in print for all to consult.

87. This statement occurs in a paragraph which was not present in the 1969 published version of this chapter.

88. The CEAA *Statement* does not take a great deal of space to make this point, nor does Thorpe, who says, "The sources of such information are so various that it is hardly worth mentioning any, except as examples" (p. 181).

A more consequential matter which Thorpe takes up is the treatment of accidentals (pp. 131-170).[89] After providing a sampling of statements from authors of various periods, stressing their indifference to accidentals, and a historical survey of printers' manuals, suggesting that printers over the years have felt an obligation to "correct" accidentals, Thorpe concludes that "probably in most cases" the author "expected the printer to perfect his accidentals" and that therefore "the changes introduced by the printer can be properly thought of as fulfilling the writer's intentions" (p. 165). It seems to me that there are two basic difficulties with Thorpe's position. The first is that quotations from authors and from printers' manuals are not comparable, because the former are statements of personal opinion (often prompted by specific situations), while the latter are public announcements of recommended general practice. Thus Thorpe's evidence from the printers' manuals[90] is sufficient to show that printers have widely regarded the alteration of accidentals in copy as part of their function; but his evidence from individual writers by no means can be generalized upon to suggest that in any given instance the chances favor an author's having been indifferent to the handling of accidentals. The conclusion would seem to follow—contrary to Thorpe—that, without convincing evidence on the other side, an author's manuscript stands a better chance of reflecting his wishes in accidentals than does a printed text. Here the second difficulty arises—in Thorpe's conception of an author's "intention." In his opening chapter—his well-known essay on "The Aesthetics of Textual Criticism"[91]—he asserts, "While the author cannot dictate the meaning of the text, he certainly has final authority over which words constitute the text of his literary work" (p. 10). As a result of this distinction between "meaning" and "words," Thorpe tends to accept at face value an author's statement about wording, without focusing on the fact that the motivations influencing such a statement may be just as complex as those lying behind a statement of intended "meaning." Although he recognizes that, in the absence of an authorial statement, the intended wording must be arrived at through a critical analysis of all available evidence (p. 193),

89. This chapter is an expanded version of a paper read at the University of Kansas on 30 April 1971 and published later that year as a pamphlet entitled *Watching the Ps & Qs: Editorial Treatment of Accidentals.*

90. Additional evidence of the freedom with which nineteenth-century compositors altered accidentals is offered in two of James B. Meriwether's contributions to the *CEAA Newsletter*: "House-Styling, Vintage 1856," No. 3 (June 1970), pp. 11-12; "'On Careless Punctuation,'" No. 5 (December 1972), p. 3.

91. Originally published in *PMLA*, 80 (1965), 465-482.

at various points he implies that the existence of a statement settles the matter—as when he says that "the personal testimony by the author as to his intentions is plainly the most primary textual evidence that there can be" (p. 109).[92] This point of view leads to an uncritical acceptance of an author's remarks about his indifference to accidentals (or his preference for those in the printed text). The upshot of Thorpe's discussion is his astonishing recommendation that "the editor will do best to spend only a modest amount of his time on accidentals— mainly a losing cause—and devote himself to matters of substance" (p. 168). It is difficult to reconcile Thorpe's readiness to believe that an author preferred the printer's accidentals with his strict view of "the integrity of the work of art" (pp. 14-32); and it is hard to see how an editor whose aim is to establish the author's intended text, in acci- dentals as well as in substantives,[93] can justify the decision in advance to spend a "modest" amount of time on the accidentals. Like the earlier discussion of bibliographical detail, this chapter on accidentals reflects a peculiar view of scholarly endeavor: it suggests, in effect, that a scholar's sense of perspective is shown less by his ability to evaluate and integrate data than by his prior decision to limit his consideration of certain clearly relevant areas.[94]

92. Thorpe's position on this question is criticized by Peckham, who points out (p. 152) that "intention" about past events must inevitably be a reconstruction, for which an author's statement is only one piece of evidence. In an essay called "The Intentional? Fallacy?", included in *The Triumph of Romanticism* (1970), Peckham states the point more fully: "Briefly, an inference of intention is a way of account- ing for or explaining the generation of an utterance; it can never be a report. The speaker of an utterance has greater author- ity than anybody else in his so-called inten- tional inference only because he is likely to have more information for framing his historical construct, *not* because he gener- ated the utterance" (p. 441). See also foot- note 81 above.

93. Although Thorpe says, "The basic principle is that the author's intentions with respect to accidentals should be car- ried out" (p. 198), he also asserts, at the end of the same paragraph, "Whether the text should be presented in old-spelling or

in modernized accidentals is mainly a mat- ter of convenience for the intended audi- ence"—as if there is no contradiction in- volved. He surveys the arguments for and against modernizing accidentals on pp. 134- 140 and pp. 169-170 and concludes, "I can say that the losses from modernization seem to me less than most textual scholars assume" (p. 170). Nevertheless, despite his reluctance to distinguish clearly the pur- poses and implications of the two kinds of texts, the primary focus is on the author's own wishes: "Our task is, I believe, to fulfill the intentions of the writer in these small details [accidentals] as well as in greater matters" (p. 165).

94. For Bowers's criticism of Thorpe's po- sition, see footnote 6 in "The New Look in Editing," *South Atlantic Bulletin*, 35 (1970), 8; for Peckham's, see *Proof*, 1 (1971), 122, 135-138, 152. See also the re- views by John Feather, in *MLR*, 68 (1973), 381-382, David J. Nordloh, in *Resources for American Literary Study*, 3 (1973), 254- 257, and G. R. Proudfoot, in *Library*, 5th ser., 28 (1973), 77-78.

If Thorpe's book, weakened by such contradictions, does not manage to serve the useful function of fairly surveying "the basic principles which underlie the practice of textual criticism" (p. vii), neither does Philip Gaskell's chapter on "Textual Bibliography" (pp. 336-360) in *A New Introduction to Bibliography* provide the kind of basic summary of current thinking which one might expect of an "introduction." Although his exposition of "Copy-Text" (pp. 338-343) does not specifically mention Greg's rationale, he does provide an accurate statement of its general application, with one important exception.[95] He is unwilling to push that rationale to its logical conclusion and recognize that a fair-copy manuscript, when it survives, becomes the copy-text, except when there is convincing evidence pointing toward the first (or some later) edition as the proper choice.[96] His argument rests on the same assumption as Thorpe's:

Most authors, in fact, expect their spelling, capitalization, and punctuation to be corrected or supplied by the printer, relying on the process to dress

95. Bowers, in his review of Gaskell, "McKerrow Revisited," *PBSA*, 67 (1973), 109-124, speaks of Gaskell's "rejection of Greg's classic theory of copy-text" (p. 122). But Gaskell does not reject it totally: his explanation of the difference between substantives and accidentals and of the reason for choosing an early text as authority for accidentals is obviously derived from Greg. What Gaskell rejects is the logical extension back to the manuscript of the steps that led to the choice of the first edition over a later edition as copy-text. Cf. my review in *Costerus*, n.s. 1 (1974).

96. The separate question of whether different versions of a work exist, each deserving to be edited separately from different copy-texts, is touched on by Gaskell in a somewhat confusing way. Near the beginning of the chapter he calls it "an anomaly of bibliographical scholarship today" that "much effort is expended" on editing works "of which the early texts differ from each other only in minor and frequently trivial ways," while "books of which we have texts in several widely different forms are either avoided by editors or edited in a single version" (p. 337). If "single version" means one of the author's versions, the process would seem to be what the situation probably calls for; if it means (as

the context suggests) an eclectic or "critical" text, one would have to say that such a text might be, but would not necessarily be, inappropriate—depending on the way in which the forms of the work are "widely different," whether as a result of a large number of changes or as a result of the nature of what changes there are. That Gaskell is thinking primarily in quantitative terms is shown later in the chapter. In discussing authorial revision of printed texts (p. 341), he states that the first edition remains the copy-text, provided that the author did not revise the punctuation and provided that "the revision [of substantives] is not extensive (say no more than a word or two in each paragraph)." Similarly, after describing the extensive revisions of *Pamela* (citing 8400 changes in the first two volumes of the last version), he asserts, "Here it would obviously be impossible for an editor to incorporate the first, the intermediate, and the final versions of the novel in a single critical text" (p. 342). Maybe so, but the reason is not the sheer number of changes; for only the nature of the differences, and not merely their quantity, can justify regarding two versions of a work as, in effect, separate works. I discuss this point further in my forthcoming article on "The Editorial Problem of Final Authorial Intention."

the text suitably for publication, implicitly endorsing it (with or without further amendment) when correcting proofs.   (p. 339)

He concludes that it "would normally be wrong, therefore, rigidly[97] to follow the accidentals of the manuscript, which the author would himself have been prepared—or might have preferred—to discard" and asserts that "in most cases the editor will choose as copy-text an early printed edition, not the manuscript" (p. 340). Later, he reiterates that "the manuscript if it survives, will be consulted but will not be followed in accidentals unless the compositor appears to have misrepresented the author's intentions" (p. 358). Although he allows for situations in which the manuscript is the proper choice, he places the presumption of authority with the first printed text. I have already commented on the difficulties of maintaining such a position, but I should perhaps call attention to the way in which Gaskell's wording itself reveals some of them. To say that an author is "implicitly endorsing" the accidentals of the proofs when he lets them stand is not at all the same as to say that he prefers them, and it ignores the economic (and other) factors which may have influenced his decision; similarly, to believe that an author "would himself have been prepared . . . to discard" the accidentals of his manuscript is not the same as to believe that he wished to discard them, and it surely does not give an editor license to carry out that discarding. Gaskell asserts that the accidentals of a first edition, despite "the process of normalization carried out in the printing house," will "still be closer both to the text that the author wanted, and to the reading of his manuscript, than the altered accidentals of the second and third editions" (p. 340). This statement is true, but the reference to manuscript readings undermines the general argument: if there is any desirability in having the accidentals resemble those of the manuscript, then the manuscript ought to be chosen for copy-text in the first place; on the other hand, if the author's preference is for the first-edition readings, then the manuscript is irrelevant in this context. Gaskell raises further doubts in the reader's mind by citing the example of Thomas Hardy, who, "in revising his printed texts for new editions, appears to have changed the normalized accidentals back to the forms of the original manuscript" (p. 342). Even though Hardy may not be a typical case, his revision illustrates the point that a writer may acquiesce in printing- or publishing-house styling without preferring it. Is not the more reasonable approach,

97. Of course, "rigidly" prejudices the case, since an editor who "rigidly" followed the manuscript, or any other text, without regard for the specific evidence involved would plainly be in the wrong.

then, to presume, until contrary evidence is adduced, that a manuscript reflects the author's intentions in accidentals, rather than to begin with the presumption that it does not?

A further confusion is introduced by the argument that an author's accidentals may stand in need of correction. Gaskell doubts "whether it is worth preserving thoroughly bad punctuation just because it is the author's" (p. 358) and later advises, "Let us carry out the author's intentions wherever we can, but not to the extent of taking pride in reproducing the manifest inadequacies of his accidentals" (p. 359). But punctuation which seems "bad" to the editor may have seemed appropriate to the author; and if the editor's aim is to preserve what the author wrote, rather than his own "improvements" upon it, he cannot very well say that he will pursue the author's intention only up to a point, and no farther. Gaskell's belief that "an editor may reasonably aim at consistency in his final version" (p. 358) suggests that he is thinking of a modernized text,[98] although most of his comments seem to be concerned with editions that aim to recover the author's intentions. At any rate, it is true that his discussion never focuses on the differences in purpose between modernized and unmodernized texts:

Printed accidentals are unlikely to have had more than the general approval of the author, and if they seem to be both unsatisfactory and in contravention of the author's usual practice, the editor will have to emend them. (Whether he will emend them according to the conventions of the author's period or to those of his own is something else which he will have to decide.)   (p. 360)

The illogic of this passage results from the fact that two kinds of editions are being talked about simultaneously. Since "unsatisfactory" accidentals may not be "in contravention of the author's usual practice," the editor is being instructed here to emend only those "unsatisfactory" accidentals which are not characteristic of the author, thus producing a partially regularized, but not modernized, text. But when he has done that, he does not still have open to him the option of

---

98. That regularizing or normalizing amounts to modernizing has been made clear by Hershel Parker in "Regularizing Accidentals: The Latest Form of Infidelity," *Proof*, 3 (1973), 1-20. Furthermore, as he says in his cogent concluding section on the dangers of modernizing, "Normalizing to satisfy an editor's instinct for tidiness or to make smooth the way of a reader is ultimately demeaning for the editor and insulting to the reader." I have made some further comments on regularizing in "Bibliographical Problems in Melville," *Studies in American Fiction*, 2 (1974), 57-74, and in "The New Editions of Hawthorne and Crane," *Book Collector*, 23 (1974), 214-229.

emending "according to the conventions . . . of his own" period—that is, of modernizing. After all, there would be no point in selecting the readings in need of emendation on the basis of whether they are uncharacteristic of the author and then to emend them on the basis of present-day practice. Either the editor decides to establish, as accurately as he can, the author's own accidentals; or he decides to make all the accidentals conform to the practice of his own time. The fact that the former approach is necessary for scholarly (that is, historical) study does not, of course, mean that there may not be occasions on which the latter is more appropriate. But the failure to distinguish carefully between the two cannot lead to clear thinking about editorial problems. It is unfortunate that Gaskell's discussion gives the impression of describing (as one would expect an "introduction" to describe) current generally accepted practice; beginners who turn to it for guidance will be puzzled and misled.[99]

This account of the CEAA's application of Greg's rationale to American literature and of the critical reaction to it suggests several observations. To begin with, one must recognize that, when Wilson expressed surprise at the "violence and venom" of the correspondence

99. A third book of a general and introductory nature which appeared in 1972 is F. W. Bateson's *The Scholar-Critic: An Introduction to Literary Research*. Although not limited to bibliographical and textual matters, as Thorpe and Gaskell are, it contains a chapter on "Textual Criticism" (pp. 126-146) which belittles the " 'biblio-textual' school" of Greg and his followers (for supposedly attempting to eliminate literary judgment from editing) and endorses modernized texts. His argument for modernization seems strangely inconsistent with his own general position. He begins by labeling as a fallacy the view that "the ability to compose great literature necessarily carries with it the ability to spell and punctuate it correctly" (p. 139). But he later makes the sensible distinction between "good English" and "correct English," and it would seem that the attempt to enforce "correct" punctuation (by whatever standard) on an author's work would reveal as petty an attitude as to wish that he had been more "correct," and perhaps less effective, in his wording. And if printed literature is to be considered a recorded form of oral language—as Bateson describes it in "Modern Bibliography and the Literary Artifact," in *English Studies Today*, 2nd ser. (1961), pp. 67-77, from which part of this chapter is drawn—it would seem that punctuation would have to be regarded as an inextricable part of the effort to convey nuances of meaning in print. When he recommends that accidentals "should always be modernized" except when "such a process affects the meaning" (p. 142), it does not seem unreasonable to conclude that his statement amounts to saying that accidentals should never *be* modernized. That we can understand Shakespeare without reading him in his own pronunciation—a point cited by Bateson in support of his position—is irrelevant; for, while the pronunciation of words does not, within limits, seriously affect their meaning, the way in which we are directed to speak them by the punctuation does frequently affect it. (Bateson has also expressed his view of modernizing in a letter to the *TLS*, 1 January 1971, pp. 14-15.)

aroused by his article, he was calling attention to characteristics which have unfortunately been manifested by a number of persons in this debate, on both sides. It may be gratifying to some editors to find that people care enough about editing to become emotionally involved in theoretical discussions, but scholarship is not advanced by arguments which rest on preconceptions or vested interests or clashes of personality. There can be no doubt that some of this debate has sunk to that level, and the opponents of CEAA policy are not the only ones at fault. What is particularly unfortunate is that so much time and energy has been poured into arguments about superficial or nonexistent issues, when there are so many issues of importance that remain to be considered. The belief that bibliographical and textual work is not humanistic simply because it tries to establish facts or utilizes mechanical aids—and that those engaged in it therefore do not really care about literature—is obviously an emotional rallying cry, not a proposition to be seriously entertained. Similarly, the view that editors who follow Greg are engaged in a mysterious, complex procedure with an elaborate, arcane terminology can only be regarded as an invention of those who are temperamentally disinclined to perform editorial work, for it would be uncharitable to believe that they actually find these concepts and terms a strain on the intelligence. As emotional reactions, these attitudes are understandable, and proponents of Greg's theory have sometimes done their part to provoke them; but as intellectual arguments, there is simply nothing to them.

I am not suggesting that the entire controversy has been frivolous; but even the more serious arguments have so often resulted from a misunderstanding of what is really an uncomplicated approach that one is puzzled to account for them in any but emotional terms. Neither am I saying that Greg's theory and the CEAA application of it ought not to be criticized and analyzed, for any serious intellectual position can only benefit from thoughtful constructive criticism. The point, indeed, is that there has been too little—scarcely any—of this kind of criticism. Yet much of fundamental importance remains to be thought about. The question of what is meant by authorial intention, of how that intention affects the treatment of punctuation, of what differences may be required in working with a typescript rather than a holograph manuscript—such matters as these, when disentangled from self-serving attacks on or defenses of particular editions, need more discussion. Now that a considerable interest in editorial matters has been aroused, a great deal can be accomplished if the collective effort of those interested is expended constructively. No one pretends to have solved all the problems, but solutions can best be approached by a positive effort to understand what accomplishments have so far been achieved and to build on them. Presumably all readers are interested in seeing reliable texts of American literary works made widely available; it would be unfortunate if those who share a common goal allowed themselves to be diverted by controversy from keeping that goal at the center of their attention and working together to attain it.[100]

---

100. While the present paper was in proof, another essay critical of Greg's theory appeared. Vinton A. Dearing, in "Concepts of Copy-Text Old and New," *Library*, 5th ser., 28 (1973), 281-293, argues that Greg's procedure, by emphasizing an early text rather than a later one, "implies that a scribe or compositor regularly puts more errors into a text than the author takes out of his copy" (p. 293). Actually, of course, it implies no more than that errors do creep into a text as it is transmitted; each variant must still be given careful individual attention. Dearing's proposed solution raises many more questions than it answers: "Count the changes certainly made by the author and those certainly made by the scribe or compositor, and assign the rest to the cause with the greater total." I trust that it is unnecessary to enumerate the difficulties which such a statement involves. Still another relevant essay which appeared too late to be cited above is "The CEAA: An Interim Assessment," by Hershel Parker with Bruce Bebb, *PBSA*, 68 (1974), 129-148, which offers succinct evaluations of the CEAA editions in respect to design, arrangement of material, textual policies, and the provision of historical essays.

Recent Editorial Discussion and the Central Questions of Editing

1974-79

THE LATE 1970s WERE AN EXTRAORDINARILY ACTIVE AND INTEResting period for those concerned with editorial matters. In addition to the continuing stream of scholarly editions, these years saw the beginning (1976) of a Center for Scholarly Editions (CSE) within the Modern Language Association of America, the inauguration of an Association for Documentary Editing (1978) and of an interdisciplinary and international Society for Textual Scholarship (1979), and the founding (1979) of a nonprofit corporation, Literary Classics of the United States, Inc., for publishing reliable texts in a form easily accessible to the general reading public. What these organizations have in common, aside from their interest in editing, is a breadth of vision. The fact that the CSE is the successor to the Center for Editions of American Authors (CEAA) is symbolic: whereas the CEAA was limited to the consideration of editing projects in American literature, the CSE is prepared to consult with editors of any kind of material from any country; in its 1977 *Introductory Statement*[1] it emphasized that editors of diverse works "have a common ground for coming together" and pledged "to promote greater understanding among editors in all fields." The Association for Documentary Editing—though the original impetus for its organization came from historians editing the papers of statesmen —welcomes as members editors from all disciplines, and editors of literary and philosophical works have been active in it.[2] Similarly, Literary Classics of the United States, although it is committed to publishing works that can be regarded as American, is not limiting its purview to works that are "literary" in a narrow sense, and it recognizes that a re-

1. *The Center for Scholarly Editions: An Introductory Statement* (1977), also printed in *PMLA*, 92 (1977), 583–597. See also Peter L. Shillingsburg, "Critical Editing and the Center for Scholarly Editions," *Scholarly Publishing*, 9 (1977–78), 31–40.

2. This spirit of maintaining "close and cordial relations" among all editorial "coworkers" was stressed by Arthur S. Link in his presidential address before the first annual meeting of the Association; see "Where We Stand Now and Where We Might Go," in the ADE's *Newsletter*, 2, no. 1 (February 1980), 1–4.

sponsible textual policy can accommodate itself to a variety of kinds of editions.[3]

This climate of openness and cooperation is highly desirable; but its increasing presence should not be taken as a sign that the editorial issues argued about with considerable vehemence during the previous fifteen years have been settled. The familiar debates—such as whether Greg's rationale is appropriate for post-Renaissance material or whether the CEAA was too rigid in its standards—have continued and have often been as ill-informed as before. It would be wrong to suggest that the late 1970s did not have their share of unpleasant and fruitless editorial controversy. But I think it can also be said that the discussion began to take on a somewhat different aspect during these years: arguments based essentially on emotional reactions did not as often hold center stage, and somewhat more commentary appeared that raised thoughtful questions about central issues. Tom Davis, in an important review of the CEAA enterprise,[4] was being overly generous when he referred to "the sophistication of the scholarly debate" that the CEAA editions generated; but there is no doubt about the sophistication of his own piece, and it is a prime example of the newer, more serious criticism of the CEAA.

When in 1975 I surveyed the editorial literature that had grown up around the CEAA,[5] I noted that much of it seemed to have arisen from conflicts of personality or temperament. Quantitatively these writings may have served a purpose, directing more attention than is customary to the activity of scholarly editing (though also reinforcing the view that editors are a contentious lot); but qualitatively this literature left much to be desired. The time now seeems appropriate to extend the survey through the remainder of the 1970s, not only to continue the record (for the development of the debate is of interest in its own right as an episode in the history of modern scholarship) but also to see if an examination of this literature cannot serve to identify and clarify certain basic issues of editing. Some of the pieces require little attention, for they are simply restatements of points of view that I have commented on in the earlier survey; but others, even if they are sometimes inept or illogical, touch on fundamental questions that are worth exploring further. The process of working through these discussions can, I trust, prove to be a fruitful way of approaching those questions. Although the specific subjects are

3. It plans to reprint CEAA or other scholarly texts when they are available; but when they are not it will reprint the texts of first editions (or other historic texts of significance, as appropriate in particular instances), explaining to its readers exactly what texts they are being offered and why.

4. Cited in note 35 below.

5. "Greg's Theory of Copy-Text and the Editing of American Literature," *Studies in Bibliography*, 28 (1975), 167–229; reprinted in *Selected Studies in Bibliography* (1979), pp. 245–307.

frequently the CEAA or Greg's rationale, the issues obviously go beyond American literature and Greg; many misunderstandings have come about through a failure at the outset to be clear about what these underlying issues are, through a failure to make certain elementary distinctions. One of the unfortunate effects of a protracted controversy can be to envelop the issues with a greater aura of mysterious complexity than they actually possess. Editors have difficult enough decisions to make in the process of producing critical editions without needlessly complicating the conceptual framework within which their activity must take place: deciding between two variant readings, for instance, may indeed be a complex affair, requiring an involved discussion, but explaining what one hopes to accomplish by making such decisions should not be a difficult task. A look at some recent editorial discussions can lead, I think, to a realization of how simply the basic questions can be framed.[6]

I

The additions during 1974 and 1975 to the debate inspired by the CEAA editions contribute little that pushes forward one's understanding and do not require any extended consideration. They are of some interest, however, in illustrating how the misconceptions and misunderstandings of the earlier discussions continue to appear and how in fact certain ill-considered arguments become almost stock responses, destined to come up whenever the CEAA is mentioned. Morse Peckham, for instance, delivered a curious paper on "The Editing of 19th-Century Texts" at a symposium on "The Nature of Linguistic Evidence" at the University of Michigan in March 1974.[7] This paper is partly concerned with repeating certain ideas in his 1971 essay, "Reflections on the Foundations of Modern Textual Editing,"[8] such as the view that "an author correcting his own work has the same relation to the text that an editor has" (p. 124). That earlier essay deserves serious attention for its analysis of the nature of written communication, but the aspect of it repeated here—and repeated without any new supporting arguments—is the weakest part of the whole. What the more recent paper emphasizes, however,

6. As before, I am surveying essays that raise general theoretical points, not reviews of individual editions or discussions that examine specific emendations. There has been a larger number of rigorous review essays in this period, however, that examine particular editions in depth: see, for instance, those by Don L. Cook and Wayne R. Kime in *Review*, 1 (1979), 13–27, 105–122, and by Donald H. Reiman in *JEGP*, 73 (1974), 250–260.

7. This paper, written with advice on statistics from David R. King, was published in *Language & Texts: The Nature of Linguistic Evidence*, ed. Herbert H. Paper (1975), pp. 123–146.

8. *Proof*, 1 (1971), 122–155. I have discussed this essay in *SB*, 28 (1975), 211–219 (*Selected Studies*, pp. 289–297).

is the "randomness" in verbal behavior and textual transmission and the problem such randomness poses for editors.[9] Because of the possibilities for variation at every stage of the transmissional process and because of the dispersal of the evidence through hundreds or thousands of copies of individual impressions of printed editions, editors cannot—as Peckham correctly observes—be in a position to know when they have seen all the evidence. But this situation need not fill one with the degree of pessimism that Peckham exhibits; his reaction is seemingly colored by his own dissatisfaction with and resignation from the Ohio University Browning edition, an event that occurred a few months before his paper and that is alluded to in it.[10] He is right to suggest that a more sophisticated statistical approach be taken to the search for variants in nineteenth-century books; but to regard CEAA texts as failures because of what he calls a "policy" of collating[11] only five or six copies of individual editions (p. 133), or to conclude that "reliable editions cannot be created" (p. 142), is to overreact to the unfortunate truth that inductive investigations are never certainly "final." To be sure, some CEAA editors have from time to time been guilty of exaggerated rhetoric, and presumably that is what Peckham is referring to when he speaks of "unjustified claims about completeness or definitiveness" and describes editors "boasting what a superb and thorough-going job they have done" (p. 136); but those editors at the same time have normally been careful to put on record just what their research consisted of and surely did not fail to understand that additional information might later turn up that would alter their conclusions. When Peckham says at the end that "the current way of making editions creates a closed or dead-end situation which requires that the effort be repeated, and must fail again," his use of the word "fail" suggests that a work is not successful if it is superseded. But of course the accumulation of knowledge proceeds precisely by building on what went before, and it is naïve to think of scholarship in terms of finality.[12] There

---

9. "The textual editor . . . is engaged in policing what he judges to be the randomness which in fact is inseparable from the process of textual transmission" (p. 129).

10. Some further remarks describing his disappointment with the Browning edition are quoted in Donald H. Reiman's thorough review of volumes 3 and 4 in *Victorian Poetry*, 12 (1974), 86–96.

11. It is not clear why Peckham believes that collating machines have served "to increase the amount of reliable data beyond the point at which it can be used" (p. 134). Indeed, his whole discussion of how "scientific instruments" serve to "undermine the theory responsible" for their invention seems a perverse way of describing how inductive investigations proceed.

12. Similarly, he objects to the "establishment theory of bibliographical analysis . . . that the history of the printing of a book can be recovered," because "the intrusion of randomness in the complex of interacting behaviors involved in printing a book is horrendous" (p. 131). But the "recovery" of any piece of history is always subject to modification by the "recovery" of still further data.

is no question that some editors are more thorough than others in their procedures, and much of what Peckham says about the importance of recognizing the human element in printing and the need for more awareness of statistical procedures in analytical bibliography is well taken. But his insistence on attacking the supposed claims of definitiveness in CEAA editions only serves to confuse the issues and weakens what could have become a helpful positive statement about the responsible handling of evidence. This is not the first, nor the last, time that the issue of the "definitiveness" of CEAA editions has diverted attention from more basic and substantial concerns.[13]

Peckham's paper—valedictory since he announces in it his resignation from the Browning edition—can be paired with another valedictory essay of the same year, Paul Baender's "Reflections upon the CEAA by a Departing Editor."[14] Baender in fact comments on Peckham's paper and makes an effective rejoinder to parts of it (see pp. 136–139). Although Baender is a "departing editor" (from the University of California Press edition of Mark Twain) because he finds himself not temperamentally suited to editorial work, he believes that the CEAA editions are "eminently worth doing" (p. 141) and places in proper perspective some of the superficial criticisms they have received. In the light of his effective exposure of certain "clichés" that continually turn up in writings critical of the CEAA,[15] it is surprising that his own criticisms also include some arguments that are clichés. For example, he objects to the "trivialities" and "excesses of trivia" that he finds recorded in some CEAA editions and suggests that if people had "taken the outrage of Mumford and Wilson seriously" the proliferation of "meaningless data" would not have occurred (p. 135).[16] To protest about the quantity of data recorded in CEAA editions has certainly become one of the clichés of criticism. But it is difficult to fathom why people become so incensed over the presence of information they do not find of use. Perhaps some editors are overly generous in supplying evidence they have considered in the

13. I should note, parenthetically, that another part of Peckham's article criticizes the typography and design of the CEAA editions, calling them "absurdities" (p. 137) and claiming among other things that "the format of most of the CEAA editions is too big, too typographically voluptuous," to serve as the basis for inexpensive photo-offset reprints (p. 138). There is no reason, of course, why large pages cannot be photographically reduced: an example is the use of the Northwestern-Newberry Edition of Melville's *Redburn* in the paperback series of Rinehart Editions (1971).

14. *Resources for American Literary Study*, 4 (1974), 131–144.

15. See his comments (pp. 142–143) on Hamlin Hill's "Who Killed Mark Twain?", *American Literary Realism*, 7 (1974), 119–124.

16. Later in the essay (p. 142) he deplores certain other arguments as "the angry knee-jerk reactions of Mumford and Wilson." Reference to Mumford's and Wilson's pieces, and some commentary on them, can be found in *SB*, 28 (1975), 198–201 (*Selected Studies*, pp. 276–279).

process of preparing an edition; but readers who are not interested in the information are free to ignore it. Criticizing an edition for containing too much so-called "trivial" information is itself a trivial complaint. Baender views this criticism more sensibly later when he says that "pedantic excesses" are "relatively minor concomitants of the editorial process" (pp. 143–144)—but at the same time he unexpectedly admits, "I too find little importance in word-division lists." These lists have been a favorite target for unreflective critics, but it is hard to see how anyone who has been involved in establishing a text could fail to understand their significance. I do not suppose that any editor regards them as particularly appealing, but editors nevertheless recognize that these lists play an essential role in the task that an edition aims to accomplish: when an editor has taken pains to establish a text—punctuation as well as words—it is illogical not to inform readers about which line-end hyphens should be retained in making quotations from the text.

Baender's essay in other respects, as in this one, does not advance the frontiers of editorial debate; but some of the questions he raises should perhaps be enumerated as further examples of his own category of "clichés." For instance, he blames the CEAA inspectors for some of the "trivia" in the published editions, noting with apparent distaste that "Generally the inspectors are greatly concerned with accidentals" (p. 135) and referring to "the inspectors' nitpicking" that causes editors "to worry over the details of their textual descriptions" (p. 136). Though some inspectors have doubtless been guilty of excesses, to regard the questioning of details as "nitpicking" suggests a lack of sympathy with the kind of attention to detail that scholarly editing necessarily involves.[17] Of more substance is Baender's dissatisfaction with the term "final intention"; but his brief discussion is no more than a gesture, for he ignores the interesting aspects of the question by taking "final" to mean "last," without regard to motive (he claims that if certain of Mark Twain's revisions of *The Innocents Abroad* for the Routledge edition are rejected as adaptations for a British audience, "the criterion of final textual intention has been compromised" [p. 140]). On another important aspect of intention—the relation to authorial intention of revisions dictated by the publisher—he makes an admirable statement ("an individual has the power and privilege of self-expression and of changing his mind," and "other individuals do not have the privilege of altering that self-

17. Baender places in a footnote to this discussion a variation of perhaps the most common cliché of criticism of the CEAA, the charge of rigidity or dogmatism. Here the CEAA inspectors are said to have derived from Greg "dogmas which are theirs, not his" (p. 135, n. 5). Baender's criticism on this point is more enlightened than many others', for he does not attribute the dogmatism to CEAA policy but rather to the approach of particular inspectors.

expression or of forcing that change of mind"); but when he adds, "I believe the CEAA has not sufficiently recognized that a writer's acquiescence in his publisher's alterations may also be construed as self-expression" (p. 141), he raises—but does not explore—what has become one of the most ubiquitous issues in discussions of modern editing. Baender's piece is essentially thoughtful, and for that reason certain stock reactions to the CEAA stand out in it all the more flagrantly; their presence in such an essay suggests how pervasive they have become.

Another paper of 1974 written by a person generally sympathetic to the CEAA but at the same time exhibiting superficial criticisms of it is Joseph Katz's paper for the November 1974 Toronto Conference on Editorial Problems. Its title announces that Katz's theme is the endlessly asserted "rigidity" of CEAA policy: " 'Novelists of the Future': Animadversions against the Rigidity of Current Theory in the Editing of Nineteenth-Century American Writers." [18] Katz offers a useful discussion of some of the textual problems in editing Frank Norris; but when he tries to show that these problems "strain a strict application of current editorial approach" (p. 69), he resorts to several of the old clichés. He is particularly concerned about the notion of a "definitive" edition, asserting that the paucity of prepublication material for Norris's novels makes a "definitive edition" impossible (pp. 70–71, 74) and stating that he cannot conceive of a "definitive edition" of any work: "Every edition with which I am familiar could be upset completely by the emergence of some document not available to the editor" (p. 67). But surely no scholar imagines that a piece of work can be produced that could not be overturned by the discovery of new documentary evidence. To claim that CEAA policy requires editors to undertake a task that everyone agrees is manifestly impossible is merely to set up a straw man. Katz does say that "the problem is in part a matter of rhetoric"; but when he adds, "so are most editorial problems," one wonders how to take other parts of his own essay. Like his comments on definitiveness, his discussion of "author's final intentions" is in fact a rhetorical exercise and does not get to the interesting aspects of the issue, but it appears to have been written under the impression that a matter of substance was being taken up. What bothers him about the phrase "author's final intentions," he says, is the assumption "that there is always and invariably a single work" (p. 67)—"that an author himself always and invariably pursues a work until it has reached its one ideal state—or that he wants to, or that he ought to want to" (pp. 74–75). It seems unlikely, however, that many people have ever held such an assumption. Certainly Greg himself and those who

18. Published in *Editing British and American Literature, 1880–1920*, ed. Eric W. Domville (1976), pp. 65–76. Domville briefly sums up the paper on pp. 4–5.

have in general followed his rationale have recognized that various "final intentions" might exist with respect to different versions of a work that deserve to be taken as independent entities.[19] By using his space on a non-issue, Katz has neglected to look into any of the intriguing questions that the concept of intention raises, such as how one decides when to treat a version of a work as if it were a separate work. Similarly, he begins with the often-repeated, but insubstantial, criticism that current editorial thinking assumes "the existence of a proven editorial routine which will produce definitive texts of works written at any time, in any place";[20] and at the end he makes the point in an equally familiar way by saying that "the problems faced by scholars concerned mainly with editing dramatic texts of the English Renaissance are not the problems that confront the editor of a nineteenth-century American text." These assertions are again matters of rhetoric and skirt the significant issues. Obviously there are differences of detail among textual situations from different periods, but there are some underlying central questions of editing that remain constant and that must be thought about before one can responsibly proceed to those details. And to claim that "current theory" entails a rigid routine is not only to confuse theory and practice but also to miss the flexibility built into the basic CEAA statements and exhibited in the various CEAA editions. This is not necessarily to argue on behalf of the CEAA editions but only to point out that Katz's paper does not go past certain stock responses to consider the real issues that are involved.

A paper that deals more seriously—but in the end no more success-fully—with problems raised by the concept of authorial intention is Hans Zeller's "A New Approach to the Critical Constitution of Literary Texts," which appeared in printed form in early 1975.[21] This paper serves as a convenient summary for English-speaking readers of a position that has been gaining acceptance in Germany. Zeller's argument essen-

19. I have made further comments on this question in "The Editorial Problem of Final Authorial Intention," *SB*, 29 (1976), 167–211 (*Selected Studies*, pp. 309–353).

20. Specifically, he says that what implies the existence of that routine is the metaphor of pouring old wine into new bottles. Presumably the allusion is to the title of Fredson Bowers's paper ("Old Wine in New Bottles: Problems of Machine Printing") at the second (1966) Toronto conference, published in *Editing Nineteenth Century Texts*, ed. John M. Robson (1967), pp. 9–36. But Bowers's paper is aimed at showing how the bibliographical analysis involved in establishing a text must deal with different kinds of complexities in different periods depending on changing printing technology. The metaphor of his title is not used to suggest "the existence of a proven editorial routine"; Katz's opening sentence ("Good editing is not just a matter of pouring old wine into new bottles") is thus not a refutation of anything asserted in Bowers's paper.

21. *SB*, 28 (1975), 231–264. An earlier version of this paper was read at a conference on editorial problems held at the Villa Serbelloni, Bellagio, in September 1973, under the directorship of Hans Walter Gabler.

tially is that any authorial alteration of a work creates a new "version" of the work and that each version is a independent entity which should not be emended by an editor with authorial variants from another version. This position, which limits the critical role of the editor to the detection and correction of errors within each version, is said to rest on the view that any alteration of a work produces a different relationship among all the elements of the work and on the belief that an author's artistic intentions cannot be disentangled from various practical and worldly concerns. Both these points have much to be said for them, but they do not necessarily lead to the conclusion Zeller draws. One can argue that the editor is in a position to attempt to discriminate among kinds of revisions and among various motivations for revision and that not to attempt such discriminations is to ignore many of the nuances of the textual situation, the result being an oversimplified picture. Presumably no one would deny the value of editions of individual versions of a work, but a more eclectic approach also has its particular merits. Zeller's position deserves to be considered as part of the recurrent challenge to the soundness of the critical editing that has followed from Greg's rationale;[22] his arguments, however, do not finally call into serious question the usefulness of an approach that allows an editor, as an act of critical scholarship, to make judgments not simply about the correction of error but also about the emendation of readings revised by the author.[23]

22. Zeller states that "the motives behind the emergence and elaboration of the new Germanist theory are not the same as those implicit in such objections as have been raised against the application of the Greg-Bowers principles to the editions of modern American authors" (p. 231). Nevertheless, in dealing with the nature of authorial intention and the relations among versions of a work, it confronts some of the same questions that have often been raised in criticizing Greg's rationale and the CEAA.

23. I have commented on Zeller's paper in more detail on pp. 329–331 of "Problems and Accomplishments in the Editing of the Novel," *Studies in the Novel*, 7 (1975), 323–360. The German position as represented at the Bellagio conference is also alluded to by G. E. Bentley, Jr., in the introduction to the volume he edited containing the papers from another conference held six weeks later, the 1973 Toronto editorial conference—*Editing Eighteenth Century Novels* (1975), p. 7. Bentley contrasts the German practice of preserving "the copytext inviolate" with the French approach, represented by Roger Laufer (who participated in both the Bellagio and Toronto conferences), of modernizing a text "to make it accessible to students and scholars who are not specialists." Laufer's Toronto paper ("From Publishing to Editing *Gil Blas de Santillane*: An Evaluation of the Rival Claims of Practical and Ideal Editing," pp. 31–48) criticizes Greg's distinction between substantives and accidentals, misleadingly asserting, "Greg's theory comes really to saying that accidentals are so trivial that an author hardly ever bothers to revise them while emending words or sentences, but, nevertheless, the original accidentals should be preserved at all costs" (p. 37). Laufer believes that an editor should attempt to distinguish between significant and insignificant spelling and punctuation, retaining the significant and modernizing the other. But nothing that Laufer says about the nature of written language refutes the standard

Later in 1975 *Studies in the Novel* devoted a special number, edited
by Warner Barnes and James T. Cox, to "Textual Studies in the Novel"
(vol. 7, no. 3). Among other contributions,[24] this collection includes an
article by John Freehafer, "Greg's Theory of Copy-Text and the Textual
Criticism in the CEAA Editions" (pp. 375–388), which the editors in
their preface describe as singling out "for specific (and often harsh) criticism many of the practical and theoretical problems inherent in the
CEAA editions" (p. 319). Freehafer does make a few valid criticisms and
helpful suggestions—such as lamenting the customary omission in CEAA
volumes of a historical record of variants in punctuation and spelling,
and pointing out the desirability of making available facsimiles of significant documents in the textual history of particular works—but these observations occur in the midst of many others that misrepresent what
Greg's rationale entails or repeat certain well-rehearsed but ill-informed
objections to it. His expression of surprise that two editors following
Greg but choosing different copy-texts of Dryden's *The Indian Emperour*
should come up with texts that vary at a great many points (p. 377) indicates the level of his response to Greg's rationale. He takes the divergence
as an indication that the editors have adhered too mechanically to their
copy-texts instead of recognizing that an expectation of identical results
presupposes a precision alien to any procedure relying on critical judgment. It is no criticism of Greg's rationale, of course, to say that it has
been misused by some editors as a means for avoiding judgment. "The
popularity of Greg's theory of copy-text as it has thus come to be applied," Freehafer claims, "may be partly because it often relieves the
textual editor of the difficult task of trying to recognize authorial corrections, afterthoughts, or revisions, especially in accidentals" (p. 382). Freehafer does recognize Greg's emphasis on critical judgment, and the
phrase "as it has thus come to be applied" makes this sentence tauto-
logical. Whether or not CEAA editors have in fact avoided making textual decisions is another matter, and one not related to Greg's rationale.
The old question of the applicability of Greg's approach to nineteenth-
century texts is one that Freehafer is inclined to answer in the negative,
but his reasoning again refers to an inflexibility that is not part of Greg's

---

arguments against modernizing. He wishes his edition to be "contemporary" (p. 38), but
serious readers will feel that modernizing puts an additional barrier between them and the
historic text they want to understand as fully as possible and is thus self-defeating. (For a
summary statement regarding the inappropriateness of modernizing in scholarly endeavor,
see *SB*, 31 [1978], 48–50, or *Selected Studies*, pp. 498–500.)

24. My survey of textual work on the novel, referred to in note 23 above, appears in
this issue, as does a useful list, "Textual Studies in the Novel: A Selected Checklist, 1950–
74" (pp. 445–471), compiled by James T. Cox, Margaret Putnam, and Marvin Williams.

own statement. The CEAA editor, he says, faced with series of authorially revised editions that are common in the nineteenth century, is likely to choose an early text "as a source of readings more often than he should" (p. 379); but Greg made allowance for selecting revised editions as copy-texts when circumstances warrant. Freehafer's piece requires little discussion and in any case has already been sufficiently analyzed in "The Center for Editions of American Authors: A Forum on Its Editions and Practices," which immediately follows his essay (pp. 389–406).[25]

Two more essays of 1975 represent extremes, one being less important and the other more important than any of the discussions thus far examined. What is probably the most uninformed and irresponsible criticism of the CEAA, Peter Shaw's "The American Heritage and Its Guardians," appeared in late 1975 in the *American Scholar*.[26] Because of its publication in a general journal, Shaw's article has perhaps reached a wider audience than any of these others. No doubt some readers without any background in textual matters have been persuaded by it; but anyone acquainted with the CEAA editions and the recent series of editions of the papers of American statesmen knows how far off the mark Shaw is when he claims that the editions of the statesmen generally show more fidelity to the historical documents than do the "eclectic" editions of literary figures. Whether or not one approves of the CEAA editions or of Greg's rationale, one can see that Shaw misunderstands the "eclecticism" of modern critical editing and does not recognize why the unrecorded alterations that occur in many of the historical editions constitute a weakness. The article is full of confusions and repeats many of the clichés about the CEAA without adding significantly to the discussion. Shaw was simply unprepared to write such a piece, and it can safely be dismissed.[27]

25. This "Forum" is made up of the following short contributions: Bruce Bebb and Hershel Parker, "Freehafer on Greg and the CEAA: Secure Footing and 'Substantial Shortfalls'" (pp. 391–394), which calls Freehafer's comments on Greg "thoughtless compared to what other scholars have been saying in recent years" but finds valuable his "criticism of CEAA textual policies"; Vinton A. Dearing, "Textual Criticism Today: A Brief Survey" (pp. 394–398); Thomas L. McHaney, "The Important Questions Are Seldom Raised" (pp. 399–401); Morse Peckham, "Notes on Freehafer and the CEAA" (pp. 402–404), which states that Freehafer's "strictures are not as severe as they could be, nor is his analysis as penetrating as it should be"; and G. T. Tanselle, "Two Basic Distinctions: Theory and Practice, Text and Apparatus" (pp. 404–406).

26. *American Scholar*, 45 (1975–76), 733–751 [i.e., 37–55].

27. I have discussed parts of Shaw's article in more detail in two other places: in "The Editing of Historical Documents," *SB*, 31 (1978), 7–8, 54–55 (*Selected Studies*, pp. 457–458, 504–505); and in "External Fact as an Editorial Problem," *SB*, 32 (1979), 31–34 (*Selected Studies*, pp. 385–388). For Fredson Bowers's comment on Shaw's piece as "the low water mark to date," employing "the Big Lie technique" beyond "all bounds of decency," see "Scholarship and Editing" (note 31 below), p. 164, n. 4.

At the other extreme is an essay by Fredson Bowers, "Remarks on Eclectic Texts,"[28] published at about the same time. This long discussion is an essay in definition: it explores, with many illustrations, what is meant by eclecticism in editing and shows the scholarly significance of critical editions. As a reaction against the unprincipled eclecticism of some editors in previous centuries, there has been a twentieth-century current of distrust of eclecticism. This distrust has taken many forms, as the essays of Zeller and Shaw suggest. Thus Bowers's discussion goes to the heart of one of the principal issues raised by critics of the CEAA editions. After examining in detail the application to various kinds of situations of an approach that aims to establish a text that will best represent its author's intentions, he arrives at an eloquent statement summarizing why the results of this approach "should constitute the finest flower of textual scholarship": "the main scholarly demand is for an established critical text embodying the author's full intentions (not merely one segment of them in an inevitably imperfect form) insofar as these can be ascertained by an expert who has had available all documentary sources and has devoted time and study to their transmissional history and authority" (p. 527). Bowers recognizes that facsimile editions have their uses and understands that in some cases two versions of a work are so different as to make any attempt to construct a single eclectic text inappropriate. But he shows that normally the expertise of the editor is not put to its highest use if it does not result in a single critical text: "Literary critics, historians, general scholars, students of all kinds—these need as authoritative a reconstruction of a full text as the documents allow, not editions of the separate documents, except when the distance is so great as to make eclectic reconstruction impossible" (p. 528).[29] Bowers's careful and thorough discussion will now be the standard reference to cite when questions are raised about the meaning or value of eclecticism in modern scholarly editing.[30]

28. *Proof*, 4 (1975), 31–76; reprinted in his *Essays in Bibliography, Text, and Editing* (1975), pp. 488–528. A shorter version of this paper was his contribution to the Bellagio conference in 1973 (cf. notes 21 and 23 above).

29. In the light of all the controversy over exaggerated claims of definitiveness, one should note that Bowers here describes "as authoritative a reconstruction . . . as the documents allow." A scholar is limited to the available evidence and knows that further evidence may later become available; thus the goal of a scholarly critical edition is "to be the most authoritative and comprehensive that can be contrived for its time and place in the history of scholarship" (p. 528).

30. Todd Bender does not perhaps take Bowers's arguments for eclectic texts sufficiently into account when he talks about the "arbitrary limits" of a "printed code system" that allows only one reading to stand at each point in the text; but he does make a number of interesting points about the way in which a text in electronic form can hold all variants simultaneously, and he argues that such a text does not amount simply to a collection of documents but that it is instead "the primary form of the *work*," for a work often implies

Another essay of Bowers's, the following year, deserves mention here both because it provides a convenient and thoughtful general summary of the approach to editing that derives from Greg and because it opens the way to the serious reconsideration of Greg that was to occur in the following years. Delivered in an abridged form before the Bibliographical Society of America in 1976, "Scholarship and Editing"[31] principally offers an authoritative statement regarding modernization, eclecticism, radiating texts, choice of copy-text (Greg's rationale),[32] and apparatus. But it also comments on "exceptions to Greg's rationale" in which "the author can be shown to have devoted as much attention [in a revision] to the formal features of his text as to its material or substantive features" (p. 179). Such texts "appear to call for a relaxation of Greg's principle," he says, "not at all for the reasons adduced for Ben Jonson [i.e., the thoroughness of the substantive revision in *Every Man in His Humour*] but instead because the author can be shown to have paid such particular care to the essentials of his formal presentation" as to make a later edition "more authoritative in its accidentals on the whole" than the first. This kind of situation can be said to offer an exception to Greg's rationale in the sense that it requires the editor to depart from the common pattern of adopting as copy-text the text closest to the author's manuscript. Calling it an "exception," however, should not lead one to infer that it is not taken into account in Greg's essay. Greg cites *Every Man in His Humour* at one point (p. 390) as an example of substantive revision, but he also uses it as an illustration of an author's supervising "the printing of the new edition," correcting the proofs and taking responsibility for the re-

a "range of possibilities." See "Literary Texts in Electronic Storage: The Editorial Potential," *Computers and the Humanities*, 10 (1976), 193–199. A good survey of the literature relating to computers and editing appeared soon afterward: T. H. Howard-Hill, "Computer and Mechanical Aids to Editing," *Proof*, 5 (1977), 217–235.

31. *PBSA*, 70 (1976), 161–188. Another essay of Bowers's during 1976, intended to provide a general summary for a much broader audience, is "Recovering the Author's Intentions," *Pages*, 1 (1976), 218–227.

32. One of his comments on Greg's rationale may perhaps prove misleading. He says that when a decision about verbal variants "seems indifferent to critical analysis, Greg suggested that the odds should favor the editorial adoption of the later reading since it appeared in a text that had general authority for its substantives" (p. 177). Greg of course, like McKerrow, did recognize that the authority for spelling and punctuation might lie in a different text from one that provides authoritative verbal revisions; but to suggest the adoption of all indifferent substantive variants from a text containing recognizable authorial revisions would amount to considering that revised text the copy-text for substantives, and Greg departed further than this from McKerrow's idea of placing the authority for all substantives in a text containing any authorial revisions. According to Greg, "a later variant that is either completely indifferent or manifestly inferior, or for the substitution of which no motive can be suggested, should be treated as fortuitous and refused admission to the text" ("The Rationale of Copy-Text," in Greg's *Collected Papers*, ed. J.C. Maxwell [1966], pp. 387–388). For Greg, the copy-text is the text to fall back on in the case of all truly indifferent variants, substantives as well as those in punctuation and spelling.

vised edition "in respect of accidentals no less than substantive readings" (p. 389).[33] Bowers issues a useful caution, in other words, against interpreting Greg with an inflexibility alien to the spirit of his essay. Whereas Greg criticized "the tyranny of the copy-text" (p. 382) by arguing in favor of the use of editorial judgment to determine authorial revisions or corrections that should be incorporated into the copy-text, Bowers points out a different kind of tyranny: Greg's concept of divided authority, he says, "has been so welcome to recent textual critics that they have had a tendency to overreact against any other rationale" and thus "have been loath to accept any suggestion of a return to unified authority even when the special situation warrants it" (pp. 179–180). This statement succinctly summarizes a situation brought about by the success of Greg's essay; but one would be incorrect to attribute the situation to a weakness or oversight in Greg's position, since Greg covers the possibility that undivided authority can reside in a later edition and emphasizes flexibility in approaching the great variety of "cases of revision" (p. 390).[34] So long as one arrives at a sensible editorial rationale, it does not of course matter whether or not one finds support for it in Greg's essay. But so much has been written, pro and con, about the relation between Greg and the CEAA editions that it is worth noting just how much is actually encompassed within his rationale. Bowers's essay, by calling attention to a new kind of textual tyranny, provides an occasion for doing this at a critical point in the history of recent textual discussion, just before the appearance of two major analyses.

These two major essays, which must be carefully considered by all who are concerned with modern editing, were published just about a year apart in 1977 and 1978, the first by Tom Davis and the second by Bowers himself. They raise more fundamental questions about the broad applicability of Greg's rationale and analyze them more cogently than all but one or two of the earlier CEAA-related discussions. Davis's piece,[35] a long review of the whole CEAA undertaking, is balanced and thoughtful: although Davis has some serious reservations, he is also able to praise the contributions to "literary, bibliographical, and historical scholarship" made by the CEAA editions (p. 63), and it is clear that, unlike some

33. Greg specifically takes up *Every Man in His Humour* in the paragraph following the one in which these phrases occur, calling it the "classical example" of what he had just described in general terms.

34. As Bowers points out, "It is obvious from some of his cautionary statements about his own rationale that Greg would have agreed"—agreed, that is, that the "mechanical measurement of authority in the accidentals must give way to the special conditions of an author's revision of these same features on an equal footing with his revision of the substantives" (p. 181).

35. "The CEAA and Modern Textual Editing," *Library*, 5th ser., 32 (1977), 61–74.

previous commentators, he is approaching the issues with an open mind.[36] If it is an overstatement to describe, as he does, the "intense textual debate" generated by the CEAA as "profoundly stimulating and valuable," those adjectives may be applied to his own contribution; and he is right to make the interesting point that the extent and prominence of the continuing discussion mark "the beginnings of a replication of the scholarly audience that the editor of classical texts can expect" (p. 61). Davis concludes with the familiar complaint that CEAA editors have been too rigid in applying what they take to be rules derived from Greg, and he advocates "greater use of editorial judgement" (p. 71). What distinguishes his essay from most of the others that arrive at similar conclusions is the quality of the analysis leading up to the conclusion. He concentrates on two CEAA "methods or rules" that are "adopted from Greg's paper" and "depend on logical inconsistencies": the distinction between substantives and accidentals and the idea of following the copy-text when variants are indifferent. Even though the careful reader is not likely to be in complete agreement with Davis, the intelligence of his analysis makes his argument a rewarding one to think through.

On the distinction between substantives and accidentals, Davis's position is that the concept, both in Greg's essay and in restatements by CEAA editors, is so fuzzy as to be useless and that, in this form at least, it should be scrapped. As he explains it, the trouble essentially is that the definition of substantives as words and accidentals as punctuation and spelling does not coincide with the further definition of substantives as elements of meaning and accidentals as elements of form. CEAA editors do, of course, recognize accidentals as having a kind of meaning distinct from purely formal features of typographic design, for they are concerned to reproduce the former but not the latter. The "absurd consequence," in Davis's words, is that "all CEAA editors are committed simultaneously to the dedicated pursuit of authorial spelling and punctuation, while being equally committed to the belief that these phenomena are meaningless" (p. 68). Obviously Davis has, for effect, made this statement sound as absurd as possible; a fairer way to put the matter would be to say that serious scholarly editors (whether associated with the CEAA or not) regard spelling and punctuation as meaningful parts of a text[37] but that

36. His essay is not, in other words, part of what Bowers calls "an extremely contentious defense of the status quo and the familiar" that has characterized many reviews of CEAA volumes ("Scholarship and Editing" [note 31 above], p. 164, n. 4).

37. Obviously the spelling and punctuation of texts many steps removed from their authors (such as those dealt with by classical and Biblical scholars) have a different significance from those in autograph manuscripts or editions (or copies) derived directly from the manuscripts.

some of them have been careless in distinguishing nonverbal elements ("accidentals") of a text from the words themselves so as to suggest that the former do not convey meaning. Davis's treatment does dramatize the sloppiness of thinking that has often been associated, from Greg onward, with attempts to define "substantives" and "accidentals." A number of CEAA editors have from the beginning been dissatisfied with these terms and their implications, and several criticisms of Greg's terminology have appeared in print; indeed, much of what Davis says on this score is inherent in Morse Peckham's 1971 essay,[38] though Davis's expression of it is clearer and more forceful. In one sense all this attention is misplaced, for in practice editors have not thought in terms of "substantives" and "accidentals" when making emendations: any variant reading in a later text, whether in wording or spelling or punctuation, has been accepted into the copy-text if it can convincingly be attributed to the author. Of course, as Greg predicted, one can less often argue with conviction about revisions in spelling and punctuation than about revisions in wording, but the same process of thought has been applied to all variants. From another point of view, however, one cannot so easily dismiss the problem, for incoherence of argument deserves to be deplored whether or not it has practical consequences; the very fact that it may not have consequences is in itself troubling. Just because Greg stresses the casualness of his distinction between substantives and accidentals and calls it "practical" rather than "philosophic" is no reason to overlook the problems it causes. On the other hand, one can tell, with a little reflection, that what Greg proposes is not as illogical as the language he uses would seem to imply: it is clear that his distinction was not meant to describe the nature of written communication but only to indicate how people have in fact often reacted to spelling and punctuation. If people who can affect textual transmission, such as compositors or publishing-house editors, think of spelling and punctuation in general as elements of form, distinct from "content," or words, their treatment of those features and the kind of attention they devote to them may be affected. It does not matter whether they are right to make such a distinction; what matters to the scholarly editor, who is a historian, is whether people have indeed acted on this conception.

Davis is quite right, therefore, to stress "the actual or inferred practice of authors and printers" (p. 68). Although he is not the first to make this point, his use of it is particularly effective.[39] Following a lucid ac-

---

38. Which Davis expresses his indebtedness to.

39. I have no desire to claim any priority in this matter and in fact do not know who may have first looked at Greg's rationale in this manner. I simply wish to repeat here, as another way of stating the same thing, what I said in 1975 in commenting on Peckham's similar criticism of Greg's distinction between substantives and accidentals: "What Greg

count of textual and typographical meaning (and the way in which printers sometimes have control over "not only the signs in a text that are not considered to generate the meaning of the work, but also many that do" [p. 64]), he provides an excellent summary of Greg that emphasizes the behavior of authors and printers, beginning with this sentence: "Greg's central insight is that both writers and printers tend to make a distinction between the words, and the spelling, punctuation, italicization, paragraphing, hyphenation, and so forth, of the text" (p. 65). After this summary (the paragraph beginning at the bottom of p. 65 should stand as a classic statement of Greg's approach), he points out that his paraphrase unfortunately does not represent the way in which Greg or the CEAA editors present the rationale, and he proceeds to show the difficulties that ensue when the equation of words with meaning, and punctuation with form, is enunciated as if it had a "philosophic" truth beyond its "practical" value in describing the behavior of writers and printers. The fact that Davis can regard his fine summary as a "paraphrase" of Greg, despite the illogicalities that he subsequently specifies in Greg's discussion, shows that he is able to see through the surface confusions to the clear-sighted position that lies beneath. Similarly, I can assert that a number of CEAA editors, regardless of how they may have worded their summaries of Greg, understand his position in the same way that Davis does and would concur in Davis's paraphrase. That does not of course excuse lack of rigor in presentation, and I am not for a moment suggesting that Davis was wrong to criticize many of the restatements of Greg that appear in CEAA editions. But I would add that to concentrate on those statements is to stop short of investigating the way in which Greg's distinction has actually been employed in editing. That there may be a discrepancy between the rhetoric employed in some editions and the editorial approach to spelling and punctuation manifested in the editing itself is unfortunate, but to dwell on the former rather than to see through it to the latter is not finally to get to the heart of the matter. Davis's incisive treatment of the distinction between substantives and

---

meant by a 'practical' distinction is one which, however mistaken it may be, has in fact operated to govern human behavior; and, since the editor is concerned with analyzing the behavior of certain individuals, such a distinction may be useful to him. . . . What I take Greg to be saying, then, is that the editor distinguishes substantives and accidentals not because he believes that he is making a valid conceptual distinction between two elements in written language but because the distinction is one which is likely to have been made by the persons who have been involved in the transmission of any given text (and which therefore may be useful in segregating different features of that text which may have been accorded different treatment)." See *SB*, 28 (1975), 213–214 (*Selected Studies*, pp. 291–292). Cf. the earlier comment, in the summary of Greg, that "the focus is pragmatic—on the habits of individuals" (p. 174 [252]); or the view that Greg's position is based on a generalization about "the behavior of human beings in dealing with written language" (p. 180 [258]).

accidentals leads one to be somewhat disappointed that his analysis ends
with criticism of the language used by CEAA editors; one would expect,
from the level of his previous discussion, that he might have examined
the extent to which the actual editorial practice of those editors is accurately reflected in their statements, just as he was able to "paraphrase"
what Greg was getting at in the "Rationale" in spite of the language in
which it was expressed. In any case, one can agree with Davis when he
says, "It is to be hoped then that we shall not hear much more about accidentals and substantives, but about words, and punctuation, and the
actual or inferred practice of authors and printers" (p. 68). A number of
editors and writers on editing have for some time now been reluctant to
use these terms or have in fact refrained from using them; and it is clear
that the time has come when the terms should in most situations be
abandoned. The real contribution that Greg makes can—as I shall suggest shortly—be taken advantage of without clouding the issues by the
use of these questionably defined terms.[40]

The second of Davis's two major points is a criticism of Greg's suggestion that the copy-text reading be retained whenever the editor finds
the variant readings indifferent. Unfortunately Davis's treatment of this
question is less satisfactory than his treatment of the previous one, for
here he only alludes to the central issue involved; he does not pursue it
at all but instead turns to a less significant aspect of the general question
and then falls short of his own standard of perceptiveness (amply demonstrated earlier) in handling it. He begins on a promising note by questioning whether Greg's generalization is applicable to later periods;
nineteenth-century novels, he points out, are "much more subject to authoritative revision than those works with which Greg was concerned" (p.
70). "It is by no means inevitable," he continues, "that in the case of indifferent verbal variants non-evident compositorial error will preponderate;
it is possible that the reverse is true." And if "such errors do not preponderate, then to treat all indifferent variants as compositorial errors
is to increase one's chances of adopting the wrong reading." Clearly the
question raised here is of crucial importance. Whether or not Greg's
rationale is valid for post-Renaissance writings has of course been frequently asked, often in trivial ways; but the real heart of the issue is to
determine whether the circumstances of publishing in certain periods
were such that textual variations in later editions were more likely to be
authorial than compositorial. If such were the case, then Greg's rationale
would obviously not be applicable to those periods, for it would lead
editors in the wrong direction, assigning presumptive authority to an

40. A very different use of the word "substantive" is carefully looked at by Bowers in
"McKerrow, Greg, and 'Substantive Edition,' " *Library*, 5th ser., 33 (1978), 83–107.

early text rather than a later one.[41] Instead of following this interesting line of thought, however, Davis lamely concludes: "in practice since there is no way of knowing which kind of reading preponderates [authorial revision or compositorial error],[42] no ascertainable harm is done by following Greg's principle, so long as its tentativeness is preserved." If it is true that one cannot generalize about the nature of the indifferent variants, then it is also true that no *ascertainable* harm would come from choosing an early, rather than a later, text as copy-text and assigning it presumptive authority in the case of indifferent variants; but neither would any ascertainable good come from it, and under those circumstances one would have no justifiable reason to follow Greg's approach. To believe that an otherwise unjustifiable approach would be permissible if its "tentativeness" were emphasized is not a very constructive position; one would do better to regard seriously Davis's earlier point that "taking the trouble to toss a coin would statistically speaking give one a better text." The fact is, however, that Greg's rationale, for all its tentativeness, is predicated on the belief that one can indeed generalize about the deterioration of successive texts in sixteenth- and seventeenth-century editions; otherwise there would be no justification for retaining the readings of an early edition at points where variants are indifferent. And if one is to employ Greg's approach in dealing with later writings, one cannot simply appeal to tentativeness but must confront the question whether the same generalization applies to other periods. This central question, brought up but not analyzed by Davis, is examined by Bowers in the essay to which we shall shortly turn.

First, however, we should note what Davis concentrates on instead. Taking as his theme the "tentativeness" of Greg, he points out the way in which CEAA editors and commentators have in his opinion hardened Greg's tentativeness into "something much nearer certainty." He calls it a "heresy" (against Greg, that is) to claim that by retaining copy-text substantives (as well as accidentals, of course) in cases of indifferent variants one maximizes the chances of incorporating the author's intended readings. It is true that Greg considers the choice of copy-text to depend "solely on its formal features (accidentals)" and says that "fidelity as re-

41. If it is accorded to the later one, the question arises whether it should be accorded for spelling and punctuation as well as for words; to do so would of course involve the belief not only that compositors more accurately reproduced copy but also that authors normally made revisions in punctuation and spelling.

42. I use the phrase "compositorial error" because that is the one used by Davis; but this term should properly include intentional alterations made by compositors or others in the printing or publishing house. Such alterations would not be errors in the usual sense, since they would have been made intentionally. The appropriate counterpart to authorial revision, in other words, is nonauthorial alteration, whether that alteration results from error or deliberate change.

gards substantive readings is irrelevant" (p. 386); but these statements are not inconsistent with his view, regarding substantive variants in revised editions, that a later variant which is "either completely indifferent or manifestly inferior, or for the substitution of which no motive can be suggested, should be treated as fortuitous and refused admission to the text" (pp. 387–388). Whether or not Greg can be interpreted as supporting the position, however, is not the principal point, as Davis realizes. What Davis argues is that CEAA editors and commentators, who believe they are acting in the best interests of preserving the author's intention by emending the copy-text with later readings (both substantives and accidentals) only when there is compelling evidence to do so, are in fact guilty of yielding to "the tyranny of the copy-text." There is some irony in this situation, since everyone is agreed that Greg's aim was to give editors freedom to use their judgment in deciding individual readings and to liberate them from feeling bound to the substantives of the copy-text (or to all the substantive variants of a later text in which it is clear that some are authorial). The crux of the disagreement lies in determining what is meant by an "indifferent" variant. If an editor describes a particular variant as somewhat suggesting an authorial rather than a compositorial hand but finally considers the suggestion not to be strong enough to justify emendation of the copy-text, Davis believes that such an editor has not really regarded the variant as indifferent and has simply retreated to the comfort of sticking with the copy-text. Naturally, different editors might make different decisions on whether to emend at a given point: allowing editors to exercise judgment ensures that there will be no uniformity of result. But just because an argument can be made for emending need not lead one to think that the failure to emend signifies a backing away from a decision and a reliance on a mechanical rule. It is crucial in scholarly critical editing, after all, for editors to distinguish between their personal preferences and their informed judgment regarding what the author would have preferred. Calling a variant indifferent, therefore, is another way of saying that the evidence for its being authorial (or nonauthorial) is not, in the editor's judgment, sufficient to settle the matter. The trouble with Davis's discussion of this point is, first, that he does not make adequate allowance for the role of scholarly judgment in the determination of what is indifferent, and, second, that he does not investigate the question whether Greg's suggestion for the treatment of indifferent variants is valid for periods other than the Renaissance.[43] Davis ends with some examples from CEAA texts, intended

43. Davis's quotation of Greg's statement criticizing the view "That if a scribe makes a mistake he will inevitably produce nonsense" (p. 71) is not to the purpose since decisions regarding indifferent readings involve much more subtle distinctions than whether or not a reading makes sense. The passage in Greg where this statement is made occurs near the

to show the need for a fuller recognition of the "subjective and critical process" involved in critical editing, and he repeats the usual points (which are not in question) about the inevitable lack of definitiveness of the products of a critical process.[44] The last part of his essay is thus less impressive than the earlier part; but that early part takes its place as one of the key passages in the whole editorial discussion stimulated by the CEAA. If more of the discussion had been on such a level, editorial thinking would now be more advanced than it is.

The other major essay of this period, and one of greater significance, is Fredson Bowers's "Greg's 'Rationale of Copy-Text' Revisited."[45] This remarkable essay confronts directly the question of the applicability of Greg's rationale to periods other than those Greg himself was familiar with and suggests that certain cautions are in order in attempting to make such a transference. Because Bowers is the most influential champion of Greg's rationale, his reservations on this score are particularly striking. Champions of causes are often regarded as being inflexibly committed to the positions with which their names are normally identified, and some superficial critics of the CEAA have looked at various CEAA editors, including Bowers, in this light. Anyone who has followed Bowers's writings carefully, however, will recognize that this essay is not the first occasion on which his concern with developing an editorial rationale for works of the last four centuries has led him to adapt or move beyond what Greg specifically says. Perhaps the most important earlier instance is his essay on "Multiple Authority,"[46] which complements Greg's "Rationale" by taking up a class of textual relationships not covered by Greg (radiating texts, standing equidistant from a lost common ancestor, as opposed to a

---

beginning of Greg's essay (p. 375) and criticizes the mechanical approach, derived from Lachmann, of considering it "scientific" to follow a copy-text whenever its readings "were not manifestly impossible." The main line of the essay, of course, is to set forth a rationale for departing from the copy-text, even when its readings are possible, if one finds later variants that can be judged authorial revisions; the rationale does indeed involve retaining copy-text readings when the variants are not convincingly authorial, but that is not the same as saying that they are to be retained whenever they are not "manifestly impossible." What Davis quotes as Greg's criticism of adhering to the copy-text when variants are indifferent is actually Greg's criticism of an earlier approach: the idea that one should follow all the readings, except those that are manifestly impossible, of the text that is "generally more correct than any other." The CEAA procedure Davis criticizes is in no way a relapse to this position.

44. He is wrong in thinking that definitiveness is "implicit in the notion of a seal of approval" (p. 73): the discussions leading to the use of the indefinite article in the wording of the CEAA seal ("An Approved Text") recognized that more than one approvable text of a work could exist. (Whether or not any kind of seal should be used is a different matter, about which there has never been complete agreeement, even among CEAA editors.)

45. *SB*, 31 (1978), 90–161.

46. "Multiple Authority: New Problems and Concepts of Copy-Text," *Library*, 5th ser., 27 (1972), 81–115.

series of texts in linear descent). In contrast to that essay, which supplements Greg, the recent essay provides an incisive analysis of what Greg does in fact say. Bowers's knowledge of Renaissance texts enables him to examine closely the illustrations cited by Greg and to explain, more precisely than had been done before, the way in which Greg's recommendations arise from the textual situations generally encountered in work on Renaissance literature. From that firm base, he can then explore how well what Greg was saying fits other situations more characteristic of later periods. It is hard to imagine anyone better equipped for this task: Bowers's extensive editing of works from many periods has provided him with an amazing range of detailed examples. This kind of knowledge is exactly what had been missing from previous discussions of the broad applicability of Greg, and thoughtful editors will need to work their way through Bowers's analyses.

As the essay makes clear, the significance of copy-text for Greg was rather different from what it has been for editors of nineteenth- and twentieth-century works. Greg was under no misapprehension that the accidentals of an Elizabethan printed book reflected much of the author's practice; for Greg the choice of an early edition to supply copy-text was simply an expedient measure designed to ensure that the edited text would have accidentals as close in time and place to the author's as possible. As one moves to works of later periods, however, with more fixed spelling and punctuation and for which more authorial manuscripts survive, the chances of choosing a copy-text that will preserve authorial accidentals increases. For the editors of later works, accidentals have "a literary interest, not merely a philological" one: these editors are likely to believe "that the accidentals are an inseparable whole with the substantives in transmitting the author's total meaning" (p. 125). Therefore for them the choice of copy-text "transcends the grounds of expediency and must be recognized as having a critical significance beyond that which Greg conceived"; and they will more often be able to exercise critical judgment in the choice of accidentals "on the same basis that Greg urges for the substantives" (pp. 128–129). Although this difference in point of view might affect the significance of particular choices of copy-text, I think one can say that it would not in itself require different general rationales of copy-text for different periods. One could operate, for instance, within Greg's general rationale, even though the different conditions associated with different periods might cause editors more often to find persuasive evidence for selecting a revised edition in certain periods than in others. What would remain the same would be the presumption in favor of an early text as copy-text over a later, except when there is convincing evidence to the contrary. But since the purpose of choosing a copy-text is solely to provide a rationale for handling indifferent variants (substantives as well as accidentals), this presumption is fruitful only if there is reason to believe that texts normally deteriorate as they are reprinted or copied. We come back, then, to this issue as the central one. Bowers's analysis of the differences between Greg's concerns in his own editing and the concerns of editors of later writings is enlightening; but the question whether Greg's rationale is applicable to all periods (or periods other than the one for which it was originally designed) is a separate question, and one that turns entirely on the validity of the idea that texts usually deteriorate as they are transmitted. Bowers's attention to this point is therefore the aspect of his paper that is of the greatest moment.

There is no need here to go over the illustrations he discusses from post-Renaissance literature; they are all cogently set forth, and I have no quarrel with the textual observations made in them. What I wish to comment on is the generalization drawn from these examples. Bowers concludes that, in cases of linear transmission from manuscript to print or from one printed edition to another,

the closer one comes to periods where compositorial accuracy improves— especially in the setting from printed copy—the more the authority grows in favor of variants in a revised edition and the more likely it is that an indifferent variant in the revised text is authorial, not compositorial. If so, a very real question arises whether Greg's advice is a good editorial principle to adopt under changed conditions from those of Renaissance compositorial and scribal free-wheeling. (p. 155)

Although this statement specifically deals with substantive variants, a similar point is made about accidentals:

it is at least allowable that from the late seventeenth century when more uniformity in spelling and in standards of punctuation began to be imposed on compositors, the uncertainty that attaches to Elizabethan conditions of transmission begins to clear. . . . With the change come certain modifications that may need to be applied to the popular interpretation of Gregs' rationale. (p. 129)[47]

The concept of "accuracy" or fidelity entailed here clearly involves more than compositors' skill in following copy; it also takes into account their conventional practices. The state of English spelling in the Renaissance was such that compositors could feel free to follow their own spelling

47. At various times Bowers argues for applying the same kind of editorial judgment to variants in accidentals as to variants in substantives. Cf. his comment from pp. 128–129 quoted earlier, or his remark (p. 128, n. 31) that Greg concentrated "on editorial freedom to deal with variant substantives" but had "little recognition of the comparable opportunities that exist with accidentals." Bowers is surely right to make this point, and in what follows I shall take up both accidentals and substantives as equally relevant to a discussion of fidelity in textual transmission.

habits or to alter spellings to facilitate justification. As a result, what they set was not "accurate" in the sense that it did not fully correspond to their copy; but the lack of correspondence was not—at least in many cases was not—owing to carelessness or lack of ability. In the same way, any attempt to assess the performance of compositors in later periods must take into consideration the practices that compositors were expected, or allowed, to engage in. As spelling became more fixed, compositorial freedom to introduce variant spellings was correspondingly reduced; but if another kind of compositorial interference took its place, the divergence between copy and print was not necessarily decreased. For example, the growing concern with "correctness" of spelling and with syntactical punctuation in the nineteenth century meant that compositors were often expected to impose the preferred forms on wayward copy; such compositors did not have the freedom of their Elizabethan counterparts to follow their own inclinations, but they might equally transform the copy they were working from.[48] Furthermore, the differences between manuscript and first edition or between one edition and the next are not entirely to be accounted for by the activity of compositors, for there may also be copy-editors or publishers' "readers" whose function it is to make certain kinds of alterations (including many that are substantive) before the compositors enter the picture. Such persons were less in evidence in earlier years, before publishing as a distinct operation had fully developed; but in later years (the last two centuries or so), during the very time when—one might argue—compositorial fidelity to copy generally increased, the structure of publishing grew in complexity, and new positions with responsibility for making alterations in printer's copy came into being. The question that must be asked, therefore, is not whether compositorial accuracy increased over the years but whether the printing-publishing process as a whole has in certain periods resulted in so little alteration of printer's copy that, in the absence of contrary evidence, one had better regard the later variants, both substantives and accidentals, as presumably authorial.

It is extremely difficult, of course, to generalize about such matters. Not all printers and publishers in a given period will have behaved the same way—nor will a single publisher necessarily have treated each author the same way. Editors must naturally search for any evidence bearing on these matters in individual cases; and the more they learn about the author and the printers and publishers involved, the less they are in need of a generalization to fall back on. But when they can find no direct evidence pertaining to a particular situation, they are forced to try to

48. The argument is sometimes made that the imposition of standard forms, when they exist, is something that authors expect. But this argument moves into the question of authorial intention, which I shall touch on below. At present the concern is solely with how much of the author's practice survives in print.

generalize about the practices prevalent in the period in parallel circumstances. The papers of other authors and publishers are one source, and another is the published comments that appear in printers' manuals, publishers' style books, authors' guides, and the like. There have recently been some surveys of these books, showing—despite many individual variations—that it was not uncommon, through the nineteenth century and into the twentieth, for printers and publishers to regard spelling and punctuation as their preserve.[49] My own unsystematic examination of such books confirms this view. Not long ago, for instance, I came across Benjamin Drew's *Pens and Types; or, Hints and Helps for Those Who Write, Print, or Read*, published by Lee & Shepard of Boston in 1872—a book that I have not seen referred to in the published surveys. Its statements may of course reflect only the policy of Lee & Shepard, but on the subject of punctuation they do coincide with those of a number of other books. The distinction it makes between words and punctuation in fact resembles Greg's generalization about the practices of printers nearly three centuries earlier. Drew, after calling punctuation "the perfection of common sense," continues:

The printer and proof-reader are to take for granted, that, in every work which falls under their supervision, the proper agreement between thought and expression has been effected by the author. He alone has the right to change the words and their collocation; and, if fairly punctuated, it is better that the manuscript be, in this respect also, closely followed.

Every person who writes for the press should punctuate his work presentably; but—since the majority of writers are inattentive to punctuation—custom and convenience, if not necessity, have thrown upon the compositor and proof-reader the task of inserting in their proper places the grammatical points, that the author's meaning may be more readily apprehended. (p. 51)

Drew's attitude toward punctuation is clearly a nineteenth-century one, but his assertion that authors pay more attention to words than to punctuation and his acceptance of compositorial alteration of punctuation as a routine occurrence are not very different from points made by Greg. Even the idea that the division between words and punctuation is expedient, not logical, emerges from this passage—since the admission is made that punctuation can affect meaning.[50] Above all, Drew makes clear

---

49. See, in particular, John Bush Jones, "Victorian 'Readers' and Modern Editors: Attitudes and Accidentals Revisited," *PBSA*, 71 (1977), 49–59. See also James Thorpe, *Principles of Textual Criticism* (1972), pp. 151–164; and *SB*, 28 (1975), 222, n. 90 (*Selected Studies*, p. 300). Hugh Williamson, in the *Times Literary Supplement*, 15 September 1978, pp. 1017–19, expresses the opinion—in regard to both past and present—that "The printer believes that he has not only a right but a duty to amend the author's copy."

50. The other standard ironies of the situation are also present: thus the compositor is not to alter words, but he revises punctuation in order "that the author's meaning may be

that the printer has authority over the punctuation: the author's punctuation is to be followed only if the manuscript is "fairly" or "presentably" punctuated. One cannot generalize from the passage, or the many others like it, and claim that the attitudes expressed there were universal. Nevertheless, evidence of this sort turns up frequently enough to make one feel hesitant about accepting a generalization for any period that would place presumptive authority in the case of indifferent accidentals with the later rather than the earlier readings. And the same can obviously be said with equal force for substantive variants, especially in the years after the publishing industry became well developed: the officiousness of nineteenth-century publishers' "readers" is notorious. What must be emphasized is that in thinking about copy-text one is concerned only with indifferent variants. Whenever one has good reasons for choosing particular readings, one has no need for a copy-text theory; and among the reasons that will prevent readings from seeming indifferent is knowledge one has about the practices of the printer and publisher involved. The question for copy-text theory is whether, in the absence of evidence that one finds persuasive bearing on a particular case, one can generalize about a period as a whole and say that the odds favor the authority of indifferent variants in a revised edition. The picture that continues to emerge regarding the processes of textual transmission in all periods suggests that it would be unwise to take such a position. Bowers's discussion confronts this central issue more directly than any other essay and ends up questioning the appropriateness of Greg's rationale for post-Renaissance literature. I do not disagree with his analyses of specific cases but would simply suggest a different emphasis: choosing readings from revised editions or selecting revised editions as copy-texts when the evidence points in that direction does not—even if such instances are frequent—negate the existence of publishers' editors who made revisions or of compositors who were trained in the tradition of certain printers' manuals and took punctuation as their domain. As long as such possibilities for nonauthorial alteration of texts exist—as they seem to in all periods—the conservative approach would appear to be to consider an early text the better choice when the editor does not judge the available evidence conclusive one way or the other.

In addition to Bowers's essay, 1978 saw the appearance of several essays and a book that ought to be mentioned here.[51] One of the essays, by

---

more readily apprehended"—which implies that he is able to understand the author's meaning despite faulty punctuation but that the reading public is better served by the compositor's punctuation than the author's.

51. Of the essays dealing with particular textual decisions in a single edition, special note should be taken of Hugh Amory's "*Tom Jones* among the Compositors: An Examination," *Harvard Library Bulletin*, 26 (1978), 172–192. See also his other related essays in the

David Foxon,[52] is principally concerned with the same point as Bowers's. Arguing from his knowledge of the texts of Pope, Foxon suggests that Greg did not sufficiently distinguish between scribes and compositors: the latter were subject, Foxon says, to "the check of proof-reading, often by the author himself" (p. 121), as well as to the general rule set forth by Moxon that compositors were to follow copy strictly. An author's passing of proofs does not of course in itself tell one anything about that author's care in proofreading or imply that the text fully conforms to the author's intention. As for the printer's rule of compositorial fidelity, there were various occasions—as we have just noted and as Foxon himself observes—for departing from that rule, even though it is no doubt true that the simpler and easier course was to make no changes. Thus to say that Pope's compositors "followed copy rather than their own habits and inclinations, and this is what we expect from modern compositors" (p. 121) is not to say that as a general rule one should rely on compositorial fidelity. Foxon is right to notice that "correctors" at the press were also responsible for alterations[53] and to emphasize that the "crucial question" is what the author's practice was in correcting proof. He rightly sees where this leads (though I am not sure why it is a "frightening prospect," since it is to be taken for granted as the scholarly approach): editing a work "may well mean studying the whole publishing career of that author, the changes in his practices when writing manuscripts and when proofreading, the conventions of his printers" (p. 123). These are useful points for Foxon to have underscored; but it is not clear how his discussion is a modification of Greg. He has established that in reading proof Pope was as concerned with accidentals as with substantives; and in later editions Pope "continued to make revisions on a large scale," with the changes in accidentals outnumbering those in substantives—"later editions refine his punctuation and remove typographical inconsistencies" (p. 119). "In this context," Foxon asserts, "Greg's proposals are not applicable, and my experience suggests that the case of Pope is by no means unusual. The cause of our present difficulties is the belief that a single generalized rule can have universal application." All one can do in the face of such a statement, made at this late date by a perceptive and learned bibliographer, is to repeat once again—by now perhaps rather tiredly—what has been said time after time before: the only "generalized rule"

same journal: "*Tom Jones* Plus and Minus: Towards a Practical Text," 25 (1977), 101–113; "The History of 'The Adventures of a Foundling': Revising *Tom Jones*," 27 (1979), 277–303; "*Jones* Papers: Envoi," 28 (1980), 175–180.

52. "Greg's 'Rationale' and the Editing of Pope," *Library*, 5th ser., 33 (1978), 119–124.

53. In connection with this point, he claims, "The corrector's role has been generally ignored by Greg and his followers" (p. 122). Whether or not this is true, the existence of the corrector reinforces the validity of Greg's general rationale.

that Greg proposes is for situations in which one has no basis otherwise for making a decision; to find that a number of authors revised accidentals as well as substantives so thoroughly for a late edition as to make that edition the best choice for copy-text in no way contradicts what Greg was saying.[54]

At roughly the same time the first of a series of articles under the rubric "Redefining the Definitive" was published in the *Bulletin of Research in the Humanities*. The inauguration of a series to examine "definitive" editions in the first number of this journal under its new title shows its intention to continue the interest in editorial methodology exhibited in 1971, when it (as *Bulletin of the New York Public Library*) contained a brief flurry of discussion about CEAA practices.[55] Although this first piece is devoted to particular textual decisions in one edition,[56] the second, later in the year, raises a general point about the treatment of punctuation in CEAA editions. In it Harry Knowles Girling argues that "CEAA-approved editors" restrict authorial freedom of punctuation by imposing printers' conventional practices on manuscripts or by preserving the compositorial practices of printed texts.[57] Authors who protest printers' regularizations of punctuation, he says, "would lament the embalming of printers' choices in a 'definitive' text of their work" (p. 303); and scholars who adhere to a printed copy-text are "expending their devoted labours in perpetuating the original flouting of authorial intentions" (p. 297). Girling's generalization here is off the mark: although some CEAA editors have in certain instances made unwise decisions about punctuation, CEAA editors for the most part would agree with Girling's insistence on the importance of authorial punctuation; the effort to incorporate authors' rather than printers' punctuation into scholarly texts has normally been one of their primary concerns. Despite this misplaced attempt to discredit CEAA editing, Girling's article is refreshing because his criticism is just the opposite of the more usual one: more often critics of the CEAA are inclined to say that authors expected their works to be styled by the printer or publisher and that selecting manu-

---

54. Another point of Foxon's, to which he devotes a short paragraph (p. 120), is to criticize what he calls Greg's assumption that authorial spelling "should be recovered regardless of an author's wishes." His conclusion that certain of an author's "idiosyncrasies" are more properly preserved in a study (or transcription) of the manuscripts than in an edition of the works is not to be quarreled with; but the general line of his argument on this score seems based on an overly simple view of authorial intention, equating authors' statements or expectations with intentions.

55. References to, and an analysis of, these articles are provided in *SB*, 28 (1975), 202–211 (*Selected Studies*, pp. 280–289).

56. Thomas Woodson, "The Title and Text of Thoreau's 'Civil Disobedience,'" *Bulletin of Research in the Humanities*, 81 (1978), 103–112.

57. "A Toot of the Trumpet against the Scholarly Regiment of Editors," *Bulletin of Research in the Humanities*, 81 (1978), 297–323.

scripts as copy-texts does not do justice to the authors' intentions. Girling, however, believes—in line with most CEAA editors—that authorial
punctuation reflects "semantic and stylistic distinctions" (p. 297) and
that "the punctuation to be observed in nineteenth-century authors'
manuscripts seems to have its own alternative consistency" (p. 303; alternative, that is, to printers' practice). He carries this position so far as
to argue that "the editing of a piece of holograph manuscript as copy-
text raises the question of the necessity of emending at all" (p. 304). Obviously a facsimile edition of a manuscript has its place; but if one is
preparing a critical edition, one cannot by definition rule out the possibility of emending. An author's manuscript may contain slips of the
pen or readings later altered by the author, and a critical editor using
the manuscript as copy-text would have to emend at those points. Emendations involve judgment and therefore are sometimes wrong; but the
goal is to establish, as Girling would wish, the readings (including punctuation) of the author.[58] The value of Girling's essay is that it provides a
forceful statement of the reasons for preserving an author's own punctuation and offers one of the most detailed analyses available within the
context of editorial discussion showing the ways in which punctuation
affects meaning. After examining the changes in punctuation in the New
York Edition of *The Princess Casamassima*, he concludes that James "had
succeeded in exemplifying a punctuation system unguided by rules or
precedents, and controlled only by a sense of taste and style" (p. 318).
James's approach, he goes on, "gives a clue to the way that all authors
(and all pen-wielders, even the most humble) might regard punctuation,
were they not bullied into accepting a system that was developed to suit
the exigencies of hand-compositors and maintained to support the con-
formist pieties of copy-editors and editorial scholars." One can overlook
Girling's inaccurate generalizations about scholarly editors in order to
have his strong argument on behalf of the determination and retention
of authorial punctuation, an argument that in fact supports the view of
a large proportion of editorial scholars.

One more publication of 1978, appearing in September, is Philip
Gaskell's *From Writer to Reader: Studies in Editorial Method*. This book
consists of a ten-page introduction on the general principles of editing,

58. When a printed edition is copy-text, Girling seems to imply that an editor can
purge it of the printers' punctuation by using standard printers' manuals or handbooks of
punctuation, like De Vinne's or John Wilson's (pp. 301–302). Even if printed punctuation
had been as regular as Girling suggests since about 1850, and therefore as identifiable, one
would still not know, in the absence of a manuscript, what the author's punctuation had
been, or whether indeed it had coincided with the printers' practice. Girling is right to say
that editors need to be aware of these manuals; but how an editor can avoid, in the absence
of a manuscript, retaining punctuation from a printed copy-text, and thus inevitably some
of the printer's punctuation, is not made clear.

followed by twelve chapters, each of which examines the textual problems in a particular work, normally focusing on a single passage and repro- ducing the various relevant texts of that passage. In his introduction Gaskell improves in some respects on his unsatisfactory treatment of editing at the end of *A New Introduction to Bibliography* (1972).[59] For instance, he now recognizes the reasons why it may be defensible to allow copy-text inconsistences to stand, and he sees that there is a difference be- tween authorial acquiescence and intention. As a whole, however, his introductory chapter unfortunately does not succeed in providing a solid foundation for editorial thinking. His eagerness to emphasize the idea that one cannot edit by rules causes him to neglect certain basic principles or distinctions that are necessary for clear thinking on editorial matters. In a single sentence he can bring together three distinct approaches to editing without explaining how radically different they are: the editor, he says, in selecting a copy-text, "may consider whether the choice of a particular version will result in a system of punctuation, spelling, etc., in the edited text which is more likely than another to represent the author's own intentions for the form of the work; whether the resulting system is better critically than one that would result from a different choice; and whether it is the system most likely to be acceptable to readers of the edition" (p. 6). He proceeds to suggest that when an editor has insufficient evidence regarding authorial intentions, "the editor might decide for instance to follow the version that is best on critical grounds." What he never explains is how such a switch would mean preparing an entirely different kind of edition; he never clearly distinguishes between scholarly critical editing—in which the editors' judgments are directed toward at- tempting to establish what the author would have wanted—and another kind of editing in which choices are based on the editors' own critical preferences. Such imprecision and lack of logic occur throughout the book.[60] The individual analyses are nevertheless useful up to a point, since they conveniently bring together some basic information about a wide range of texts; but any commentary Gaskell adds to the factual in- formation must be taken with great caution.

Given Gaskell's declared "message" that "the editor should not base his work on *any* predetermined rule or theory" (p. vii), it is perhaps not surprising that he should have joined those who look on the CEAA as

---

59. For some comments on that treatment, see *SB*, 28 (1975), 224–227 (*Selected Studies*, pp. 302–305).

60. Other weaknesses seem less important in comparison. One of them is Gaskell's seemingly irrational aversion to extensive apparatus. He repeatedly criticizes what he re- gards as excessive documentation; but characteristically his principal objection to a detailed record of variants is that it is "unreadable" and "unattractive" (p. 25). (Davis similarly refers to "massive lists of variants" that "invite themselves not to be read" [p. 74].)

rigidly doctrinaire, inflexibly insistent on a single rule. A number of his observations appear to stem from this image of the CEAA, but the one chapter that directly involves a CEAA edition is the chapter on Hawthorne's *The Marble Faun* (pp. 183–195). That chapter is particularly relevant in the present context and can represent the kinds of problems that occur elsewhere in the book.[61] After a brief account of the surviving textual evidence, pointing out that the compositors of the first edition "normalized the text freely" (p. 185), Gaskell discusses the choice of copy-text. The Ohio State *Marble Faun*, he says, "is based, in accordance with the principles of the series, on the manuscript, not on the first printed edition" (p. 189). The manuscript is indeed the copy-text, but otherwise this sentence is misleading, for it suggests that the CEAA required surviving manuscripts to be used as copy-texts. What the CEAA guidelines in fact say is that a finished or printer's-copy manuscript would "normally" become copy-text but that an author's habits of revision in proof "may modify this choice."[62] Gaskell, however, is convinced of the rigidity of the CEAA and describes the CEAA application of Greg's rationale as "both more comprehensive and less flexible than Greg's pragmatic approach," asserting incorrectly that "it denies the editor much critical discretion in the choice of copy-text" (p. 190).[63] In extending Greg's rationale from Renaissance works, for which manuscripts do not often survive, to later works, the CEAA has —according to Gaskell— adopted the "very dubious" assumption that, "in the absence of evidence to the contrary, a nineteenth- or twentieth-century author 'intended' the manuscript rather than the printed version of his work" (p. 191). Gaskell does not pursue the meaning of authorial intention or explore reasons why students of an author might legitimately prefer to read a text with that author's punctuation rather than a compositor's or copy-editor's. Instead he shifts the grounds of the discussion: because, he says, we often cannot know whether authors "specifically approve or disapprove the normalization of the text" that occurs in the process of printing and pub-

---

61. Even though the focus of the chapter, as Gaskell himself points out, is somewhat different from the others, for here the principal subject is the CEAA edition, whereas in the others the emphasis is on the textual questions raised by the work, not on a particular scholarly edition (though some discussion of a particular edition is often appended). This shift of emphasis in this one chapter is itself revealing. I am limiting myself to this chapter here, because I have commented on Gaskell's book in considerably greater detail, giving some attention to each chapter, in a review in the *Library*, 6th ser., 2 (September 1980).

62. This passage in the CEAA *Statement of Editorial Principles and Procedures* (rev. ed., 1972), p. 5, goes on to describe two situations in which a surviving manuscript would not become copy-text.

63. Vinton A. Dearing, in a helpful review of Gaskell's book (*Analytical & Enumerative Bibliography*, 3 [1979], 105–116), provides an effective criticism of this statement (p. 111). He also offers a fresh summary of Greg's rationale and concludes that it is "perfectly general," not limited in its application to Renaissance books.

lishing, all we can state is "that this version is to be preferred to that on other—perhaps critical—grounds." Just what he means by "critical" becomes clear in the next paragraph, when he explains why he agrees in this instance that the manuscript should be copy-text. The manuscript, he says, has "excellent punctuation" that contributes to the rhythm of Hawthorne's prose "in a way that the mechanical details of the normalized printed texts do not"; thus "there is a good critical case for basing an edition on the text of the final manuscript, which is that it offers the most convincing punctuation of the text" (pp. 191–192). The implication is that if the printed text had contained more "convincing" punctuation, it would become the copy-text, regardless of whether it was the author's. What Gaskell has done here—as he does repeatedly—is to confuse the attempt to establish an author's own words and punctuation with the attempt to produce the artistically "best" text of a work. He claims, "There is no need to introduce the assumption, which cannot be supported by evidence, that Hawthorne intended or would have preferred his own punctuation to that of the first edition" (p. 192). But if one is engaged in producing a *scholarly critical* edition, one is by definition attempting to establish an author's own words and punctuation, not one's own preferences, and part of the "evidence" is one's developed sensitivity to the author's characteristics. Whether the punctuation is "excellent" and "convincing" is beside the point, unless it is excellent and convincing in a way that the editor has learned, through close study of the author, to associate with that author's punctuation.

The central issue Gaskell attempts to deal with here—the choice of copy-text as between manuscript and first edition, and the assessment of authorial intention in relation to this choice—deserves careful attention, but Gaskell's treatment only confuses the question.[64] He then turns to an evaluation of whether the emendations in the CEAA *Marble Faun* are "both necessary and right." In objecting to what he regards as excessive regularization, he makes some good points. But he nowhere alludes to the practice of other CEAA editions; and since at the beginning of the

64. His discussion of this issue in other chapters does not help. For instance, in the cases of *The Heart of Mid-Lothian* and *David Copperfield*, Gaskell recommends choosing the first editions over the manuscripts, despite publishing-house normalization, on the grounds that the authors were "content with the result" (p. 114) or "did not prevent these alterations from being carried out" (p. 152); but when he comes to *Henry Esmond* he is much more sympathetic to the manuscript, without explaining what makes this situation different in his view from the other two. (For some further relevant discussion of authorial intentions and expectations, see Jane Millgate's "The Limits of Editing: The Problems of Scott's *The Siege of Malta*," *Bulletin of Research in the Humanities*, 82 [1979], 190–212. This unfinished manuscript, she says, brings into focus the question of "judging the kind and degree of supplementary intervention an author assumes his manuscript will receive, and how far it is legitimate for an editor to seek to recreate that intervention and regard it as in a sense part of the text" [p. 210].)

chapter he calls this volume "a typical CEAA edition" (p. 184), he leaves the impression that the kind of regularization he describes is characteristic of CEAA editions—which is not the case. Indeed, the final two paragraphs of the chapter consist of entirely unwarranted generalizations, coming at the conclusion of a discussion of a single volume:

The CEAA and its editors have been noble in vision, rich in good intentions as well as in funds, indefatigable in industry, and scrupulous in accuracy. These qualities, and the features of the CEAA editions that derive from them, are applauded even by the CEAA's critics. Yet the whole great enterprise seems to have gone astray. CEAA editions are not and never can be "definitive"; their main editorial principle is unsound yet inflexibly applied; and individual editions sealed by the Center can be grossly imperfect.

It would seem that editing—which is at least as much a part of literary criticism as of bibliography—cannot well be regimented, and that editors should always consider the why and the wherefore and the how of their work according to the circumstances and the needs of each individual case. Books of rules can prove delusive guides. (p. 195)

The idea that one volume—regarded for whatever reason as "typical"— can lead to such conclusions derives from Gaskell's view of the inflexibility of the CEAA and the resulting assumption that all volumes in the series are identical. Actually, the "main editorial principle"—if by that is meant Greg's rationale—liberates editors to use their judgment; so even if it were "inflexibly applied" it would result in a great deal of variation, which in fact is what exists. I would certainly not wish to defend all CEAA volumes or every decision made in them. But whatever opinion one holds of individual volumes, one must deplore the kind of glib generalization that Gaskell indulges in here. It is sad to have to recognize that his book, which one might reasonably have expected to be an important statement, marks no advance in editorial thinking and indeed does not rise above the level of many of the less satisfactory contributions to this continuing discussion.[65]

---

65. Another book of 1978—*Editing Nineteenth-Century Fiction*, ed. Jane Millgate, containing the papers from the 1977 Toronto editorial conference—includes some essays that should be mentioned here. Peter Shillingsburg, in "Textual Problems in Editing Thackeray" (pp. 41–59), makes a clear and succinct statement of the unexceptionable view that scholarly texts require judgment and that "there can be no such thing as *a* definitive text" (p. 47). His decision to "present first intentions" in his text of *Pendennis* is justifiable; whether he should do the same thing "even for works without the dramatic revisions of *Pendennis*" (p. 46) is less clear from the information furnished in the essay. If, in every case, what revisions there are serve to alter the overall effect of the work, he would of course have the choice of editing either the first or the later version; but if the rationale is to present first intentions in the text and later readings in the apparatus simply because that arrangement provides a more orderly chronological register of the variants, one could raise the same questions that come to mind in connection with Zeller's approach. Shillingsburg also includes an interesting discussion of Thackeray's "approval" of first-edition punctuation in

It remains to note briefly one or two comments from 1979, which unhappily show what little effect all this editorial debate has had on improving the caliber of some of the discussions that get into print. F. W. Bateson prefaces a textual discussion of *The School for Scandal*[66] with some remarks on Greg's rationale that exhibit the same mixing up of distinct approaches to editing already observed in Gaskell. Greg's "mechanical ruling," he says, growing out of work on Elizabethan drama, was more concerned with printers' corruptions than authors' revisions (p. 323), and he believes that "biblio-textual" research is "helpless before authorial *revision*" (p. 322)—an argument that obviously ignores the central role Greg gives to editorial judgment in detecting authorially revised readings. The novel aspect of his criticism of Greg, however, is his opinion that "Such textual philistinism as Greg's may be ultimately social in its origin" (p. 324); his astonishing view is that Greg, because he was wealthy and therefore interested in property, looked on literary works as the "private property" of their authors and wished to tie later editions and readers to authors' revised readings even when those readings were inferior. Everyone would agree that authors can be whimsical and unsystematic in making revisions: "A revision . . . may stay or go or revert to its original form as the author decides—on the inexplicable spur of

---

Vanity Fair (pp. 55–57). He is aware that such tacit approval is not the same as intention, but he regards the manuscript as "inadequate" and in need of additional punctuation. A critical approach to this problem leads him to a sensible conclusion, one that is perfectly standard but nevertheless worth repeating: "the editor cannot hope to say that his edition *recovers* Thackeray's intentions, but only that he has tried to fulfil those intentions as his judgment and imagination have led him to understand them" (p. 56). Michael Millgate's paper, "The Making and Unmaking of Hardy's Wessex Edition" (pp. 61–82), provides a perfect demonstration of the way in which authors' acceptance of house-styling does not amount to their actually wishing to have their writing so punctuated. Hardy's texts, punctuated "carefully and deliberately in manuscript," went through a long process of "erosion and accretion"; he accepted "the heavier and more rigid punctuation imposed on his work" because in "his early years he must have felt too insecure and too busy to protest" and "later on it must have seemed unnecessary to worry over details that had been so long established" (p. 68). And the final paper in the volume, Hershel Parker's "Aesthetic Implications of Authorial Excisions: Examples from Nathaniel Hawthorne, Mark Twain, and Stephen Crane" (pp. 99–119), is an effective plea for further examination of the concept of authorial intention in the light of recent work in aesthetics, speech-act theory, creativity theory, and related fields. He shows that when writers "merely delete passages without rethinking and rewriting extensive parts of the book" they "often do more harm than good" (p. 101); editors must therefore investigate the circumstances surrounding any authorial revision and be aware of the aesthetic implications of accepting the last revision as the one that best reflects the author's wishes.

66. "The Application of Thought to an Eighteenth-Century Text: *The School for Scandal*," in *Evidence in Literary Scholarship: Essays in Memory of James Marshall Osborn*, ed. René Wellek and Alvaro Ribeiro (1979), pp. 321–335. My comments on some earlier related statements of Bateson's can be found in *SB*, 28 (1975), p. 227, n. 99 (*Selected Studies*, p. 305).

the moment, or in the light perhaps of the passage's immediate context, or reconsidered to conform to the general pattern of the work or his writings generally (or even his life)" (p. 323). Of course an editor could continue this process, but the result would not be of particular interest to students of the author; the scholarly editor must be concerned with what the author did. Bateson does not seem to realize that scholarly critical editors are not limited to believing that last is best; they must, and do, try to assess the motivation underlying revisions and decide when revisions produce essentially new works, and they will not always adopt the last revision. But they could not agree with Bateson that the "responsible editor" will select "whatever after due consideration he (the editor) believes the best authorial version to be, whether it happens to be early, middle-period, or last" (p. 324). Editors of most authors will sympathize with Bateson when he says that Sheridan "was continually questioning himself—and very often coming up with the wrong answer!" (p. 333). But for a scholarly editor to choose, in each case of authorial revision, the reading that seems preferable "considered as meaning, good English, good literature" (p. 335) is not the way to be "responsibly eclectic" (p. 324). The place to make those judgments is not within the text of a scholarly critical edition.[67]

Another comment from 1979 that reflects an unfortunate misconcep-

---

67. Another essay in the same collection that touches on some theoretical aspects of editing is Tom Davis and Susan Hamlyn's "What Do We Do When Two Texts Differ? *She Stoops to Conquer* and Textual Criticism," pp. 263–279. The authors repeat a familiar criticism of Greg: that his rationale is unsatisfactory because it tries to substitute a rule of thumb for aesthetic judgment. They say that an editor who must "choose between two equally authoritative variants . . . can do so only on the basis of subjective and aesthetic judgement: there may be no possible objective rationale or scrap of external evidence to relieve him of this responsibility" (p. 275). But if "aesthetic judgement" is taken to mean a decision as to what the author would have wished and if there are grounds for making this decision, Greg certainly did not believe that a rule should stand in the way of such a judgment. The issue turns on whether editorial judgment is conceived of as being directed toward establishing authorially intended readings or readings that appeal to the editor's own literary sensibility. Davis and Hamlyn seem to be leaning toward the latter approach when they say that an editor, after consulting all the evidence, constructs a text "that represents his subjective perception of the work itself" (p. 277). Confusion about the role of subjective judgment in scholarly editing has been a principal problem with many such discussions, and the situation is not helped here by the introduction of the idea that a literary work is a "subjective construct, any physical manifestation being an approximation" (p. 276). Although one can argue that "The symphony—the play—does not exist wholly in any of its performances or published forms," the relation between a performance and a printed text is a very different matter from the relation among various printed texts of the same "work." One can agree that an editor produces *a* text, not *the* text, without agreeing with the reasoning that leads Davis and Hamlyn to that position. (Some brief additional consideration of authorial intention in relation to performed dramatic works occurs in John Bush Jones, "Editing Victorian Playwrights: Some Problems, Priorities, and Principles," *Theatre Survey*, 17 [1976], 106–123.)

tion—one that is perhaps more widespread—occurs in J. F. Fuggles's essay reviewing the bibliographical research of 1978.[68] In the course of this review he says that the argument for the exact transcription of historical documents would be strengthened by examples showing how "the meaning or significance had been affected by modernization" (p. 10).[69] Presumably he means "normalization" as well as "modernization," for the issue is broader than the question of whether or not to modernize. But the principal, and troubling, point is his implication that tampering with the punctuation and spelling of the original is unacceptable only if it can be shown to alter the meaning of the text. The burden of proof, however, should be the other way round. If an alteration is thought not to change the meaning (or "clarify" it, as some editors prefer to say), then what is the purpose of making it? Readers are not normally prevented from understanding a text by oddities and inconsistencies of punctuation and spelling, and when these irregularities are characteristic of the author what is the point of altering them? It is hard to see why editors think they are accomplishing anything by straightening out the details of spelling and punctuation in a letter or journal simply for the sake of tidying up.[70] To say that the tidying up does not alter the meaning is no defense, since it provides no reason for making any change at all. In fact, of course, any shift from the author's spelling and punctuation is likely to affect nuances of meaning. But even if that were not the case, why should one not prefer to read a document as its author wrote it? Fuggles proceeds to repeat an argument that should have been discredited long before now, one that attempts to make a distinction between historical documents and works of literature: "scholars come to different kinds of texts for different reasons," he says, and "inevitably this will influence editorial procedures. The historian will come to the letters of Lord John Russell because he is interested, perhaps, in what Lord John said to a cabinet colleague on a particular subject. Milton's punctuation

---

68. "A Review of the Year's Research," *Direction Line*, No. 8 (Spring 1979), pp. 1–32. The review includes some comment on the articles by Davis, Foxon, and Bowers discussed above, largely stressing the importance of "editorial freedom" and suggesting that Fuggles concurs with those who believe that the application of Greg's rationale to later literature has somehow restricted such freedom.

69. His discussion of this point is a part of his remarks on my essay "The Editing of Historical Documents," *SB*, 31 (1978), 1–56 (*Selected Studies*, pp. 451–506).

70. Fuggles's view that "it is easier to edit texts transcribing exactly" would not be agreed to by some historians. In a report on an April 1979 Mellon Conference on historical editing in *Annotation*, 7, no. 2 (July 1979), 8–9, William B. Willcox is reported to have said of literal transcription that it "takes too much time to do it properly." He is quoted as calling it a "theological approach" and "going wrong with confidence." (This report cites several other opinions, including the claim that "changing a dash to a period does not affect meaning, but adds clarification." It is reassuring to know that "The session ended without any clear consensus.")

will excite interest in a way that Lord John's will not" (pp. 10–11). It is no doubt true that Milton's punctuation is of greater interest than Russell's, but not for the reason Fuggles implies. Fuggles seems to be saying that historians are interested in "content" and that students of literature are concerned with "form" as well. But both groups wish to understand as fully as possible what is being communicated by certain pieces of writing. In approaching that task one can no more rule out Russell's punctuation than Milton's; the punctuation in each case is part of the essential evidence that scholars must have before them. The notion that punctuation is of more significance in "literature" than in other writing cannot be supported, even if what constitutes "literature" could be identified. That it still has its adherents shows that there is yet some way to go before fruitful communication among editors in all fields can be achieved.

This glance over editorial discussions of the past six years has revealed, I trust, certain recurrent issues that have proved particularly troubling to those who have been moved to write about editorial matters. Some of the discussions have been irresponsible and others carefully thought out, but whatever their quality they keep returning to a small number of basic problems. Evaluating those discussions amounts to working out a coherent theoretical approach to editing, as I hope my remarks illustrate. But analyzing particular arguments as they come up in a chronological survey does not produce a systematic statement, though it can provide the underlying argument to support such a statement. As a result of working through these discussions, therefore, one should be in a position to formulate, and to read with understanding, a summary statement of editorial rationale.

II

The central questions of editing can be simply put. Answers to them require thought and do not always come easily. But the editorial debate that has appeared in print in recent years has sometimes made the search for answers more complicated than necessary by diverting attention to issues that exist only as a result of misconceptions. Although there has thus been a certain amount of wasted effort, one at least can now be fairly sure of the problem spots. I shall therefore take advantage of the existence of all this discussion, and analysis of the discussion, by offering a compressed statement regarding the basic areas of difficulty. I need not elaborate on the points here, because the arguments have been rehearsed in detail, and often more than once, in what has appeared during the last several years. A concise expression of some basic propositions can serve a purpose, indeed, because of the very voluminousness of the published discussion. And I think that a further purpose can be served, at this stage, by making no reference to the CEAA or to Greg's rationale. Such a body of emotional reactions and stock responses has by now grown up around them that simply to mention them in a theoretical discussion deflects some readers' concentration in unprofitable directions.[71] Whether or not some ideas have been attributed to Greg that are not actually to be found in his writing is obviously a different question from whether or not those ideas are sound; but sometimes the two questions have become confused. There can be no doubt that Greg's rationale has been of crucial importance in the development of modern editorial thinking; but that thinking has carried Greg's line of reasoning beyond the point at which he left it. To keep returning to the question of whether Greg's rationale is applicable to periods later than the Renaissance, as some critics do, is a rather pointless way of proceeding, or at least places the emphasis on the wrong part of the issue. The important question is whether a particular way of thinking (which happens to have been influenced by Greg, but that is beside the point) offers a reasonable approach to editorial matters. The published debate suggests, I think, that the principal problems fall into three groups, and I shall describe what appears to me to be a reasonable approach to each of these three areas.

The first set of questions consists of the preliminary ones that any editor must decide at the outset, questions about what kind of edition is to be undertaken. The most basic distinction is between editions in which the aim is historical—the reproduction of a particular text from the past or the reconstruction of what the author intended—and those in which the editor's own personal preferences determine the alterations to be made in a copy-text. Scholarly editions conform to the first approach, and presumably scholarly editing is what this whole debate has been about. Yet elementary as this distinction is, it has been lost sight of in some of the discussions. Historical scholarship naturally involves judgment and subjective decisions. But there is a difference between using one's informed judgment to attempt to decide what readings reflect the author's intention and making subjective decisions reflecting only one's own tastes and inclinations; and this difference has sometimes been ignored by those who are eager to stress the subjective element in critical editing. After one has decided to undertake a scholarly edition, and understands what that means, one still has to decide whether the edition is to be critical (that is, using editorial judgment to determine when, and whether, emendations are to be made in the text) or noncritical (that is, reproducing exactly one particular text, without alteration). Choice

71. Examining the decisions made in particular CEAA volumes naturally continues to be a valuable scholarly activity; but many of the comments about "CEAA editions" in general are of little use because they assume a uniformity among CEAA volumes that does not by any means exist.

between these alternatives will be affected by the nature of the text to be edited: pieces of writing to be presented as documents are most appropriately provided in noncritical texts, whereas those to be presented as finished works are most usefully offered in critical texts.

This is really all that needs to be said in a general way about the choice among different kinds of editions—the absence of any reference to modernizing, to the nature of the intended audience, or to whether or not writings are "literary" being meant to suggest that these matters need not be taken into account. However, so much has been said about them—they have proved to be the most prominent red herrings of editorial debate—that it now seems impossible to pass over them with no comment at all. Regularizing and modernizing (their aims may be different, but they amount to the same thing) are ahistorical in orientation and therefore have no place in the historical approach to texts—which is to say, in scholarly editions. Punctuation and spelling have been the subject of a disproportionately large amount of editorial discussion, principally as a result of a doubly-mistaken assumption: that punctuation and spelling are somehow not full-fledged elements of a text, giving an editor license to be freer with them than with the words, and that most readers will have difficulty reading—or may refuse to read—texts that do not exhibit in punctuation and spelling the consistency or the particular practices they are accustomed to. The defensible position in each case is the opposite: that punctuation and spelling are integral parts of a text, affecting its meaning and impact,[72] and that readers do not generally find it a great difficulty or inconvenience to read a text containing spelling and punctuation from an earlier time. If readers are not so easily put off as some editors think, and if there is at least a chance (to understate the case) that alterations in spelling and punctuation may distort the meaning, then why should editors go to the trouble of regularizing and modernizing? And if one follows this line of thinking, the question of intended audience becomes irrelevant, because a text prepared for scholars will also be the appropriate one to present to students and to the general public. The intended audience may indeed be a factor—for economic reasons—in deciding whether a detailed apparatus is to be published with the text; but there is no reason why it should be a factor in determining the treatment of the text itself.[73] Neither should the question whether the work is belletristic have a bearing: it is delusory to think that punctu-

72. This point applies to all texts; but obviously the editor's approach to the spelling and punctuation of an ancient text, the earliest surviving form of which is a scribal copy centuries later than the time of the author, will be different from the approach to be taken when texts survive that are contemporaneous, or nearly so, with the author.

73. Except possibly for some of the earliest works in a language, which might be said to require "translation," rather than simply "modernization," for the general reader.

ation is more crucial to written "literature" than to the written communication of historians, philosophers, or scientists. That the line between "creative" writing and "factual" writing cannot be clearly defined is well illustrated by Hayden White's comments on what historical narratives "most manifestly are"—"verbal fictions, the contents of which are as much invented as found and the forms of which have more in common with their counterparts in literature than they have with those in the sciences."[74] Even scientific writing, though it may be different in some respects, uses words and punctuation to communicate ideas, and anyone wishing to understand a scientific work will need—just as much as readers of "literary" works—a text that is reliable in its punctuation as well as in its words.

The second large group of questions concerns the nature of authorial intention and how one is to handle the difficult distinction between intention and expectation. First it should be said that these are questions entailing critical judgment and are relevant only to critical editing. If one is producing a noncritical text, one is concerned to reproduce what actually appears in a particular document or impression, regardless of the extent to which it reflects the author's intentions. Of course, critical judgment about intention may enter into the choice of document or impression to reproduce in the first place and into the annotation supplied with the noncritical text, but it will not have a bearing on the readings of the text itself. In a scholarly critical edition, on the other hand, the aim is to emend the selected text so that it conforms to the author's intention; one can never fully attain such a goal (or know that one has attained it), but at least one can move toward it by applying informed judgment to the available evidence. Obviously many writers have different intentions at different times, and in such cases one must decide which version of a work one wishes to edit, for no one critical text can reflect these multiple intentions simultaneously. But when an authorial revision does not indicate a new conception of a work but simply a continuation of the process of perfecting the expression of the same conception, that revision can legitimately replace the earlier reading in a single critical (that is, eclectic) text. Judging when such eclecticism is justified and when it is not remains a difficult decision, but it is central to critical editing.[75] A related and equally basic problem is determining

74. "The Historical Text as Literary Artifact," in *The Writing of History: Literary Form and Historical Understanding*, ed. Robert H. Canary and Henry Kozicki (1978), pp. 41–62 (quotation from p. 42).

75. To argue, as some do, that such eclecticism is always improper because it violates the historical integrity of individual texts is effectively to eliminate the possibility of critical editing, even though it is sometimes asserted that each text individually can still be critically edited. Each one can, in the sense that critical judgment can be applied to the problem of detecting errors; but to rule out the adoption of revised readings from later

what relation authorial expectation bears to intention. Sometimes one hears the argument that a first-edition text should be preferred to the manuscript printer's copy because the author expected certain alterations to be carried out in the publisher's office. Each case must of course be looked at individually, but two general considerations should be kept in mind: first, that readers of a scholarly critical text are primarily interested in what the author did rather than what a publisher's editor did; and, second, that authors give their "approval," in various ways and for various motives, to alterations that they do not really prefer (as anyone who has written for publication knows all too well). Whether one is speaking of changes in wording or changes in punctuation, it is too simple a view to claim that a particular author expected certain kinds of alterations to be made and therefore that the published text takes precedence over the manuscript text; in a specific instance the published text may indeed deserve to take precedence, but one must be extremely cautious about attributing authorial intention or preference to alterations simply because they were passed, in one fashion or another, by the author. Thus scholarly critical editors frequently find themselves trying to reverse the activities of earlier publishers' editors. In this connection, some comments recently made by Robert Gottlieb, president of Alfred A. Knopf, are particularly striking because they emphasize respect for the author's text and define the role of the publisher's editor as essentially one of encouragement and support. "Even now," Gottlieb says, "it irritates me to know that Dickens changed the end of 'Great Expectations' because someone told him to. It's bad enough that the change was a mistake, but it's even worse to know that someone convinced him to make it."[76] What the scholarly critical editor must do, as Gottlieb does here, is to consider the motivation underlying textual changes; such an editor must try to disentangle the author's own wishes from the other elements

---

texts artificially restricts the critical process, for some of the superseded readings may, from the author's point of view, have been errors as surely as the typographical errors are. To begin the critical process of emending a text but to stop short of adopting any revisions from a later text on the grounds that all those revisions belong to a subsequent period seems to imply the untenable proposition that all readings of a text except for the undoubted typographical errors (or slips of the pen) are the ones intended by the author at that particular time. Clearly, revisions in later editions do not necessarily reflect second thoughts; they can be readings intended all along but for one reason or another not previously substituted for the erroneous readings. The artificiality, therefore, of beginning the process of emendation but not carrying it through makes the resulting text rather unsatisfying in comparison with the alternatives of either reproducing the historical document without change or constructing a critical text that draws on all available evidence.

76. Quoted in Tony Schwartz, "Mixer of Elite and Pop," *New York Times Book Review*, 24 February 1980, pp. 7, 40–41. The fact that in this particular instance it was not a publisher's editor, but Dickens's friend Bulwer Lytton, who convinced Dickens to alter the ending is irrelevant to the main point being made.

that shaped the published text. Authorial intention cannot be equated with expectation or with acquiescence, nor can one accept an author's statement of intention at face value. A critical edition, if it is to be worthy of its name, must examine such matters critically.

The third of these large central questions is the problem of the so-called "indifferent" variant: that is, how is the editor to choose among variants in those cases in which critical analysis of the evidence finds the variants equally balanced and provides no basis for a critical choice of one over another? This problem has been much discussed under the guise of examining how to select a copy-text. It is not necessary to have a copy-text at all, of course, unless there are in fact some indifferent variants. If at every point of variation in wording, punctuation, and spelling one is able to make a critical decision as to which variant represents the author's wishes, one has no need to fall back on the concept of a text with presumptive authority. Obviously one might, in such a case, choose a particular text to mark up to reflect these editorial decisions, but that text would only be serving as a convenient basis for producing printer's copy for the new edition and as nothing more. The reason so much attention has focused on the choice of copy-text is not that it is a necessary first step in critical editing but that in most cases variants appearing to be indifferent do seem to occur, so that one needs a principle for favoring one text over another. Generally speaking, an editor has less to go on when judging variants in punctuation and spelling than when judging variants in wording, and for that reason the text chosen as copy-text often supplies most of the punctuation and spelling for the critical text. But the editor is free, of course, to make rational decisions regarding spelling and punctuation when the evidence permits; conversely, variants in wording can sometimes seem indifferent, and the impasse is resolved by adopting the copy-text reading. It is not logically necessary, therefore, to distinguish spelling and punctuation from wording in arriving at a rationale for selecting a copy-text, for a copy-text is simply the text most likely to provide an authorial reading (in spelling, punctuation, or wording) at points of variation where one cannot otherwise reach a decision. The way in which spelling and punctuation may sometimes usefully be segregated from wording results from the fact that persons involved in textual transmission have frequently regarded spelling and punctuation as elements that they could alter more freely, or be less careful about, than the words; in situations where this generalization can be thought to apply, therefore, it will be one of the factors involved in editorial decisions. As for a general rationale for choosing a copy-text, one can draw on testimony from all periods, as well as on common sense and everyday experience, to show that texts can be expected to deteriorate as they are transmitted. It follows, therefore, that a copy-text should be an early text—one as near to the author's manuscript as possible, if not that manuscript itself—whenever the individual circumstances do not suggest a different text as the more reasonable choice. When they do, then by all means another text should be chosen: the purpose of the general guideline is not to restrict thought or to force particular situations into a common mold. One begins with the variants about which one can reason (from both external and internal evidence) and reach a conclusion; for any remaining variants, one must be guided by the trustworthiness—in general or in particular respects—that one can attach to each text. If this process leads to the choice of a later rather than an earlier text as more trustworthy, then one of course chooses the later text; accepting the general observation that texts deteriorate in transmission does not mean that individual decisions cannot constitute exceptions to the generalization.

These comments on three central questions have been, as I say, intentionally brief and unadorned, both to show that the issues are essentially clear-cut (even though carrying out a responsible editorial policy may require some difficult decisions and certainly requires knowledge and insight) and also to demonstrate the cumulative effect of recent editorial discussion, for these comments, after all, grow out of that discussion and try to build on it. However ineffective some of the discussion has been, the level of discussion now is undoubtedly higher than it would have been without these years of debate. I hope that my summary can serve to suggest the most fruitful directions in which the discussion can proceed from here.

Historicism and Critical Editing
1979-85

ALL SCHOLARLY EDITORS MUST DECIDE TO WHAT EXTENT THE TEXTS they present in their editions can be permitted to depart from the documentary texts that have come down to them; no more basic theme runs through the history of scholarly editing than the perennial debates over the role of editorial judgment (necessarily subjective, to a greater or lesser degree) in the production of responsible texts. Even those who acknowledge the value, under certain circumstances, of critical texts (that is, texts incorporating the results of critical judgments as to whether alterations are required) sometimes wish to restrict as much as possible the operation of individual judgment. They may say, for instance, that emendations should be limited to the correction of what are thought to be printers' errors in a given text and should not be drawn from the variant readings of other texts, which represent different stages in the history of the work. Critical editing by definition moves one away from documentary texts, because it admits the possibility of emending those texts. This process need not be unhistorical, for the scholarly goal of emendation is to recreate texts that once existed, even if in some details they existed only in their authors' minds. But the fact remains that critical texts (if emendations have actually been made in them) do depart from the particular texts that have survived from the past; and any recreation of something that does not exist is conjectural and inevitably reflects, to some degree, later attitudes. These issues—which, taken together, might be called the question of historicism—have been discussed at length by generations of editors, and they will always be discussed. It comes as no surprise, therefore, to recognize that they have been prominent in editorial debate in the early 1980s; but they have, I think, been approached in these years from some neglected directions, offering new twists to old dilemmas.

This trend in editorial theorizing is not unrelated to what has been happening in scholarly literary criticism. Although recognition of the interdependence of textual scholarship and literary criticism has not advanced as far as one could wish, there is no doubt that recent writers have increasingly explored the connection. Editors have always known implicitly that any actions they took as editors reflected particular assumptions about the nature of literature and of verbal communication; but over the years they have not been inclined to confront this fact very explicitly. An age of criticism that has emphasized theory, however, has naturally provided a setting in which editorial discussion becomes more self-conscious regarding the theory of literature underlying it. That editors must be critics and that critics must understand textual history are truisms just beginning to be understood beyond a small circle of scholar-critics. The elements of a new historicism emerging in literary study have recently been usefully surveyed by Herbert Lindenberger,[1] who contrasts the "suspiciousness and self-conscious playfulness" of the new history with the "detachment and self-effacement" of the old, pre-New Criticism, variety. One of the reasons for this shift of tone, he suggests, is directly connected with textual scholarship: the theoretical questioning of the organic unity of individual works has been supported by some of the evidence produced by editors, evidence showing (as he says the Cornell edition of *The Prelude* of 1798–99 shows) that a literary work "consists essentially of layers of text—often, in fact, unfinished layers— none of which necessarily commands more authority than the others." This line of thinking leads to suspicion of "authorial authority" (p. 17)[2] and in turn to rejection of "objectivity" and "permanence" as attributes of historical scholarship (p. 22). Another link between critical and textual work is the recent critical interest in reading (that is, in readers' "responses"), which encourages a concern with the texts available to readers in the past and the reception accorded them (p. 20). Although Lindenberger's account does not emphasize textual matters, it does illustrate some of the ways in which developments in critical and in editorial theory and practice have begun to feed each other.

The new historicism in textual matters that I wish to examine has a somewhat different emphasis, however. After all, the "new history" Lindenberger describes is new in part because it recognizes the importance of historical context in literary analysis and comes after a period in which historical considerations were slighted. But textual study has always been, and is in conception, historical. The recent concern with

1. "Toward a New History in Literary Study," *Profession 84* (1984), pp. 16–23.

2. Lindenberger lacks precision in making this point. His complete sentence is, "Given the suspicion we have developed in recent years toward authorial authority, even an author's authorized text need have no more authority than we choose to give it." However, it is not necessary to question the authority of authors over their texts in order to be wary of "authorized texts," which for many reasons may not fully reflect their authors' intentions. The long tradition of critical editing has involved questioning authorized texts but not normally doubting the authority of authors.

historicism among editorial theorists does not result from a rediscovery of the value of historical research (which was never lost) but from new approaches to the nature of literature that dictate new limitations on an editor's freedom to be eclectic. In the pages that follow, I propose to examine the literature of editorial theory of the late 1970s and the first half of the 1980s from this point of view. This report is conceived as a continuation of my previous surveys of recent editorial discussion.[3] That its focus is on historicism reflects the way the field has developed, for the most significant discussions of the last five or six years can profitably be examined in terms of their stance on this issue. I begin with some discussions (largely by historians) that cannot be considered to have advanced editorial thinking but that are representative of an unsophisticated attitude toward historicism still often encountered. I shall then turn to the two extreme positions that define the recent debates: the view that literature is social and collaborative in nature and therefore that the historical forms in which a work was presented to the public are of primary significance; and, at the other end of the spectrum, the view that literary works are the products of discrete private acts of creation and therefore that their essential forms do not include alterations by

---

3. The previous two brought the story from the time of W. W. Greg's "The Rationale of Copy-Text" (*SB*, 3 [1950–51], 19–36) to the late 1970s: "Greg's Theory of Copy-Text and the Editing of American Literature," *Studies in Bibliography*, 28 (1975), 167–229 (reprinted in *Selected Studies in Bibliography* [1979], pp. 245–307); and "Recent Editorial Discussion and the Central Questions of Editing," *SB*, 34 (1981), 23–65. As in those pieces, I am again concentrating on general theoretical discussions and normally exclude essays on textual problems in particular authors' works and reviews of individual editions. During the period under review several useful checklists appeared that do include such material: T. H. Howard-Hill, *British Bibliography and Textual Criticism: A Bibliography* (2 vols., 1979, continuing the series that also contains *Shakespearian Bibliography and Textual Criticism: A Bibliography* [1971]); Ross W. Beales, Jr., "Documentary Editing: A Bibliography," *Newsletter of the Association for Documentary Editing*, 2, no. 4 (December 1980), 10–16; Laurel N. Braswell, *Western Manuscripts from Classical Antiquity to the Renaissance: A Handbook* (1981); and David Madden and Richard Powers, *Writers' Revisions: An Annotated Bibliography of Articles and Books about Writers' Revisions and Their Comments on the Creative Process* (1981). There were also several anthologies of essays on editorial matters (other than those mentioned later in this essay), such as N. John Hall's collection on editing the Victorians (volume 9 of *Browning Institute Studies*, 1981) and recent volumes in the Toronto Editorial Conference series: e.g., William Blissett (ed.), *Editing Illustrated Books* (1980); A. H. de Quehen (ed.), *Editing Poetry from Spenser to Dryden* (1981); Trevor H. Levere (ed.), *Editing Texts in the History of Science and Medicine* (1982). Also during this period Donald H. Reiman published two perceptive accounts of editorial history: "The Four Ages of Editing and the English Romantics," *Text* 1 (1981), 231–255; and "Romantic Bards and Historical Editors," *Studies in Romanticism*, 21 (1982), 477–496. And two general introductory treatments of textual and editorial scholarship came out in Modern Language Association publications: my essay on "Textual Scholarship" in *Introduction to Scholarship in Modern Languages and Literatures*, ed. Joseph Gibaldi (1981), pp. 29–52; and William Proctor Williams and Craig S. Abbott's chapter on "Textual Criticism" in *An Introduction to Bibliographical and Textual Studies* (1985), pp. 52–90.

others nor even later revisions by the authors themselves. Finally I shall look at some efforts to assert the validity of multiple texts, recognizing that different historical interests may require different approaches to editing.

I

What I am calling a debate about historicism has chiefly engaged the editors of writings by literary figures, not the editors of statesmen's papers and other historical documents. The reason is that the debate is primarily concerned with critical editions, in which the principles underlying an editor's emendations determine how far the critical text departs from the documentary text[4] that served as its basis. Historians[5] have not generally dealt with these issues because the material they have typically edited consists of letters, journals, and other similar manuscripts, which are more likely to call for literal transcription than critical emendation. For them, the issue of historicism in editing is apt to be whether eclectic texts (products of critical editing) can ever be preferred to diplomatic transcriptions of single documentary texts. Even though many historical editors have practiced critical editing in the sense that they have normalized or regularized certain features of their texts, and have not simply produced diplomatic transcriptions, many of them have not been able to see the value of the further step that literary editors have often taken when dealing with multiple texts of a single work, the step of emending one text with variants from another. Not having progressed beyond this elementary stage in the process of thinking about editing, they have not been in a position to enter into the more sophisticated discussions of historicism in critical editing. It is an unfortunate fact that what historians have published on the subject of editing has not contributed to the development of editorial theory.[6]

4. A "documentary text" can of course be the text of either a manuscript or a printed item: in either case the text is documentary in that it is what has been preserved in the historical record.

5. Editors of literary works are historians, too; but for convenience I use "historians" to refer to editors of the documentary texts largely used by students of history.

6. I do not mean to suggest that all historical editors think alike: I am aware that there are many who do understand what the literary editors have been discussing in recent years. But the most vocal historical editors, and those who publish their views, have not generally come from this group. An exception is John Y. Simon, who showed his open-mindedness in his ADE Presidential address, "Editors and Critics," *Newsletter of the Association for Documentary Editing*, 3, no. 4 (December 1981), 1–4. Jon Kukla, in his review of the Kansas conference volume (see below), recognized the irony that "as the so-called literary editors push for more thoughtful handling of textual evidence, they are forcing all scholars to confront the fundamentals of *historical* method" (*Newsletter*, 4, no. 1 [February 1982], 5–7).

Just prior to the period under review here, in September of 1978, a Conference on Literary and Historical Editing was held at the University of Kansas, under the joint sponsorship of the National Endowment for the Humanities and the National Historical Publications and Records Commission. That such a conference took place was encouraging, for it was the first organized effort to open the lines of communication between literary and historical editors.[7] But the title of the conference, like the title of the 1981 volume collecting some of the conference papers, *Literary & Historical Editing* (edited by George L. Vogt and John Bush Jones), was misguided in suggesting that the nature of editing shifts at disciplinary boundaries (assuming they can be located). It is perhaps permissible, if not very felicitous, to speak—in convenient shorthand—of "literary editors" and "historical editors," when referring to the editors who deal with the writings of literary[8] and historical figures; but it is surely illogical to speak of "literary editing" and "historical editing," as if differences in editing arise more from the subjects involved than from the kinds of materials. Letters pose similar problems, if they are from the same period and country, whether they are written by statesmen or by novelists;[9] and works published in a series of editions pose a different set of problems, regardless of whether the author is a politician or a poet. I endeavored to make this point in my contribution: although it was entitled "Literary Editing" (pp. 35–56) because that was the assigned topic, it explained that the real distinction is between writings of the kind normally intended for publication and those of the kind normally not so intended (critical editions often being most appropriate for the former, diplomatic transcriptions for the latter). Blurring this distinction in the title and organization of the conference was effectively to discourage participants from recognizing the extent of their shared concerns.

The paper that represented "historical editing"—at the conference and in the volume—set forth a viewpoint, largely through implication,

7. Other lines, within the field of literary studies, need to be opened as well: see Conor Fahy, "The View from Another Planet: Textual Bibliography and the Editing of Sixteenth-Century Italian Texts," *Italian Studies*, 34 (1979), 71–92. On the need for interdisciplinary discussion, see also my comments in *Text*, 1 (1981), 1–9.

8. This shorthand use of "literary" encompasses works in other genres as well. Much of the recent scholarly editing of philosophical works, for example, is in the tradition of "literary" editing. See Fredson Bowers, "Editing a Philosopher: The Works of William James," *Analytical & Enumerative Bibliography*, 4 (1980), 3–36.

9. Recent discussions of letters include J. A. Dainard (ed.), *Editing Correspondence* (1979); Robert Stephen Becker, "Challenges in Editing Modern Literary Correspondence," *Text*, 1 (1981), 257–270; A. R. Braunmuller, "Editing Elizabethan Letters," *Text*, 1 (1981), 185–199; Norman Fruman, "Some Principles of Epistolary Interpretation," *Centrum*, n.s., 1 (1981), 75–94; and Ernest W. Sullivan II, "The Problem of Text in Familiar Letters," *PBSA*, 75 (1981), 115–126.

that has not yet died out from its own illogic and therefore must be glanced at here. George C. Rogers, Jr., entitled his paper "The Sacred Text: An Improbable Dream" (pp. 23–33) and seemed by the title to be implying that too much attention can be paid to texts, an interpretation borne out by his reaction to an essay of mine: "The text, the text, it is always the text!" (p. 33). One gathers that he believes textual details to be less important for historical than for literary scholars, for he seems to think that the former deal with ideas (and are presumably above such minutiae), whereas the latter deal with language. This astonishing position (which, I hasten to add, Rogers is not alone in holding) is apparently what underlies his statement that the "work to preserve the words of the founding fathers . . . provides us with an understanding of our republic," whereas "the work to find out what Shakespeare himself had to say" provides us "with an understanding of our language" (p. 27). On this basis, presumably, he can report with approval that the texts in the *Papers of Henry Laurens* incorporate silent alterations to increase "readability"—dashes, for example, are deleted "unless it is obvious that they should be retained as they would be in modern writing," and commas are added "only when the editors are sure that the addition will clarify the meaning of a passage" (p. 29). More important to him than offering a record of such alterations is the provision of historical annotation, for a textual apparatus "tends to confine thinking to the text at hand" (mere language, that is), but annotation "tends to release thinking in a thousand new directions" (p. 31). The connection between nuances of language (including punctuation) and nuances of thought is not made, and thus there is no recognition of the fact (which follows from it) that textual details are of equal importance to all who wish to read with the fullest understanding, regardless of the nature of the writings to be read. Much of Rogers's paper—after an introductory section explaining incorrectly what literary editors do[10]—sets forth the practices of the

---

10. He begins by saying that the literary editor "usually works with materials quite different from those with which the historical editor works, for the latter is interested in manuscripts" (p. 23). Literary editors do frequently deal with works that have been printed; but, if manuscripts survive, these editors not only are "interested" in them but often make them the basis for a new edition. Not realizing this fact, Rogers proceeds to assert, "Literary editors now agree that the first printed version has the best claim to be the copy-text." There is no hint here of the extensive debate, then and now, over this point, and no suggestion that individual situations might affect the choice of copy-text. Literary editors, he claims, make "no attempt to present a facsimile version" (in fact, of course, they often do). instead preferring critical editions, in which "the editors take liberties with the copy-text in order to obtain what the editors consider a text closer to the authorial intention" (p. 24)—a statement that would have been fair enough if the process of emendation had not been misunderstood and trivialized as "taking liberties." In the collation of texts that provides some of the evidence for emendation, we are told, substantives "receive more attention than

Laurens edition, as an example of what historical editors do. But nothing in that account explains how the "work to preserve the words of the founding fathers" (or other historical figures) is furthered by concealing certain details of the manuscripts (and depriving readers of the opportunity to arrive at their own evaluations of the significance of those details);[11] nor is any coherent rationale offered for preferring annotation, however stimulating, to information about the words and punctuation of the text itself, the text presumably being the reason for the existence of the edition.[12]

Rogers's Kansas paper makes no contribution to editorial thinking nor—unfortunately, given the occasion for which it was prepared—to the promotion of mutual understanding among editors in different fields.[13] Resuscitating it here is no doubt unkind; but its essential position, however ineptly set out in this instance, continues to be argued. Two years later, at the Williamsburg conference of the Association for Documentary Editing (which had been founded a few weeks after the Kansas conference, with the same goals), Robert J. Taylor still found alterations for the sake of readability to take precedence over the presen-

---

accidentals" (the naivete of expressing this view without further elaboration clearly goes unrecognized). "In this scheme of editing," Rogers adds, "there tend to be no silent changes" —as if the mechanical reporting of emendations is a part of a theory of editing. There is no point continuing this recital: nearly every statement he makes about the work of literary editors is incorrect or seriously askew. Similar misunderstandings crop up elsewhere in the conference volume: in one of the two introductions, George L. Vogt says, "Most historical editors probably still balk at the literary editors' idea of a completely 'recoverable' text, with all the back-of-the-book baggage that that implies" (pp. 4–5); but no one would claim that every feature of a manuscript text can be recovered from any edition, and the most detailed transcription imaginable need not have any appended apparatus, either at the back of a volume or at the foot of a page.

11. In a review of the conference volume in the *Bulletin* of the Bibliographical Society of Australia and New Zealand (7 [1983], 188–190), Harold Love agrees that the faithful reproduction of manuscript texts is desirable but adds that "the overriding considerations must always be the kind of use such documents are to be put to by historians"; it is hard to believe, however, that any serious use of the texts of documents is well served by the elimination of evidence that could play a role in their interpretation. Gordon S. Wood has concisely said, "For historians, convenience of use apparently overrides their concern for literal accuracy" (p. 875 in "Historians and Documentary Editing," *Journal of American History*, 67 [1980–81], 871–877).

12. I am not in any sense denigrating annotation, which is one of the kinds of commentary that an edition should set in motion (whether within the covers of the edition or elsewhere). Textual and other kinds of historical annotation are not, in any case, easily separable entities, since textual questions cannot be handled sensitively apart from the historical context.

13. Rogers, as a historian, is surely going out of his way to be hostile when he claims not to understand that the value of research is not determined by how dramatic the results are: he asks (irrelevantly, but with an implied answer that is incorrect), "Have the editors of nineteenth-century texts come up with any earth-shaking discoveries?" (p 25).

tation of literal transcriptions.[14] He claims that the inclusion in the edited text of "inconsequential" authorial deletions, "incomprehensible" authorial punctuation, and "superfluous" authorial dashes "could well annoy a modern reader" and that "reader annoyance itself could block the reader from sensing a writer's mood" (p. 5). It does not seem to have occurred to him that any serious reader will be more annoyed by an editor's officiousness in withholding documentary evidence and will find incredible the idea that the "burden of proof" should be on those who introduce no alterations rather than on those who do.[15] Curiously, Taylor presents an excellent statement explaining why anyone who is bothered by unfamiliar or inconsistent spelling and punctuation reveals thereby "an unhistorical attitude"—for he does not see that this point demolishes his own argument. He proceeds to say that "slavish copying" can sometimes "get in the way of the meaning of the words and the spirit of the document" and that the "main objective" is "the illumination of history" (p. 6). We thus come back to the same basic misunderstanding that was present in Rogers's paper, but Taylor is more explicit: "the aesthetic interest is central in the study of literary documents," whereas the "overriding concern" in the study of historical documents is "their contribution to the understanding of history" (p. 6); therefore "the principle of the sanctity of the text" is "not necessary for many, perhaps most, of the documents that an historical editor works with" (p. 7). Aesthetics has nothing to do with the issue, of course; what is being missed here is the simple fact that a careful reading of any piece of writing involves attention to details of wording and punctuation, whether or not the writer is generally considered to be an effective user of the language.[16]

14. "Editorial Practices—An Historian's View," *Newsletter of the Association for Documentary Editing*, 3, no. 1 (February 1981), 4–8. The counterargument was provided by Don L. Cook, in "The Short Happy Thesis of G. Thomas Tanselle," pp. 1–4 (the reference being to my piece on "The Editing of Historical Documents," *SB*, 31 [1978], 1–56—reprinted in *Selected Studies in Bibliography* [1979], pp. 451–506).

15. It is no defense of editorial interference to take the line (implied by Taylor on p. 5) that such alterations do not affect the meaning. As I have previously pointed out (*SB*, 34 [1981], 58), why then go to the trouble of making the changes at all?

16. Literary historians will be surprised to hear that "No one feels the need to study the poems of mediocre poets or to run through their letters, unless they made better friends than they did poems" (p. 6). A number of historians have made statements similar to Rogers's and Taylor's. Fredrika J. Teute, in "Views in Review: A Historiographical Perspective on Historical Editing," *American Archivist*, 43 (1980), 43–56, says that "the historical editor treats the document as a fact. While perhaps slighting the nuances which literary editors appreciate, he does not produce bowdlerized versions claiming to represent the author's true, though unexpressed, intent" (p. 49). And Nathan Reingold, in "Reflections of an Unrepentant Editor," *American Archivist*, 46 (1983), 14–21, states that "the literary editors have a sense of the sacredness of the words they process. The historical editors, even those imbued with origins and essences, have a belief in the importance of the pur-

Those inclined to agree with the views expressed by Rogers and Taylor often make a further point, which in fact renders their brand of historicism rather paradoxical. They are likely to disapprove of eclectic texts on the grounds—as Taylor puts it—that such texts have "no *historical* validity," not having "a real existence" and not representing "what was" (p. 7). Wayne Cutler has concisely stated this position by saying that "the historical editor speaks only for one document at a time"; "conflation," he says, "breaks down the time factor that is so important in linking written witnesses to particular past events."[17] These editors therefore put themselves in the peculiar position of saying that one loses the evidentiary value of individual documents by any conflation of the texts of two or more of them but that certain kinds of editorial alteration within the texts of single documents are permissible, and indeed can even assist readers in seeing the historical significance of those documents. An additional irony is that the editors who produce eclectic texts generally provide records of variants and emendations (thus recognizing the importance of documentary evidence), whereas those who favor individual documentary texts often (especially in the field of history) furnish no detailed records of their normalizations (thus suggesting a less rigorous concern with such evidence). But the issue should not be how important documentary evidence is: obviously it is fundamental, whether or not one decides to take the next step and make critical use of that evidence. Some editors who do not wish to take that step, however, are not willing to think about its potential usefulness. The result is the sad spectacle of scholars asserting—sometimes with a touch of pride—their own closed-mindedness. Cutler unfortunately serves as an example:

> To what uses literary critics may put bastard documents is for them to say, but the saying of the same will not likely change the historical discipline's rules of evidence and citation. I am far from being convinced that a common definition of terms would inform our dissimilar approaches to editing, for it may well be the case that on the subject of methodology we have little of consequence to exchange. (p. 9)

It would be a great misfortune if editorial discussion were to stall for long at this level.

Yet attempts to deal with the supposed differences between "histori-

---

port of the words" (p. 18). In the first number of the *Newsletter of the Association for Documentary Editing* (March 1979), William B. Willcox had referred to the "high priests of *ipsissima verba*, who bemoan our textual impurities" (p. 5).

17. "The 'Authentic' Witness: The Editor Speaks for the Document," *Newsletter of the Association for Documentary Editing*, 4, no. 1 (February 1982), 8–9. Cutler's piece was written in reply to David J. Nordloh's 1979 conference paper, "The 'Perfect' Text: The Editor Speaks for the Author," printed in the *Newsletter*, 2, no. 2 (May 1980), 1–3.

cal" and "literary" editing persist in getting off the track. An egregious instance is Claire Badaracco's proposal for a paper for the first conference (1981) of the Society for Textual Scholarship.[18] One can readily concur in her dissatisfaction with the use of the words "historical" and "literary" to designate two kinds of editing, but it is hard to see what is gained by her substitution of "documentary" and "textual," based on "principles emerging from one's philosophical stance in relation to the problem of VALUE" (p. 43). When she explains that "textual" editors[19] value "the author's intention," whereas for "documentary" editors "it is not the text but the document itself which is of the greatest value" (p. 42), she is merely perpetuating a misguided approach, adding to it some new confusions. Her piece would not be worth mentioning except that it elicited from Fredson Bowers a splendid reply, which in memorable fashion cuts through to the heart of the whole question and says what needs to be said. Naturally the reporting of evidence is central. Bowers concisely makes the essential criticism of historical editors' common practice of omitting any record of the authorial deletions and revisions present in the texts of the documents being transcribed: "All one can ask is, Is this documentary?" (p. 65).[20] These editors, he notes, have repeatedly "turned a blind eye to the superior possibilities for the transmission of information that have come to characterize the new school of editing making its way in the humanities" (p. 49). The emphasis is on the "possibilities for the transmission of information," not on the nature of the edited text, since "for the purposes of historical interpreters it may be moot whether an eclectic conflated text made up from multiple authorities is better suited than a transcript of a single document, provided *in both cases* an apparatus records the variants" (p. 66). Critical editors, Bowers rightly insists, place just as much value on documentary evidence as diplomatic editors do, but the kind of edition they generally construct, containing both a critical text and an apparatus, meets the varying interests of different audiences and releases the editor from being "the victim of the requirements of only one segment of an audi-

18. "The Editor and the Question of Value: Proposal," *Text*, 1 (1981), 41–43. Although the paper she actually delivered at the conference was different from the one foreshadowed by this proposal, the proposal is printed in *Text* because Fredson Bowers based his commentary for the conference ("The Editor and the Question of Value: Another View," pp. 45–73) on it.

19. Bowers properly objects to the solecism "textual editor" and points out that a "documentary editor" must also be concerned with texts (e.g., p. 50).

20. Or, as he puts the point more explicitly, alterations occurring within the text of a document "are as much an integral part of the document as the final form of its inscription" (p. 49). By neglecting such alterations, and variants between separate drafts, historians have not learned as much as they might have from "the writer's veerings of thought" and "changes of mind" (p. 48).

ence" (p. 73). Bowers's essay—as this brief summary of a few key points suggests—deserves a wide readership among those who have had suspicions about the scholarly seriousness of critical editors in the field of literature and who have not been able to see that all who deal with texts confront the same problems. The observations he makes are in fact self-evident, as he several times suggests; but past debate does not give one grounds for hope that they will be soon understood, in spite of his effective statement to ease the way.

Even David Hall, who is particularly interested in the history of books and reading, found it possible in his 1983 Wiggins Lecture to refer sarcastically to "the work of analytical bibliographers and their holy of holies, the text."[21] The depth of his misunderstanding is revealed by his further saying, "The very concept of a perfect text is an invention of the twentieth century, and cannot be imposed upon the past" (p. 335).[22] Students of the history of reading and of the role of books in society are rightly interested in the texts available to readers at particular times in the past; but so are students of the history of literature, and no critical editor of a literary text would pretend that a newly constructed critical text (as opposed to its apparatus) would be appropriate for analyzing earlier readers' reactions.[23] Whether historians are in fact as concerned with past texts as they ought to be is a question one cannot avoid raising, if Rogers's exasperated exclamation "always the text!" and Hall's slighting reference to "holy of holies" are at all representative of a common feeling. The truth of the matter is that, because analytical bibliography developed primarily among literary scholars, many historians have not yet come to understand the lessons it has taught about the role of physical evidence in uncovering textual problems (lessons relevant to the study of manuscripts as well as of printed books) and therefore have not recognized that the task of identifying "the text" read at a given time is often more complicated than the simple location of a single copy. Indeed, the growing numbers of historians interested in what is often referred to

21. "On Native Ground: From the History of Printing to the History of the Book," *Proceedings of the American Antiquarian Society*, 93 (1983), 313–336 (and reprinted as a pamphlet, 1984). I have made some further comments on Hall's views in "The Bibliography and Textual Study of American Books," *Proceedings of the American Antiquarian Society*, 95 (1985), 291–329. Hall once described Charles Francis Adams's 1894 "literal reproduction of the texts" of some antinomian documents and then observed, "Scholarship no longer rests upon such antiquarian exactness" (*The Antinomian Controversy, 1636–1638: A Documentary History* [1968], p. 21).

22. He states that American printers and readers of the past "were quite indifferent" to the question of authorial intention. But that observation, however true it may be, has no bearing on our legitimate interest in discovering what a particular author meant to say at a given time in the past.

23. Though of course present reactions are only the latest stage in the history of the reception of various texts of a work.

(following the lead of the French in this field) as *histoire du livre*, dealing with books in their broadest social contexts, have surprisingly often failed to see how important analytical bibliography and textual study are for their endeavors.[24]

Despite extensive discussion of these matters in recent years, encouraged in part by the activities of two organizations devoted to fostering interdisciplinary communication among scholarly editors, the split between literary and historical editors regarding the responsible handling of historical evidence has not grown significantly smaller. That so much energy has been invested in debating such elementary—such essentially undebatable—points is regrettable; there are, after all, real issues waiting to be further explored. No one doubts the importance of making transcriptions or reproductions of the texts of certain individual documents (both manuscript and printed); and it seems scarcely credible that anyone would question the desirability, in connection with such transcriptions or reproductions, of reporting as much as possible of the textual evidence those documents contain.[25] Similarly undebatable, one would think, is the idea that in certain instances a further usefulness might result from the production of a text embodying alterations made at the editor's discretion[26] (with the alterations recorded).[27] Both literary and historical editors acknowledge this point, but some do so only in a limited way. Many editors who disapprove of eclectic texts nevertheless produce critical texts, for they make certain kinds of alterations, aimed at bringing a text to what in their judgment is a higher standard (whether of readability, mechanical correctness, correspondence to the author's intention, or something else). Any editor who normalizes or modernizes

24. I have tried to set forth this point in my Hanes Lecture, *The History of Books as a Field Study* (1981)—also printed in the *Times Literary Supplement*, 5 June 1981, pp. 647–649.

25. As much as possible, that is, within the limits imposed by typography and photography. Some evidence, of course, cannot be reproduced.

26. Stephen E. Wiberly, Jr., in discussing the interesting question of the editing of maps does recognize critical editions; indeed, he asserts—without qualification—that "edited maps are superior to facsimiles" (p. 509). But although he refers to the debates over the editing of verbal historical documents, he seems not to have grasped some of the issues involved in them. It does not seem promising, for example, to distinguish maps from personal papers on the grounds that "a map purports to tell us something about a reality outside the mind of its creators" and to conclude that it is therefore "logical to correct the contents of old maps" but "not logical to change the contents of personal papers" (p. 502). What he advocates is to "take an old map, accept some of its data without reservation, verify and correct other of its data, and then include both types of data in the edited map" (pp. 501–502). See "Editing Maps: A Method for Historical Cartography," *Journal of Interdisciplinary History*, 10 (1980), 499–510.

27. Whether variant readings and emendations are noted within the body of an edited text or in appended lists is a mechanical matter—not unimportant, but certainly not of the same order as the considerations just mentioned.

a documentary text is obviously engaging in critical editing, for the resulting text departs from all the historical witnesses through the operation of the editor's critical judgment. Some of these editors balk at the idea of drawing any of their alterations from another text of the same piece of writing, labeling such a practice "eclectic" and charging that it destroys the integrity of individual documents. But that integrity has already been violated by the editor's own intrusions; "eclecticism" only alludes to a particular source of such violation. No one would argue that editors have any obligation to produce eclectic texts when they find such texts inappropriate; but surely editors who understand the usefulness of even one kind of departure from absolute fidelity to a documentary text can also conceive of the usefulness, under some circumstances, of such eclectic texts. Whatever the field, scholars must engage in interpretation of the raw materials of history, and eclectic texts are one product of such interpretation.[28] Literary scholars may have more occasions for producing them than scholars in other fields; but it seems inconceivable that any scholar can fail to comprehend the rationale for and function of such texts. Yet that is precisely what much of the argument has been about. We are not talking here about which materials are most appropriate for eclectic treatment or what the principles for emendation ought to be but simply whether eclectic texts can ever be justified as historical scholarship. Clearly they can be: critical (including eclectic) texts have a place in the scholar's repertory as surely as diplomatic texts do. And in either case the scholar has an obligation to report the details of the documentary evidence. On this level, there is nothing to debate.

II

The more interesting and potentially fruitful discussions of textual theory begin at the point where these unsophisticated complaints of his-

28. Bowers says of documentary texts: "Students of history may read these texts to gain a firsthand acquaintance with the undigested material, but at higher reaches these documents provide professional scholars with the necessary data from which formal eclectic interpretation can be made in written histories and biographies" (p. 46). The essential role of subjective judgment in the historical enterprise of reconstructing past texts out of the documentary texts that happen to have survived is affirmed (with somewhat different emphases) by two recent essays on the textual study of early manuscripts: my attempt to show that recension is no less conjectural than "conjectural emendation," in "Classical, Biblical, and Medieval Textual Criticism and Modern Editing," *SB*, 36 (1983), 21–68; and Lee Patterson's demonstration that the standard dichotomy between external and internal evidence does not coincide with the distinction between objective facts and interpretations, in "The Logic of Textual Criticism and the Way of Genius," in *Textual Criticism and Literary Interpretation*, ed. Jerome J. McGann (1985), pp. 55–91. (For a more traditional summary of some of the flaws in the stemmatic approach, see Paul Oskar Kristeller, "The Lachmann Method: Merits and Limitations," *Text*, 1 [1981], 11–20.)

torical editors leave off. They start from an acceptance of the value of eclectic texts and consider the problem of historicism from a higher plane. The issue is not whether eclectic texts as a genre are defensible but how best to produce them: when to be eclectic, how much departure from a documentary form of a work is allowable and desirable, whether editors should introduce emendations of their own in addition to readings drawn from other texts, and what principles or standards should underlie alterations of either kind. Discussions of these matters are usually concerned with works of the kind normally intended for publication (usually, in fact, with works actually published, after the fashion of their times), for critical editing is more likely to be of service in connection with such works than with private writings. How one conceives of the nature of such works and what concept of authorship it entails are therefore crucial questions, the answers to which determine the goal one is aiming toward in making alterations to a documentary text of a work.

One family of answers to these questions proceeds outward from the author to the author's social context, tending to make authorship more a social than a private activity and sometimes expanding the concept of text. In some of his recent work, D. F. McKenzie has been moving in this direction, calling for a "sociology of the text." For instance, the paper he presented at a 1977 Wolfenbüttel symposium (the proceedings of which were published in 1981)[29] deals with "Typography and Meaning" and argues, as one illustration of the connection, that Congreve's altered treatment of scene divisions and stage directions in his collected *Works* of 1710 was inextricably tied up with their typographic presentation, which resulted from "a new and intimate form of teamwork" (p. 110) between Congreve and his publisher (and friend) Jacob Tonson. McKenzie is saying, in other words, that in this instance features of a printed book that are often regarded as nontextual cannot in fact be separated from the words and punctuation in considering the author's textual intentions. Congreve is a particularly interesting case, for the contrast between the original quarto editions of his plays and the *Works* of 1710 marks the transition between the seventeenth-century "*dis*junction of playwrights and printers" (p. 82), which resulted in printed forms "insensitive to the problems of mediating a theatrical experience" (p. 83), and the eighteenth-century effort to give "typography a voice in the handheld theatre of the book," which made the printed form more than a

---

29. *Buch und Buchhandel in Europa im achtzehnten Jahrhundert*, ed. Giles Barber and Bernhard Fabian (1981), pp. 81–125. McKenzie's paper, as he states, "extends the argument" of the third of his unpublished Sandars Lectures for 1975–76 ("The London Book Trade in the Later Seventeenth Century").

makeshift report of something that had its real existence elsewhere. Despite the special circumstances of the Congreve example, McKenzie intends it to be emblematic of a broader point, not limited to Congreve, the eighteenth century, or printed drama: that the book itself is "an expressive means," in which "the substance of the text" cannot be divorced from "the physical form of its presentation," for the book conveys "an aggregation of meanings both verbal and typographic" (p. 82). As he concisely puts it, "A book's total form is itself a significant historical statement" (p. 99). In support of this generalization he offers a wide-ranging survey, filled with characteristically acute observations.[30]

No one, I think, would dispute the view that every detail of a printed book carries historical meaning, though few critics have adequately integrated the evidence offered by format, paper, type design, and page layout into their readings of works, and McKenzie is quite right to stress the seriousness of this failing.[31] But we can all agree that readers' responses are affected by typography and book design without feeling that such features of books are necessarily inseparable from the works conveyed by the books. The issue turns on whether one is willing to admit the legitimacy of being interested in the artistic intentions of authors as private individuals rather than as social beings accommodating their intentions to various pressures emerging from the publishing process. On this fundamental question McKenzie wavers, and his imprecision weakens the foundation of an essay that is admirable in so many ways. A distinction has to be made between the books that were available to be read and reacted to at particular times in the past and the forms of works as intended by their authors. If one wishes to reconstruct how earlier readers reacted or to analyze their written reactions, there is no doubt that the physical features of the books they read are relevant and can in that

30. James McLaverty, who acknowledges the influence of McKenzie, has also found the early eighteenth century to be the time "when authors first became conscious of the anomalous nature of literature and of the importance of printing" (p. 95). He examines the *Dunciad Variorum* as Pope's "exploitation of the medium" of the scholarly edition, as "an imitation not of spoken discourse but of written discourse" (p. 96). Like McKenzie, he argues that the visual presentation of a text "can carry special associations, and that a richer understanding of the relation of author, book trade, and public may lead to better interpretation of literary works" (p. 105). See "The Mode of Existence of Literary Works of Art: The Case of the *Dunciad Variorum*," *SB*, 37 (1984), 82–105. Another writer who is concerned with the effect of typographic layout, especially lineation, on the "reader experiencing the play in the 'theater of the mind'" (p. 69) is Paul Bertram, in *White Spaces in Shakespeare* (1981).

31. Analytical bibliographers, of course, have used physical evidence in an attempt to uncover facts about the printing history of individual editions (and this activity can be regarded as one kind of "reading"—see Ross Atkinson, "An Application of Semiotics to the Definition of Bibliography," *SB*, 33 [1980], 54–73). But the concern here is with the way in which the physical characteristics of a book play a role in the reader's reaction to the piece of writing contained in it.

sense be considered part of the "texts." But if one is more concerned with assessing a writer's mind and ideas than in examining how they were perceived by the contemporary reading public, some or all of the elements of book design may be nontextual, if the writer was not interested in them or did not put any of them to special use. Even in these cases, a scholar should not ignore such features of original printings, for they are part of the historical setting;[32] but the physical arrangement of the scholar's critical text need not be affected. Situations will vary: there are writers, as Congreve apparently was, who are so intimately involved with the design of the printed presentation of their works that the design (or some parts of it) must be regarded as textual; for other writers, the design does not reflect authorial intention. Critical editors must judge which is true in each case, just as they must make judgments about words and punctuation.

McKenzie's essay suffers from not being built on this distinction.[33] His insistence on the necessity of eclectic texts, for example, is confusing in the context of a concern with the "sociology" of the text. In discussing Congreve's revisions for the 1710 *Works*, he says that an editor "must seek to serve the play at its fullest and best[34] by restoring a reading when he believes its suppression to reflect a narrow moral, rather than a literary, judgement on Congreve's part": "Conflation is inevitable" (p. 109). Although his defense of eclectic editing is well stated, it is likely to leave readers puzzled. Congreve's self-censorship, he believes, resulted sufficiently from "external pressures" (p. 107)—legal constraints on coarse language and Tonson's attitude toward it—to justify an editorial decision to restore the canceled language; but such a decision emphasizes the author's own wishes over the product that emerged from the social process of publishing. Of course McKenzie is right to assert that responsible textual decisions must be based on an understanding of the "complex of attitudes—personal, social and trade—" (p. 109) that lie behind variant readings; presumably he is referring to the same broad range of considerations later when he says that variants should be "interpreted in the context of book trade history" (p. 117). Editors must naturally be as informed as possible about all aspects of the historical context; but

32. Scholars should, after all, be aware of the shifting conventions in the use of particular formats and page layouts.

33. It is implicit in his reference to decisions that authors and booksellers "take, or impose on one another" (p. 103), but the point is not developed.

34. The word "best" is troubling here and recalls his earlier statement, "Every variant must of course be scrutinized for what it adds or loses in vitality of character and acuity of language" (p. 108). One has to wonder whether this way of stating the matter sufficiently distinguishes editors' own preferences from their judgments regarding what authors preferred.

being so informed does not determine what view of authorship they should take as a basis for textual decisions. For in many—no doubt in most—instances one cannot accommodate both the private wishes of the author and the collaborative product of the publishing process simultaneously.[35] If McKenzie can speak of interpreting variants in the light of book-trade history and still opt in the case of Congreve (who worked closely with his publisher) for restoring readings that the author deleted under the publisher's influence, then he is not claiming that one must necessarily give preference to the historical product of the book trade (the "historical statement" conveyed by a "book's total form").[36] He is saying only that editors' knowledge should include book-trade and typographical matters, and he does not go on to confront the fact that more than one responsible approach to critical editing can be followed by editors who have this knowledge.

What he recommends for Congreve is the same, in the end, as what many of the editors who are considered followers of Greg would have done in this situation. All McKenzie is really saying is that editors have frequently had insufficient historical knowledge to recognize the textual role that typography can play. It may be fair to call this lack a "failure of historical imagination," but it is an overstatement to assert that "most recent work in textual bibliography" (p. 105) is guilty of it, for editors routinely consider which (if any) typographical features of the printings of an author's work must be defined as textual; and a decision not to classify them as textual, in an edition focusing on authorial intention, does not necessarily signify that the editor has failed to take the whole book, or the whole historical context, into account. McKenzie's misunderstanding of Greg's rationale[37] has led him to think that "current

35. McKenzie does not acknowledge this point when he refers to "an historic and contextual accuracy in the recovery of every possible element of meaning as intended by the author and perceived by an intelligent and sensitive reader of his time" (p. 92).

36. Though it may seem that he is at other times, as when he speaks of "the most important one [concern] of all—what, exactly, an author in his own age did say to his readers and how he and his printers directed them to respond" (p. 123). What the author did say and what the author wanted to say are not always the same.

37. McKenzie devotes the first section (pp. 83–92) of his paper, rather irrelevantly, to a critique of Greg and three commentators on him (Morse Peckham, Hans Zeller, and Tom Davis). The ostensible relevance is that Greg dealt with the drama of a period in which typographical care was not bestowed on printed plays; and the argument is that recent editorial theory, greatly influenced by Greg, is therefore not equipped to handle situations in which text and presentation are integrated. McKenzie gets off the track in emphasizing the distinction between substantives and accidentals and treating it as a distinction between meaningful and formal elements, which (at least in its use by Greg's followers) "has been utterly divisive, shattering any concept of the integrity of the book as an organic form, a material statement in which all its elements participate" (p. 84). Although he is right to find the criticisms of Peckham, Zeller, and Davis deficient, his own analysis fails to recognize that the distinction between substantives and accidentals is actually based not on meaning

theories of textual criticism" are "quite inadequate to cope" with the connections between typography and meaning; actually there is no theoretical problem on this score at all, and the value of McKenzie's piece is rather to have provided us with some illuminating examples of these connections and to have reminded us forcefully how essential a knowledge of typographic and book-trade history is to editors (not to mention other things they must know). He makes no case in this piece for the necessity of what he grandiosely calls "a new and comprehensive sociology of the text" (p. 118). But in his impressive Presidential address to the Bibliographical Society five years later, he more calmly and more stimulatingly defines the "sociology of texts," not in relation to a supposed crisis that it can rescue us from but as the "substance of bibliography" (p. 365), thus expanding bibliography to include the study of orality, literacy, and "the recording function of memory" (p. 333).[38] His encompassing view enables him to offer one of the most eloquent testimonies we have to the indispensability of textual eclecticism in reaching some understanding of the past, showing that it in no way violates "historicity" (p. 334).[39] Even those bibliographers who feel uncomfortable with the idea of becoming anthropologists (as well as sociologists) will come away from McKenzie's humane manifesto with an enriched understanding of their role as textual historian-critics.[40]

---

but on a generalization about human behavior in the past, that it comes into play only when one has no other means of reaching a textual decision, and that accidentals are in fact treated as extremely important elements in texts. There is nothing in Greg's approach, even as extended and followed by others, that prevents one from regarding typography as a textual matter or from preserving the integrity of particular texts (late or early), if one believes the typography or integrity to have resulted from authorial intention; Greg's rationale is no more divisive than any other plan for critical editing, because it recommends eclecticism only when a unity of elements does not exist and only to bring about greater unity. It perfectly well accommodates McKenzie's demands for a textual theory, and there is thus some irony in his charge that the tradition deriving from Greg suffers from "intellectual timidity" (p. 92).

38. "The Sociology of a Text: Orality, Literacy and Print in Early New Zealand," *Library*, 6th ser., 6 (1984), 333–365. Another sensitive treatment of oral texts—of "the pleasures and advantages of preliteracy"—is John Miles Foley's "Editing Oral Epic Texts: Theory and Practice," *Text*, 1 (1981), 75–94.

39. Indeed, it moves outside books and for him becomes a pattern in life. There is, he believes, "a principle of textual criticism operative in the real world which implies the concept of an ideal text that the versions have failed fully to express": "The physical versions and their fortuitous forms are not the only testimonies to intent: implicit in the accidents of history is an ideal text which history has begun to discover, a reconciliation of readings which is also a meeting of minds. The concept of an ideal text as a cultural and political imperative is not imposed *on* history but derives *from* it and from an understanding of the dynamics of bibliography as a study of the meanings 'books' make" (p. 364).

40. Another writer who has stressed the importance of original typography is Randall McLeod, but his point is different from McKenzie's. His concern is not primarily with the way typographic layout carries historical meaning or with the possibility that it is an

Although McKenzie's position emphasizes the social settings in which authors work, it does not deny the primacy of unconstrained authorial intention as a guide for critical editing. Others who focus on the social side of authorship go farther and believe that the collaborative nature of the publishing process makes artificial any attempt to isolate an author's uninfluenced intentions. Jerome J. McGann has become the most prominent advocate of this point of view, particularly as a result of *A Critique of Modern Textual Criticism* (1983).[41] He attacks the approach developed by Bowers (and derived from Greg) for editing works of the last two centuries because it emphasizes authorial intention; he believes that it has "tended to suffocate textual studies" by limiting them to a narrow "psychological and biographical context" (pp. 119–120). In its place he calls for an editorial theory that would recognize literary works to be "fundamentally social rather than personal" productions (p. 8). Locating authority in authorial intentions, he says, causes works

---

integral part of a literary work; rather, he has shown in a series of articles how typographic evidence can be essential in making textual decisions (as when a particular spelling was caused by the necessity of inserting a type between two kerned types that would not fit together) and how scholarly editions that fail to report such evidence deprive readers of information they need for evaluating editorial judgments. Unmodernized (or "old-spelling") scholarly editions, in other words, do not go far enough toward providing historical evidence, for they separate spelling and punctuation from typography. Facsimile editions are desirable, in this view, not specifically because the original typography is part of the text or is what emerged from the original process of publication but because they make available to readers the evidence present in the original typography (that is, all of it that is reproducible). Whereas McKenzie is concerned with determining what details constitute a literary work, McLeod is talking about the presentation of evidence. If we are to have critical editions at all, we must resign ourselves to the fact that their apparatuses will not contain every piece of evidence used by their editors; but we have a right to expect that editors will recognize, take into account, and comment on the kind of evidence McLeod discusses, and his articles are valuable in calling attention to uses of typographic evidence often neglected. His criticism of the practices of some editors is well taken, but it does not in fact invalidate the concept of critical editions in modern typography. See his "Spellbound: Typography and the Concept of Old-Spelling Editions," *Renaissance and Reformation*, n.s., 3 (1979), 50–65; "Editing Shak-speare," *Sub-Stance*, no. 33/34 (1982), 26–55; and *"Gon.* No more, the text is foolish.", in *The Division of the Kingdoms* (see note 68 below), pp. 153–193.

41. He had earlier expressed some of the same ideas in essays, as in "The Text, the Poem, and the Problem of Historical Method," *New Literary History*, 12 (1980–81), 269–288, where he says that "every work of art is the product of an interaction between an artist, on the one hand, and a variety of social determinants on the other" (p. 275). In two other papers presented at textual conferences in 1981 and 1982 (but not published until after his book) he explores the "social nexus" of literary works and the relations between "historicist textual criticism" and literary criticism: "Shall These Bones Live?", *Text*, 1 (1981 [published in 1984]), 21–40; and "The Monks and the Giants: Textual and Bibliographical Studies and the Interpretation of Literary Works," in *Textual Criticism and Literary Interpretation*, ed. McGann (1985), pp. 180–199. The latter piece presents a useful (if rather melodramatic) statement of the role of textual criticism in literary study, depicting textual criticism as a broad field of historical scholarship, in which the production of editions is only one of many agenda (a view I agree with, though McGann believes I do not).

to be seen in "the most personal and individual way," and "the identity of the author with respect to the work is critically simplified through this process of individualization":

The result is that the dynamic social relations which always exist in literary production—the dialectic between the historically located individual author and the historically developing institutions of literary production—tends to become obscured in criticism. Authors lose their lives as they gain such critical identities, and their works suffer a similar fate by being divorced from the social relationships which gave them their lives (including their "textual" lives) in the first place, and which sustain them through their future life in society. (p. 81)

This passage sets forth, as effectively as any in the book, the view that "words do not by themselves constitute a system of communication" and that "literary works are not produced without arrangements of some sort." Thus, for him, the very existence of works (and not merely their publication) depends on collaborative effort: "the authority for the value of literary productions does not rest in the author's hands alone" (pp. 47–48).

McGann's book serves a useful purpose in asserting the importance of seeing one's own scholarly endeavors against the background of the historical evolution of the field and in focusing renewed attention on the social context of literary production. The treatment of the latter is disappointing, however; the book does not achieve its aim of developing "a fully elaborated argument for a socialized concept of authorship and textual authority" (p. 8). Such a book would be valuable, for—despite increased interest in the historical study of the profession of authorship—scarcely any careful and thoughtful analysis has been made of the implications, for textual criticism, of the social structure of authorship. McGann does provide several interesting examples, often drawn from the writings of English Romantic poets, to illustrate some of the ways in which works become collaborative enterprises, and he offers from time to time variations on his fundamental observation that "an author's work possesses autonomy only when it remains an unheard melody" (p. 51); but he expends much of his energy on a criticism of the position of Bowers and those who, in one way or another, have followed his lead. Even if this criticism were well-founded,[42] it is hard to see how the dis-

---

42. It is not, however. But the fact that his criticism of this school of editing is often superficial or incorrect is a secondary point; the more fundamental matter to be examined is his general attack on an author-based approach to editing (whether or not he has the details of the Bowers line right). I shall simply note here three of the deficiencies in his treatment of the Bowers position. The most serious flaw is his failure to acknowledge its flexibility, for it does not demand that a manuscript be used as copy-text in preference to a first edition, or a first in preference to a later edition, when the circumstances suggest

crediting of one approach amounts to a "fully elaborated argument" for another. The underlying assumption, of course, is that there are only two alternatives and that only one of them is valid. A far more productive way to proceed would be to recognize that a variety of approaches is justifiable and then to concentrate, with positive arguments, on the merits of the one under discussion.

McGann obviously believes that the structure of modern publishing does not admit of any approach to authorship that stresses individual artistic creation and that to take such an approach would be a falsification of history. But surely it is a legitimate (and natural) historical pursuit to be interested in the minds of particular persons from the past, particularly if their writings (or other accomplishments) have any reason to command our attention. However much those writings as published and read were a collaborative effort, we are not being unhistorical in wanting to know just what the initiating mind contributed to that effort. The initiator, by virtue of being the initiator, is forever set apart from those who follow, however necessary they may have been for the completion of the act of communication (and, indeed, however beneficial we judge their ministrations to have been); and if we are concerned with more than one work "by" the same person because we feel that they may illuminate one another, the creating mind is the link between them. The attempt to establish what an author thought and wrote when not making concessions to pressure from others is an essential activity for understanding history.[43] But those who engage in it are not thereby

---

otherwise, and it is capable of handling the examples he cites. A prime instance of this flexibility is Bowers's own practice in his William James edition and his own theoretical statement in "Greg's 'Rationale of Copy-Text' Revisited," *SB*, 31 (1978), 90–161—an essay cited once by McGann but not really used in his analysis. It is thus incorrect to state flatly, without qualification, that "the Bowers position is that the author's manuscript is a higher authority" than the first edition (p. 55). McGann also stresses the word "final" in "final intention" in an extremely literal way that I think the editors following Greg have not normally done; in practice the term has excluded the intentions reflected in unfinished drafts but it has not been taken to rule out the possibility of different intentions manifested in different completed versions. And several times he speaks of "the rule of final intentions" governing "the choice of copy-text" (as on p. 55), without recognizing that an early copy-text chosen for its accidentals may be very far indeed from the author's "final intentions" with respect to substantives.

43. McGann's unwillingness to accept this point underlies his belief that the Bowers system, based on a classical model (derived, via Greg, from Lachmann), is inappropriate for dealing with modern materials: because the textual critic of modern works "actually possesses the 'lost originals' which the classical critic is forced to hypothesize, his concept of an ideal text reveals itself to be—paradoxically—a pure abstraction, whereas the classical critic's ideal text remains, if 'lost,' historically actual" (p. 57). The force of this observation as a criticism is not clear, for a "pure abstraction" can be a valid goal; and textual critics of classical works (or works of any other period) have the option of attempting to construct texts reflecting their authors' intentions, as well as attempting to recreate lost documents.

denying the value of examining as well the forms of works that came off the presses and went into readers' hands. No one can reasonably claim (and I am not aware that anyone has tried to claim) that the texts of works as they in fact appeared in successive printings and editions over the years are not important for historical study or that publication is not a social process. The opposite in each case is a truism, and McGann in these respects is stating the obvious (which is not a bad thing to do). But it is equally a truism to say that intellectual (and thus literary) history is concerned with the private as well as the public, with the minds and ideas of individuals as well as with the transmutations of those ideas in their passage through the world. The two approaches are complementary and both are necessary, though one may be more appropriate than the other for certain purposes.

These observations, I believe, provide the proper context for reading McGann's book; with them in mind, one immediately recognizes the fallaciousness or narrowness of many of his statements. It is ironic, given his emphasis on breadth and on the need to free textual study from constricting ideas, that his own position is narrow-minded in limiting the acceptable approaches to a single one. Studying literature as a social product is only superficially more inclusive than studying it as the product of a single creator, since one must explore all the same areas of concern in either case; but one is clearly taking a restricted view if one is not open to the values of both approaches. There is nothing wrong, of course, with being an advocate of one position, so long as one is not blinded to the contribution of the other. Insofar as McGann is committed to denying the usefulness of an author-centered conception of editing, his argument is doomed to failure; and his advocacy of a society-oriented one is weakened by his lack of balance.

It also suffers from a lack of clarity. The role of authorial intention is central to the whole discussion, and yet at the end one does not quite know what McGann is suggesting about its place in editing. In an appendix called "A Possible Objection," he reports that a reader of his manuscript objected to his generalization that a first edition "can be expected to contain what author and publishing institution together worked to put before the public" (p. 125), by citing instances in which D. H. Lawrence was "an unwilling partner in a downright repressive process." One might well wonder how this is a "possible objection" to

---

The concept of "final intention" is not merely a device to help guide editors of modern materials through "the mass of documentary evidence" that often confronts them (p. 56); it leads to a goal worth working toward, regardless of the simplicity or complexity of the surviving documents, a goal that is historical whether or not the text being sought ever existed in written form. (Cf. McKenzie's point in note 39 above.)

McGann's general line, for if a work achieves its existence through the interaction of author and publisher, then an expurgated work must be accepted as readily as one we might regard as improved, for both can be the result of the particular chain of historical events that constitute the publishing process.[44] But McGann surprisingly replies that the collaboration of author and publisher does not always turn out well and that "the editor must examine carefully the early publishing history in order to arrive at a reasonable decision" regarding the choice of a "textual version" (p. 127).[45] He adds that authorial intention is "only one of many factors to be taken into account, and while in some cases it may and will determine the final decision, in many others it cannot and must not be forced to perform that function" (p. 128). Similarly, he had earlier stated that "Shelley's manuscripts frequently assert a strong demand to be adopted as copy-text, whereas Byron's rarely do": despite the fact that Shelley "published in a fashion that was normal for his period," it would be "a disservice to Shelley's work . . . if a critical edition today neglected to consider, in the matter of copy-text, the sincerity and integrity of Shelley's manuscripts" (pp. 108–109). If McGann's point is that we should accept the results of the publishing process only when we feel that the work has benefited from it, we are then being asked to engage in a very different kind of editing, in which our choices are dictated by our personal preferences; the results may be admirable artistically but are not designed to increase readers' understanding of the past.[46] If he is saying that we are to follow a published text only when (or at those points where) the author can be thought to have sincerely approved of and desired it, then the focus is on authorial intention after all, and the procedure is not really different from the one that editors in the Bowers tradition have been using. They have habitually made judgments to distinguish which revisions made or suggested by others (whether publishers or other acquaintances) were fully accepted by the

44. Even to summarize McGann's position, as McGann himself does, in terms of an author and publisher working together to put something before the public does not, one would think, catch the spirit of McGann's argument, if what is implied here is that they necessarily worked together harmoniously and cooperatively. To think of the production of literature as a social or collaborative process is, one supposes, only to say that a number of people are involved and that any of them may influence the published text—not that they are never in conflict with one another.

45. He says that instances of the kind under discussion "go to the issue of textual versions rather than to the rationale of copy-text," but he is in fact talking about the choice of copy-text, and his summarizing paragraph speaks of "the decision on copy-text." At another point he distinguishes, without explanation, between "copy-text" and "version of a text we choose to work from" (p. 56).

46. They are thus not the product of historical scholarship, in the usual sense that it attempts to reconstruct past events. Of course any activity in the present is historical in the sense that it in some degree reflects its own time (as I shall note further below).

author in the spirit of active and welcome collaboration, and they have rejected only those revisions that the author appears to have accepted grudgingly or been forced into accepting. These editors have normally recognized the social side of authorship by acknowledging that an author's intentions can sometimes include the results of collaboration.

Of course these matters require subjective judgments, based on historical evidence, but so do most decisions in critical editing. In the Bowers tradition, however, those judgments are made in a clear conceptual framework, with authorial intention at its center; but McGann offers no equally clear alternative, for he seems to waver in regard to what is at the center. It is not very helpful to be told that authorial intention is one of "many factors" to be taken into account and that sometimes it will be the "determining one": when the author's intentions and the publisher's actions are in conflict, what does one do? Naturally, one can go either way, but these are two different approaches to editing. McGann believes that "to see 'author's intentions' as the basis for a 'rationale of copy-text' is to confuse the issues involved" (p. 128); one should rather say that confusion is promoted by maintaining that an undefined mixture of two distinct approaches constitutes a useful rationale.[47] Clear thinking is better served by recognizing at the outset that individual desires and social pressures, though they may in specific instances be in harmony, are conceptually irreconcilable and that an editor's guiding principle in textual decisions must favor one or the other. It is understandable that many editors have regarded authorial intention as the more sensible choice for a scholarly critical edition, since one can argue that to represent the historical results of the publishing process a diplomatic edition or photographic facsimile would be pre-

47. Another example of the attempt to mix these approaches is Donald Pizer's "Self-Censorship and Textual Editing," in *Textual Criticism and Literary Interpretation*, ed. Mc-Gann (1985), pp. 144–161. Pizer's four " 'tests' for accepting the belief that self-censorship has occurred and that restoration of an earlier state of the text is required" are: evaluating evidence regarding the composition and publication history of a work, evaluating evidence bearing on the author's motives in making revisions, deciding through critical analysis whether one version is "better" than others, and considering whether "the first published version of a major work" is "a historical artifact that should continue to occupy the role of general reading text even if it has been subject to self-censorship" (pp. 150–151). The latter two are not in fact relevant to "accepting the belief that self-censorship has occurred"; they do represent two possible approaches to making textual decisions, but neither can be combined with the first two to provide a coherent rationale for choosing a single text. Pizer recognizes the value of publishing editions of alternative texts, but he still thinks ultimately in terms of a single text that he would like to see "generally read" (p. 155). (In itself, his account of "the interaction between self and world, which is inseparable from the expressive process" [p. 154], and of the "historical resonance" [p. 156] of long-established texts, is well stated.)

ferable. But I do not mean to suggest that there are no possibilities in between: one could decide, for example, to accept all the publisher's alterations but to correct typographical errors, thus producing a critical text representing the publisher's intention; or one could decide to remove from the text of a single printing the textual features imposed on it against the author's wishes, thus producing a critical text reflecting the author's intentions at that particular time (regardless of any later authorial revisions). Such alternatives, however, have clear aims, giving priority either to the author's intentions or to outside influences. McGann's account contains no hint of this rational structure of possibilities within which critical judgment can operate purposefully.[48]

The issue here is not subjectivity, for all critical editors—in the Bowers line or any other—make judgments (which are inevitably subjective) at every turn. It is difficult to understand why McGann thinks that "Giving up the rule of final intentions" will "introduce a subjective factor into the critical process" or that his proposal involves "the re-emergence of a 'subjectivity' " (p. 107), as if subjectivity had not always played a central role.[49] Because one of the factors influencing subjective decisions in a given instance is, he believes, the history of the previous editing of the work and what needs the present audience for the work has, it is not surprising that he welcomes modernizing as a legitimate scholarly activity.[50] He accuses those who reject modernizing of not understanding that all editions, even unmodernized ones, are—like all other literary efforts—time-bound, reflecting the concerns and attitudes of the age in which they were produced. All thoughtful people, including many

---

48. The "set of interconnected guidelines" he refers to at one point (p. 107) is not the same thing: it consists of considerations to be taken into account in choosing a copy-text, considerations that include "the character of the audience of the edition," "the early printing history" of the work, and "the current state of textual criticism" (p. 106).

49. He seems to think that he has opened up a wider range of options and thereby increased the area in which subjectivity can operate, but editors have always faced the same options, for there have always been valid alternatives to critical texts reflecting authorial intention (which in themselves present many alternatives).

50. The opening sentence of his chapter on modernizing betrays some confusion in terminology, if nothing else. He says that a "sharp distinction" is usually made "between the scholarly or critical edition on the one hand, and modernized or noncritical editions on the other" (p. 95). Generally the term "critical edition" is used to mean an edition containing a critical text, which is a text that does not agree precisely with a single documentary source because it incorporates alterations reflecting the editor's critical judgment (exercised to make the text more nearly conform with some desired goal). Thus an edition can be scholarly without being critical, and all modernized editions contain critical texts. Of course one can define these terms anew if one wishes, but it seems inappropriate to associate the word "noncritical," which already seems to refer to the absence of critical judgment, as in a facsimile, with "modernized," which involves a great deal of judgment and refers to editions that are at the opposite extreme from facsimiles.

scholarly editors, are perfectly well aware of this fact, but it is irrelevant. If one engages in historical scholarship, one is attempting, through an informed imaginative effort, to escape into the thinking of another time, even though one knows that the escape is never complete and that it will have to be reattempted by others in the future. Scholarly editors of critical editions do not really imagine that they are packaging up textual history for all time or preventing the further alteration of the text (see p. 93). But these realizations do not invalidate the effort of historical reconstruction. Modernized texts, like some kinds of critical essays, are attempts at elucidation, which may be more or less helpful to the readers of a given time; but those readers (even the "nonspecialist" ones)[51] who are interested in a work as testimony from the past will need to have the best results that historical scholarship has achieved in the recovery or imaginative reconstruction of particular texts and versions of that work.[52] McGann considers his discussion of modernized editions to be "the final phase of the argument" (p. 94), and it does epitomize his dual conviction that literary production is "not an autonomous and self-reflexive activity" (p. 100) and that critical editions, like all other works, are "always produced under the pressure of contemporary demands" (p. 96). But it also perpetuates the blurring of essential distinctions that permeates the book. One must deeply regret that a book offering the hope of a sys-

51. McGann continually refers in this discussion to "nonspecialist editions," by which he means "nonspecialist texts," for he is referring to the adjustment of the text, not just the apparatus, for different classes of readers.

52. Arguments for modernizing are always doomed to failure, just as the practice of modernizing is bound to be inconsistent. Yet defenses of it continue to appear. Stanley Wells, in *Modernizing Shakespeare's Spelling* (1979), believes that modernizing "removes unnecessary barriers to understanding, making it possible for the reader to concentrate on the text itself, undistracted by obsolete and archaic accidentals of presentation" (p. vi). This view of "the text itself" links Wells with generations of compositors and publishers' editors that preceded him in feeling free to alter spelling and punctuation but less free to alter words (the behavior Greg described in his "Rationale"). But after going through Wells's discussion of the problems with which modernizing is fraught, readers are likely to be convinced that the real barrier between them and the text is being erected by the modernizer. Wells ends by explaining that modernizing editors have to give "hard thought" to the meaning of each word, and their choice of a form in each case "communicates the results of such thought." Modernization, he concludes, "may thus be seen not, as some would have it, as a work of popularization, even of vulgarization, but as a means of exploring Shakespeare's text that can make a real contribution to scholarship" (p. 34). It is difficult to see how the case for modernization is strengthened by saying that it forces editors to think hard about every word, for responsible editors of unmodernized critical editions must do the same thing. Editors who modernize, Wells says, "may be surprised to find how much that is of interest in Shakespeare's language has gone unnoticed." But modernizing seems too high a price to pay for a promise that editors have done the work we expect them to do anyway. (Other unconvincing arguments for modernizing have recently come from R. M. Flores in "The Need for a Scholarly, Modernized Edition of Cervantes' Work," *Cervantes*, 2 [1982], 69–87.)

tematic exposition of a social view of authorship and its editorial implications must finally be judged to have left the issues more confused than clarified.[53]

III

A convenient pairing was brought about the following year by the publication of Hershel Parker's *Flawed Texts and Verbal Icons: Literary Authority in American Fiction* (1984),[54] for that book locates the other pole of the debate over authorial intention and its place in the historical study of texts. Parker takes the position, with a vengeance, that authorial intention is central: he believes that the important intention is what authors manifest during the creation of works and that even authors' own later revisions often have no more right to become part of those works than the alterations initiated by others. His and McGann's books, therefore, serve to define the limits of the area under discussion. What they share is a sense of urgency about the need for a renewed historical orientation in literary studies and a conviction that textual criticism is central to literary criticism. From there on, of course, they are in contrast, and in more ways than one might anticipate. For McGann's book, despite its incoherence, calls attention to a fundamental theoretical issue, whereas Parker's book, though far better written and organized, is principally of interest for its detailed case histories, not because its basic thesis is of theoretical significance.

Parker begins with the assumption that "All valid meaning is authorial meaning" (p. ix);[55] he is concerned not with arguing this general point but only with proceeding from it to a more precise definition of authorial meaning. Drawing especially on John Dewey's *Art as Experience* (1934) and Albert Rothenberg's *The Emerging Goddess* (1979), he describes the creative process as one that "begins, continues (as clinical

53. In "Shall These Bones Live?" (see note 41 above), McGann has shown how powerfully he can write about the role of history in literary understanding. I believe that what I have suggested here regarding the validity of two fundamentally opposed emphases in textual criticism is analogous to his acceptance of the necessity for two approaches to literature ("two classes of men [scholars and critics] are always upon the earth of humane letters, and whoever seeks to reconcile them seeks to destroy the existence of their shared world" [p. 25])—and indeed seems to me more in the spirit of his comments than his own *Critique* is. But he also notes that a productive symbiosis, rather than a sterile co-existence, requires constant prodding from each side. His *Critique*—and, I hope, my remarks here—can be seen as part of this constructive process.

54. Some parts of the book had been published earlier, as in (among other places) "The Determinacy of the Creative Process and the 'Authority' of the Author's Textual Decisions," *College Literature*, 10 (1983), 99–125.

55. Thus "some perfectly real aesthetic frissons" are "spurious" (p. 11).

observation records, with varying admixtures and sequences of excitement, arousal, boredom, anxiety, and determination), then ends—ends
with stubborn finality" (p. 34). Because this process is "by nature determinate, revising authors very often betray or otherwise blur their
original achievements in ways they seldom intend and seldom become
aware of" (p. ix). He therefore concludes that Greg's rationale of copy-
text is not an appropriate guide to the establishment of texts reflecting
their authors' intentions because it assumes that authors' later revisions
are, as a general rule, to be accepted in preference to the earlier readings.[56] According to Parker, "all empirical evidence should tell us that
Greg is wrong, that in any mature human being, writers included, a state
of indefinitely sustained arousal toward one object is unnatural" (p. 35).
Thus authors' later revisions—as illustrated by a number of examples,
particularly Henry James, Mark Twain, Stephen Crane, and Norman
Mailer—may introduce inconsistencies (of detail, characterization, tone,
or theme) and produce "maimed" texts. Critical editors, he believes,
should not assume that "every author retains full authority over anything
he has written for as long as he lives" (p. ix); they should instead reject
later revisions that result in "unreadable texts" (p. x).

    This argument, as set forth by Parker, is not a helpful or clarifying
one. The key to the problem is the fact that even if the creative process is
granted to be "determinate," in the sense that it comes to an end, one
is not provided by Parker with any historically oriented guideline for
defining that ending point. It does not make sense, as he recognizes, to
fix any quantitative limit: obviously one cannot say that any revision
made within twenty-four hours, or three days, or six weeks, of the writing of the last sentence of a work emerges from the heat of the creative
process, and that later revisions do not.[57] Even during what seems a

---

56. His criticism of Greg, the Center for Editions of American Authors, and Bowers is
often unfair, so much so that it is self-defeating: for example, he speaks of editors who were
moved "to stake their reputations on the validity of the rationale of copy-text set forth by
W. W. Greg" (p. 59), as if reputations were the dominant concern; he says that "no editorial formula, even one as appealing as Greg's, can substitute for the expertise which
comes only from years of conscientious (and preferably loving) biographical and critical study
of the author whom one presumes to edit" (p. 67), as if editors who follow Greg substitute a
formula for knowledge; he complains about certain critical judgments by CEAA editors
"with well-nigh limitless federal funds" (p. 82), as if the magnitude of funds (which he
knows he is exaggerating) were relevant to this issue; and he refers to the "hubris of the
Newest Bibliography which at its worst barricaded editing within a mad-scientist laboratory
more isolated from the author than any critic or theorist had yet been" (p. 240).

57. Of course one cannot limit the discussion exclusively to whole works, because the
process of original composition may be spread out over a long period, or may be interrupted,
with the result that the earlier and the later parts of a work may be the products of separate
bursts of creative activity and may conflict with each other in various ways. (John McClelland, in "Critical Editing in the Modern Languages," *Text*, 1 [1981], 201–216, takes a position
somewhat akin to Parker's in advocating as copy-text a text representing the point "where

single period of creative intensity, writers going back to an earlier paragraph may not be fully in tune with its context and may make revisions
that seem to weaken or confuse the passage. Furthermore, as Parker admits, it is possible for some revisions to appear successful even though
they were made at a time when one would assume the creative process to
have ended. "No hard and fast limits can be drawn," he says, and he
offers a few of the obvious reasons: "some writers have better memories
than others" or refresh their memories with more rereadings of their
works, and "a great deal always depends on how prolonged and overwhelming the creative process had been and how thoroughly the author
is compelled to put it behind him and go on with a new work" (p. 40).
The creative process is as various as are the temperaments of creators.
Therefore none of Parker's generalizations about late revisions can be
unqualified (he says that writers "very often"—but not always—"blur
their original achievements"), for some late revisions are not inappropriate. If satisfactory revisions do sometimes occur after the creative
process has ended, then clearly some factor other than the heat of sustained creativity is responsible for their success. Alternatively, one could
define the creative process so as to include all satisfactory revisions;
thus one could say that the existence of such revisions shows that the
creative process had not yet ended at the time they were made. Either
way, how has the introduction of the idea of a "determinate" creative
process been of assistance? The focus of attention has been placed on
distinguishing revisions that are satisfactory, or not inappropriate (or
however one wishes to describe them), from those that are the opposite;
and, it turns out, the concept of the creative process is not the analytical
element that enables these distinctions to be made.

What does underlie them is the editor's aesthetic judgment. Deciding whether a revision is successful (or satisfactory, or simply makes sense
rather than nonsense) depends on individual judgment. Some revisions
that produce clear inconsistencies are indubitably blemishes (when one
can be sure that no authorial purpose is served by them), but many of
the revisions that Parker discusses can be (and have been) the subject of
disagreement as to their worth or effectiveness. The fact that he is asking
editors to make literary value judgments is not in itself a problem, for

---

the work has acquired its definitive structure, either as the result of the accumulation of
variants or by a dramatic revision" [p. 206], for "we are probably being more faithful to the
text itself by presenting it in the state at which it was receiving the author's closest attention," since "extensive revision requires as much concentration as does composition" [p. 207].
McClelland, however, is more optimistic than Parker about the possibility of coherent later
revision and thus would approve later copy-texts more readily than Parker. In a dubious
argument, McClelland also claims that the variants would be "easier to handle" if the
copy-text were "the text that will actually be read" [p. 204].)

all critical editing requires editorial judgments, which involve literary sensitivity.[58] Nor can one accuse him of simply telling editors to choose whatever variants happen to please them, for he explicitly couches his proposal in historical terms, with its goal the establishment of the author's—not the editor's—intended wording and punctuation. Yet on a more sophisticated level there is a sense in which this accusation is justified. One must remember that Parker is concerned only with revisions that authors made of their own free will; naturally those they were forced into making do not reflect their uninfluenced intention. The essential issue, then, is whether revisions that seem to the editor to introduce inconsistency or incoherence can be considered to represent the author's intention. Normally one is safe in assuming that authors do not intend to make their works incoherent or to make revisions that damage their works. But the kind of intention Parker is rightly concerned with is the intention in the act of writing, the intention to place a certain word or mark of punctuation next, not the intention to produce a particular effect. By definition, then, authors who make revisions of their own free will are producing intended texts (which may of course contain slips), even if those revisions, in the opinion of some or all critics, were executed with insufficient thought and are damaging in their effect. Everyone agrees that authors can make mistakes. But their revisions, however mistaken, are historical facts, and we cannot deny that unsatisfying versions of works are what authors have sometimes left to us as their finally intended texts. Parker believes that in such cases we should be concerned with the earlier intentions that produced better results. In effect, therefore, he is saying that—even as scholarly editors, who inform ourselves with historical facts—we should reject authorial revisions that do not strike us as successful.

This position is not necessarily untenable, but we are not likely to be persuaded of its cogency by an argument enveloped in an irrelevant discussion of the creative process (interesting concept though it is). The more direct way to justify such an approach is to say that, if one is producing a critical text (in which the choice among variants involves the editor's judgment in any case), one should present the work in the most successful of the various forms dictated by the author's shifting intentions. (If the goal is to remain historically oriented, the editor must be

58. Thus it is no objection to his line of reasoning to say that in rejecting late revisions the editor may not see what the author was getting at. Undoubtedly it does happen that editors find revisions thoughtless or damaging because they fail to follow an author's changed, and perhaps unconventional, mode of expression. But all critical editors take the risk of misunderstanding the authors they hope to serve well. (And they are not to be blamed—as Parker suggests on p. 12 and elsewhere—for trying to make sense of the texts they encounter: literature *can* be hard to make sense of.)

limited by what the author wanted at some point, whether at the last stage of revision or not.) One way this decision has previously been approached[59] is in terms of whether a set of revisions can be judged to have turned a work into a different work (or an independent version): if grounds do exist for believing that particular revisions (regardless of their extent) affect a work so profoundly that the result ought to be thought of as a separate work, then one is free, if one chooses, to edit the earlier work rather than the later. This approach gives editors considerable scope for exercising their literary judgment—first, in making the subjective decision that the revisions produce a new work and, second, in valuing the earlier work more highly. But there is a great difference between this line of thought and Parker's, even though both rely on editors' aesthetic judgments. This one places those judgments squarely within a historical framework (admittedly, and necessarily, a subjective historical construct): one can reject later revisions if they appear to represent a new departure and turn a work in a new direction, for the result is being postulated as a historically separate entity requiring independent editing. If, however, one cannot make such a case, one must then consider the revisions as attempts to perfect or complete the work along the general lines already manifested in it, and one cannot reject some of them, simply because they seem misguided, if one's historical aim is the author's last intentions for each work (or aesthetically independent version).[60] Parker's approach, on the other hand, reverses the priorities and places the editor's aesthetic judgments above the historical succession of authorial revisions: those revisions considered by the editor to damage the work are not, in Parker's plan, allowed a place in a critical text meant to show the author's intentions. This way of proceeding involves shifting "final intention" in one of two ways: either the term means artistically final intention (however early or late such intention revealed itself) rather than the chronologically final intention of each independent version, or else it refers to the intended results, thus excluding revisions that do not, as they turned out, promote the intention of improving the work. In either case editors are asked to determine when authors' free-willed revisions were not in the best interests of their works and to construct their critical texts accordingly. It is not uncommon for critical editors to have to decide what authors "really" wanted, as opposed to what they actually did, in situations where their freedom of choice is suspect; but to protect authors from the literary consequences

59. See G. T. Tanselle, "The Editorial Problem of Final Authorial Intention," *SB*, 29 (1976), 167–211; reprinted in *Selected Studies*, pp. 309–353.

60. An interest in such last intentions does not of course mean that there is no legitimate historical interest in earlier stages of a work.

of their unconstrained textual decisions, as Parker recommends, is in fact to remove the author from the center of attention.

The role of subjectivity in Parker's plan is thus fundamentally different from its place in the approach that requires—to justify the absence of late revisions from a critical text—a demonstration that they actually produced a new work (or an independent version, whichever one wishes to call it). Parker's rejection of that approach is characteristic of his reasoning. In discussing the 1907 text of James's *The American,* he asks whether a work can be "new" when "a good many lines at a stretch, occasionally, are wholly unrevised, while some other revisions respect the structure of a long paragraph while altering it stylistically sentence by sentence" (p. 107)—as if the presence of unrevised passages, or passages with unrevised structure, are incompatible with the existence of a different work. He later ridicules critics who seem to think that an author "confers meaning on a completed text with the wave of a hand or by ripping a book apart and reordering a hunk of it" (p. 218). When "hunks are re-used, unaltered or only slightly altered," he asserts, "what goes unrevised to a greater or lesser extent goes unrethought, unrestructured, carrying its original intentionality in a new context where that intentionality is more or less at war with the different intentionality in the altered or newly written passages" (pp. 228–229). These comments suggest a quantitative test, implying that a new work must be largely constructed of new sentences: "If unaltered or scarcely altered hunks of the original text remain in the later text, that later text is not truly a 'separate' one" (p. 229). Of course unaltered passages do sometimes clash with their new contexts, but at other times they do not. A writer may make only a few crucial changes in a work, leaving the rest unrevised, and yet the import of the whole may be changed; the unaltered passages will have taken on altered significance, and the fact that they are unaltered does not necessarily mean that they are "unrethought." Parker's firm belief that "textual meaning is not something living in a text" as an autonomous entity (p. 219) should be seen to argue against, not for, his view: a passage, not being autonomous, will not necessarily carry its original meaning into a new context. If it seems to fit successfully into the new context, are we to say it has been rethought and that the result is a new work? And if it does not, that it is unrethought and the result not a new work? Parker is really saying that a new work can come only from successful revision, making "new work" an evaluative term referring to a successful work. His argument seems to run as follows: writers infuse meaning into works in the process of composition; moving passages around is not a part of the composition process unless the shifted passages are thoroughly rethought; we can tell that they have been thoroughly rethought if they function well in their new contexts; if they do not function well, we cannot consider the new versions to be new works, regardless of the nature of the revisions that were made, but only botched versions of the original work. Ironically, if he could accept the idea that revisions can produce unsuccessful new works, he would have a stronger argument for offering—what he favors—a critical text containing unrevised readings.

Parker's main thesis is built on a patent inconsistency. He repeatedly insists that the only meaning we should be interested in is what the author put into the text: we must think of the author as "a human being who worked meaning into the text line by line and page by page," for "authorial power is the only literary power there is" (p, 219). Nevertheless we are also told that authors frequently do not know when to stop revising their work and that what some of their revisions produce is nonsense rather than valid meaning: "the creative process, like any other process, has bounds, beyond which no author, however fine a craftsman, is apt to intervene with impunity" (p. 51). There is apparently a higher authority than the author, after all. Because Parker believes that unrevised passages in new contexts, not having been built up word by word anew, exemplify the doomed effort to prolong the creative process and are thus unlikely to succeed, he is scornful of authors and critics who claim—as in the instance of *Tender Is the Night*—that a rearrangement of sections has resulted in dramatic improvement. "It is," he says, "as if the right order were latent in what Fitzgerald wrote, awaiting only a magic touch to restore it to a platonic ideal which had had no reality during the years of composition" (p. 219). But Parker, too, has his platonic ideal, for he states that "the working assumption of any student of the creative process is that the direction of any developing aesthetic object is toward unity" (p. 217). The creative process has an end, and the work is then at its most unified, though authors do not always realize that they have reached this point and may try to make further improvements. Parker professes to put the author back into literary criticism: he deplores the tendency to see a work as "a verbal icon, a unique, perfect, and essentially authorless entity" (p. ix). But he also attacks the idea "that an author had the right to do whatever he wanted to do to his text" (p. 60),[61] and he believes that allegiance to the unity of the created work (whether or not we call it an "icon") finally takes precedence over a concern with what the author in fact did to the work.

61. He also attacks—a different matter—"the superstition that the author is infallible" (p. 51). Whether very many people have ever taken the position that the author could make no mistakes in revision is a real question, but is beside the point here. (Parker does understand that a "maimed text" can still retain power: see p. 8.)

Parker surely senses the trap he has set for himself, for at one point he says that we often "revere" the creator and the icon at the wrong times, the creator "after he has gone from creator of his own work to merchandiser or promoter of it" and the icon "not in the form it had when the artist was most in control of it" (p. 49)—a statement that epitomizes all the inconsistencies of the argument, even while it almost acknowledges them. The theoretical scaffolding collapses; but we are left with a series of incisive discussions of individual works, showing how a knowledge of their compositional and publishing histories (including what can be inferred about them through close reading) brings one in touch with basic critical questions about each work. These analyses, along with similar ones that Parker has published separately,[62] stand on their own, and it is regrettable that he tried to erect a theory around them. He thinks of himself as promoting a new movement and wishes he had found a name for it, recognizing that his earlier term, "the New Scholarship," was not right (p. 241).[63] In fact his achievement is to have provided some telling examples of the connections between good textual scholarship and good criticism; no label is needed to dignify that accomplishment, and his awkward attempt at a unifying theory of the creative process only detracts from it.

Once we see that Parker's approach actually moves away from the author, we should not be surprised to find that a reader-response critic takes the same general line.[64] Steven Mailloux is a rarity among such critics in feeling the need to discuss "Textual Scholarship and 'Author's Final Intention' "—as he entitles one chapter (pp. 93–125) of his book *Interpretive Conventions: The Reader in the Study of American Fiction* (1982).[65] He sees himself as offering a "third alternative" for the editor

62. Such as "Evidences for 'Late Insertions' in Melville's Works," *Studies in the Novel*, 7 (1975), 407–424; "Aesthetic Implications of Authorial Excisions: Examples from Nathaniel Hawthorne, Mark Twain, and Stephen Crane," in *Editing Nineteenth-Century Fiction*, ed. Jane Millgate (1978), pp. 99–119; and three articles by him and Brian Higgins: "Sober Second Thoughts: Fitzgerald's 'Final Version' of *Tender is the Night*," *Proof*, 4 (1975), 129–152; "Maggie's 'Last Night': Authorial Design and Editorial Patching," *Studies in the Novel*, 10 (1978), 64–75; "The Flawed Grandeur of Melville's *Pierre*," in *New Perspectives on Melville*, ed. Faith Pullin (1978), pp. 162–196.

63. See "The 'New Scholarship': Textual Evidence and Its Implications for Criticism, Literary Theory, and Aesthetics," *Studies in American Fiction*, 9 (1981), 181–197; and Brian Higgins and Parker, "The Chaotic Legacy of the New Criticism and the Fair Augury of the New Scholarship," in *Ruined Eden of the Present*, ed. G. R. Thompson and Virgil L. Lokke (1981), pp. 27–45.

64. Parker is not receptive to reader-response criticism: see, for example, pp. 219–220.

65. He admits that this discussion "will temporarily submerge the issue of reader response" (p. 94), but he believes that reader-response theory can finally contribute to the concept of authorial intention. Not surprisingly, he characterizes the kind of intention editors are primarily concerned with as "operative intentions," encompassing not only "the actions that the author, as he writes the text, understands himself to be performing in the

between the "originating view" of the author as an "isolated figure freely expressing his uniquely individual and privileged intention" and the "collaborative view of the writer as merely one among many text-producers": the "convention-based" view, in which authorship is a "convention-governed role" (and thus "socially constituted") but one that "individuals can take on" (p. 107). Although this approach combines some aspects of the other two, he considers one "advantage" of it to be that "it preserves scholarly editing's traditional emphasis on the 'author's intention' " (p. 108). There is no question that he takes the author's side when external pressure is involved; changes made under such pressure are invalid, he says, and editors are "fully justified" in rejecting them (p. 118). From there on he gets himself into the same predicament as Parker. Some revisions freely made by the author result in an "illogical or inconsistent restructuring of reader response" (p. 117), which "provides an aesthetic reason for giving the original version priority" (p. 120). In other words, "editors can take control of the intended text out of the author's hands if justified by an examination of historical evidence and the intended structure of the reader's response" (p. 121).[66] This approach "preserves" the "traditional emphasis" on authorial intention in a strange way, by shifting textual authority from author to editor (who is also a reader). Mailloux, in the end, makes editorial decisions the same way that Parker does, but he does not begin from the same premise, since he believes that "literary authorship is socially constituted" (p. 107).

text" (or "active intentions") but also "the immediate effects he understands these actions will achieve in his projected reader" (p. 99). (He unnecessarily elaborates his set of definitions by introducing "inferred intention" to "characterize the critic's description" of what the author is aiming to achieve, even though he recognizes that "operative intentions" are also necessarily inferred. "I am trying," he says, "to emphasize the inferential process an editor uses to posit a specific authorial intention." Surely this process need not be called an "intention" or brought into the definition of authorial intention at all. Mailloux's confusion is shown by his illustration of how the term is useful: it allows him, he says, "to talk about the operative intention an author claimed he had and a perhaps differing inferred intention an editor arrives at after evaluating all the relevant evidence." But the first of these is simply an author's "stated intention," which editors are always wary of, and the latter is the "operative intention" that the editor infers on the basis of all evidence, including the author's claims.) The upshot of his discussion hardly seems a revelation, because editors have regularly been able to understand, without being schooled by reader-response theorists, that authors use language conventions and therefore have expected their readers to react in certain ways to certain locutions. Explicitly defining the concept of authorial intention so as to include the "immediate effects" to be produced in the reader during the reading process is, perhaps, unobjectionable, but it is also unnecessary; it represents no shift in what has always been meant by the concept of the author's intention to convey a meaning through writing down particular words and punctuation. (Why a concept of authorial intention should imply a "specific rationale for critical interpretation"—a point made several times, as on pp. 108, 110, 112, 113—is puzzling.)

66. Or, perhaps more straightforwardly: "it is possible to reject some authorial revisions because they deface the text *after* it was finished" (p. 112).

Here we have a social view of authorship that nevertheless sanctions editorial interventions on the supposed grounds of authorial intention. And thus have we come full circle.

IV

These proposals to treat literature either as a social product or as the outcome of a private creative process are marred by various flaws of argument, but the weakness they share is their assumption that only one approach is valid. Editorial theorists who recognize (as most of them do) that a critical text is based on critical judgment should also see that no one critical text can be the best one from everyone's point of view or for all purposes. If there is a legitimate interest both in a writer's process of creation and in the vicissitudes that writings undergo in the process of initial and subsequent publication—as there obviously is for any historically minded person, since both are historical processes—then various approaches to textual criticism, emphasizing one or the other of these interests, must be acknowledged to be acceptable, depending on their own internal logic. Thoughtful editors have long recognized this point, and even if they have become advocates of a particular approach they have not denied the usefulness of multiple editions reflecting different approaches.[67] Yet the lure of the single text is so strong[68] that it has made many, perhaps most, editorial debates less fruitful than they might have been. Among recent writers on editorial matters, two—Hans Walter Gabler and Peter L. Shillingsburg—have particularly addressed them-

67. Certainly those editors responsible for the wording of the CEAA emblem ("An Approved Text," not "The Approved Text") felt this way; but this gesture has not been taken as seriously as it deserves to be. Tom Davis, in a thoughtful review of the Lawrence and Hardy editions ("Textual Criticism: Philosophy and Practice," *Library*, 6th ser., 6 [1984], 386–397)—which begins with promise and descends to anticlimax—describes two models of "a text and its history": one emphasizes growing deterioration and corruption, the other a positive process of collaboration. Both, he says, are "equally 'true'" (p. 389).

68. As Randall McLeod puts it, "our tradition is unwilling to allow multiple textual authorities to rest as a simultaneous set of existential entities to be encountered absurdly by the reader" (p. 422 of "The Marriage of Good and Bad Quartos," *Shakespeare Quarterly*, 33 [1982], 421–431). He goes on to speak of "the *infinitive* text, which we may define as a polymorphous set of all versions, some part of each of which has a claim to substantive status." The recent controversy over the text of *King Lear* calls attention to the perennial competition between the attractions of a single text and the messier possibilities of independent versions. Although those who believe that the *Lear* variants provide evidence of Shakespeare's revision have overdramatized their case, there is no doubt that the possibility of authorial revision must always be in the editor's mind in evaluating variant readings. See Steven Urkowitz, *Shakespeare's Revision of "King Lear"* (1980); Gary Taylor and Michael Warren (eds.), *The Division of the Kingdoms: Shakespeare's Two Versions of "King Lear"* (1983); and Ernest A. J. Honigmann, "Shakespeare as a Reviser," in *Textual Criticism and Literary Interpretation*, ed. McGann (1985), pp. 1–22.

selves to the question of how to accommodate multiple texts of a work. For both of them a theory of literature supports the argument for the necessity of multiple texts; but they both also give serious thought to the practical matters of apparatus, because the chief problem for this capacious view is the challenge of adequately displaying variant readings.[69]

Gabler's position, far less well thought out than Shillingsburg's, serves to focus some of the issues. In a paper for the 1981 Society for Textual Scholarship conference,[70] Gabler argues that we take too limited a view when we concentrate on the "synchrony" of a particular version of a work and that we ought to be alert to the "diachrony" of the evolutionary stages through which a work develops. We must distinguish, he says (and few would contradict him), between transmissional variants (which are deviations from what the author intended) and authorial variants (some of which are too often regarded as further deviations from an ideal text). The former should be corrected through emendation, but all of the latter, he believes, have a place in the literary work, which "may be said to comprise all its authorial textual states." What Gabler calls "a natural condition of the literary work" is "the manifest existence of discrete authorial versions of a text." In his pretentious language, the "total text" of a work "presents itself as a diachronous structure correlating the discrete synchronous structures discernible." The variant is not an "extraneous irritant" but an "integral textual element of pivotal significance in the textual totality of the work" (p. 309). One sees what he is getting at here, despite the expression and despite two serious conceptual flaws: first, he continually refers to transmissional errors in such a way as to suggest that it is no problem to separate them from authorial revisions, when of course making that distinction is in many instances a central editorial activity;[71] second, he repeatedly speaks of "discrete textual states" (even claiming that "there

69. Fredson Bowers has recently summarized his views on apparatus in "Notes on Editorial Apparatus," in *Historical & Editorial Studies in Medieval & Early Modern English, for Johan Gerritsen*, ed. Mary-Jo Arn and Hanneke Wirtjes, with Hans Jensen (1985), pp. 147–162. (He and Paul Werstine have also had an exchange on historical collations that include readings from posthumous editions: Werstine, "Modern Editions and Historical Collation in Old-Spelling Editions of Shakespeare," *Analytical & Enumerative Bibliography*, 4 [1980], 95–106; Bowers, "The Historical Collation in an Old-Spelling Shakespeare Edition: Another View," *SB*, 35 [1982], 234–258.)

70. "The Synchrony and Diachrony of Texts: Practice and Theory of the Critical Edition of James Joyce's *Ulysses*," *Text*, 1 (1981), 305–326. As the title makes clear, this paper is intended to provide the rationale for the plan followed in Gabler's edition of *Ulysses* (1984); but it also includes illustrations from Faulkner and Milton and is meant to be a theoretical statement of wide applicability.

71. At one point, for example, he distinguishes between "the authoritative text free of corruption" and "the critically constituted text of final authorial intention established by bibliographically controlled editorial eclecticism" (pp. 310–311; see also p. 318).

must always have been discrete textual states, in temporal succession, of a literary composition") without facing the fact that revision frequently does not proceed in readily separable "discrete" stages and that—when it does—such stages do not necessarily coincide with those represented by surviving documents.

Having set forth this view of the nature of literary works, Gabler proceeds to outline a method for presenting the evidence, for he believes that the traditional apparatus is at odds with that view. Since "revisional variation" is "meaningful only in its contextual relations," we need to "devise modes of apparatus presentation which leave the contextuality intact": "Lemmatised fragmentation is categorically not suitable for the purpose" (p. 311). Instead, what "would seem an absolute necessity" is "some manner of 'integral apparatus' for the visualisation of revisional variance in invariant contexts, which in this case should display the work's entire shape, or sequence of variant shapes, in apparatus form before the critic's eye." Whatever form is chosen, it must not lose sight of "essential tenets, such as those of the situatedness in context of the revisional variant and its integrity to the work's total text" (p. 313). The point that emerges from this verbiage is that authorial variants, being part of the literary work, are more appropriately reported in the running text than in an appended list. He illustrates some of the possibilities, such as texts in parallel columns and the "synoptic" text he has adopted for *Ulysses*. However much Gabler wishes to make the presentation of variants a matter of theory, it remains a practical issue. All editors, whatever their theory of literature, recognize that variant readings, to be understood, must be placed in context; and when editors decide that the most suitable form of report under the circumstances is an appended list, they are not suggesting that the variants are somehow less significant than those that other editors choose to print (marked with various symbols) in the text. Readers who have used texts with integrated apparatuses (such, indeed, as the *Ulysses*) know that they are not necessarily easier to follow than appended lists.[72] Gabler implicitly recognizes the difficulty

---

72. A distinction should be made between a "genetic" text and the kind of "synoptic" text that Gabler is recommending. A genetic text aims to show the development of the text or texts present in a single document by providing a running text that indicates cancellations, interlineations, and other alterations. Gabler's synoptic text, on the other hand, aims to bring together in a single running text the authorial readings from all relevant documents. The symbols in the synoptic text, therefore, have to serve two functions: to indicate (as in a genetic text) the status of alterations within documents and also (as the sigla in a list do) to identify the various source documents and show their sequence. Furthermore, the synoptic text contains editorial emendations, for it is concerned only with authorial revisions, not with "corruptions"—which are therefore to be corrected in the synoptic text and recorded

of reading such texts when he provides for "an orientation text for the apparatus," or a "reading text" (p. 316), or even "the edition text" (p. 318).[73] But why, one is bound to ask, should there be a separate "reading" text if all the variants are an essential part of the work? Why should "the object of scholarly and critical analysis and study" (which is "the totality of the Work in Progress") be seen as "opposed" to "a general public's reading matter"? If the "work of literature possesses in its material medium itself, in its text or texts, a diachronic as well as a synchronic dimension" (p. 325), does it make sense for the "general public's reading matter" to be something less than the whole work? Is Gabler saying that scholars and critics need the real work, but ordinary readers can make do with what amounts to an abridged version, offering less than the full aesthetic pleasure that the work in its entirety provides? Gabler's position has obviously not been carefully thought through, but it is worth noticing here because it calls attention to questions that must be faced by anyone who hopes to defend the idea of multiple texts.

Peter Shillingsburg handles these issues with far greater sensitivity. His book, *Scholarly Editing in the Computer Age: Lectures in Theory and Practice* (1984),[74] is so thoughtful and refreshing that one hesitates to mention its problems, for they (as opposed to the flaws in so many more limited efforts) do not stand in the way of the salutary effect it can, and should, have. Like Gabler, Shillingsburg believes that "literary works of art, unlike some other forms of art cannot safely be treated as single end-products" and that variants resulting from authorial revision form "an important part of a reader's experience of the work" (p. 31);[75] thus he, too, considers the handling of apparatus crucial to the reader's understanding. In contrast to Gabler, however, Shillingsburg bases his conclusions on a thorough reexamination of all the concepts that underlie textual and editorial work, and he does not limit his recommendations to a single approach. His rethinking of the whole process of editing gives weight to his recognition that the various approaches to

---

"in the type of subsidiary apparatus best suited to the purpose, i.e., an appended lemmatised emendation list" (p. 318).

73. In his edition of *Ulysses* he calls his "reading text" a "new, critically established text," consisting of "the emended continuous manuscript text at its ultimate level of compositional development" (p. 1903).

74. Issued as Occasional Paper No. 3 by the English Department of the Faculty of Military Studies, Royal Military College, University of New South Wales. A revised version will be published by the University of Georgia Press in 1986.

75. As he states this point elsewhere, "reading a single text of a work of art as if it adequately represented the work or was in fact the work may limit the reader's access to the whole work of art" (p. 71).

editing, and the various approaches to literature from which they arise, are irreconcilable and must all be accepted.[76] He deplores the "single-mindedness of each school in thinking theirs is the higher course" and urges that editors "acknowledge, not the correctness, but the legitimacy of opposing viewpoints." Editors ought to "explore the felt needs that the different approaches seek to fulfill" and then to "create editions that at least acknowledge the potential of other approaches" (p. 73).

Since a single critical text can represent only one approach, it falls to the apparatus to show that potential. Shillingsburg does not object to appended lists, but he strongly believes that variants should be identified more fully than they normally are in lists, associating each one not only with a "source document" but also with a "source agent (author, editor, compositor)" and a "source time" (p. 32). He argues that lists in which all variants, authorial and nonauthorial alike, are indistinguishably mixed do not encourage readers who are interested in a different approach to explore the evidence: "trivialized tables confirm critics in the habit of not using the apparatuses of critical editions because they cannot imagine what to use them for" (p. 75).[77] Shillingsburg's view here is analogous to Gabler's, both in its emphasis on the separation of authorial and nonauthorial variants and in its feeling that lists can sometimes make information seem less important than it is. Everyone naturally is in favor of making apparatuses as useful and convenient as possible, but whether the segregation of authorial from nonauthorial variants will always help readers is far from obvious: because the distinction between the two is by no means clear-cut and thus depends on critical judgment, readers will have to examine both categories in any case to determine whether their own judgment agrees with the editor's. And even when, as usual, only the documentary source of variants is identified in the apparatus, readers normally know—from the explanation of textual policy for the edition—the agent (or class of agent)[78] to whom the editor has attributed each type of variant in each document. I would not deny that in some instances dividing a long list of variants into categories could be helpful, but the gain does not seem as dramatic as Shillingsburg suggests;

76. He does not, however, always give adequate recognition to the fact that critical editing is a form of literary criticism—as when he says that "textual critics tried to provide texts that would deserve the new scrutiny" of the New Critics (p. 7), as if the providing of a text is a pre-critical activity.

77. Shillingsburg forsakes his usual even-handedness here by calling lists that include nonauthorial variants "trivialized"; to the person interested more in the text that emerged from the publishing process than one reflecting authorial intention, these variants are not trivial.

78. Often it is not possible to identify the agent more precisely than "publisher's editor or compositor" or "someone other than the author."

and it is hard to believe that readers who do not understand the purpose of apparatus in one form will readily see it when the form is shifted. The impulse to use apparatus is not instilled in readers by the inviting qualities of the apparatus but by those readers' habits of mind; readers who are interested in history will want to examine the evidence, and whatever form it is presented in will not deter them (though of course they are glad to have it in as convenient a form for their particular purpose as possible).

One can accept Shillingsburg's advice on apparatus or not, as one chooses: the issue is one of convenience, not substance. His significant point is simply his emphatic reaffirmation of the essential function of apparatuses as supplements to reading texts. Justifying a reading text without interpolated variants poses less theoretical difficulty for Shillingsburg's position than for Gabler's. Although Shillingsburg does not deal directly with this matter, the rationale would be, I think, that in order to accommodate all approaches one has to recognize that for some of them alternative readings cannot be considered part of the text. Apparatuses, then, must be looked at in two ways, as Shillingsburg's varying manner of speaking about them suggests: they may be seen as recording "utterances that were or remain a part of the work"[79] or else as presenting "significant information about the work" (p. 75). Some readers will see them one way, and some the other. What Shillingsburg is saying could be reduced to the standard point that editors normally profess: apparatuses are crucial because they enable readers to take different approaches and make different judgments from the editors'. But this point has not always been made in a spirit of tolerance. Shillingsburg's contribution lies not in his advice on constructing apparatuses but in his restatement of an old truth in an uncommon context, one that stresses genuine openness to alternative approaches.

He also makes a contribution in his sane review of the fundamental theoretical issues that all editors must take a position on. Even when they cannot fully agree with him, editors and other readers will benefit from working through his intelligent analyses of such matters as intention, ontology, and what he regards as the four basic approaches to editing. His discussion of intention, for example, is helpful in its emphasis on a writer's "intention to do" (that is, to write "a specific sequence of words and punctuation") rather than an "intention to mean" (pp. 27–29); but in the process Shillingsburg overstates the recoverability of the intended sequence of words and punctuation (he says it is "almost completely

---

79. Or, as he puts it elsewhere, editors should shift their "emphasis from 'the right text' to 'the whole work' " (p. 42).

recoverable")[80] and underestimates the degree to which establishing an "intention to do" involves postulating an intended meaning.[81] In his

80. If there were as little doubt about this kind of intention as Shillingsburg suggests, those editors whose aim is to establish authorial wording would not disagree as often as they do. Since manuscripts, as Shillingsburg recognizes, may contain "scribal error, Freudian slip, or shorthand elision" (p. 27), one must use critical judgment, based on an interpretation of intended meaning, to determine where these flaws occur.

81. Editors who talk about authorial intention do in fact generally mean an intended sequence of words and punctuation, but it is understandable that their discussions often contain references to intended meaning: the one is inextricable from the other. Recognizing this point in no way leads editors away from the active authorial intention they should properly focus on and toward such other levels of intention as "an intention to be brilliant or successful, or to write a novel or poem." But Shillingsburg oversimplifies the issue when he adds to this series: "or to convey an idea or emotion or attitude" (p. 26). Of course he is right to say that "several alternative texts of more or less satisfaction to the author" might convey the same meaning; nevertheless, the intention to convey a particular idea is not irrelevant to the intention to write down a particular sequence of words. Shillingsburg (p. 28)—like Mailloux (pp. 96–97) and Parker (p. 22)—complains that my concept of active intention in my 1976 essay (see note 59 above) does not encompass the author's intention in the process of composition. All I can say is that I meant for it to: when I spoke, for example, of "the intention of the author to have particular words and marks of punctuation consti-tute his text" (p. 182 [324]), I was assuming that such intention manifests itself continuously throughout the writing of a work (and often shifts, producing revisions—a problem I took up in the later parts of the essay). (I am aware of the irony: this situation illustrates the fact that a writer's statement of intention does not always match what readers find in the work.) Shillingsburg himself, though he emphasizes the composition process, is inclined to think in terms of "stages" (as on p. 24) rather than—more realistically—a continuous process, in which any pronounced points of stability that do exist grow out of numerous subordinate stages. Another writer who defines the intention relevant to editors as what the author "intended to *write* or what he intended to constitute his text" (p. 127) is James McLaverty, whose article on "The Concept of Authorial Intention in Textual Criticism," *Library*, 6th ser., 6 (1984), 121–138, is an unusually intelligent, if occasionally mistaken, treatment of the subject. McLaverty believes that every published version of a work reflects a different intention and that an editor must choose one version (not necessarily the "final" one) to edit (p. 130); but he does not understand that the editor can draw emendations from the texts of other versions without necessarily mixing versions, for in many cases the only documentary evidence of corrections in one version is the report of them embedded in the documentary text of the next version (cf. note 85 below). His reluctance to allow such eclecticism springs from a general tendency to wish to restrict the area in which editorial judgment operates. Thus he finds a way to argue against any correction of errors of external fact: an author's intention to be correct, he feels, is outside the scope of the kind of intention (to have a certain sequence of words and punctuation) with which the editor is concerned (p. 129). Critical editors, however, if their approach is to be truly critical, cannot eliminate any part of a text—such as references to external fact—from critical scrutiny, even though there will be no universal agreement as to which factual errors are, and which are not, expressed in words that the author intended to write. (See also my comments on "External Fact as an Editorial Problem," *SB*, 32 [1979], 1–47; reprinted in *Selected Studies*, pp. 355–401.) His complaint that no principle has been established for determining which versions of a work are so different as to require separate editions similarly represents a desire for rules that would replace judgments. In another interesting essay on intention, James E. May ("Determining Final Authorial Intention in Revised Satires: The Case of Edward Young," *SB*, 38 [1985], 276–289) attempts to identify those revisions in satires that "presuppose an audience and state of affairs different from those for which the work was originally in-tended" (p. 277) and to show that they (unlike the ones "compatible with the work's original

chapter on "Ontology," Shillingsburg makes thoughtful distinctions among the concepts of *work, version, draft,* and *text* and shows how the entities envisaged in each case have no material existence,[82] though they may be stored in a physical medium (each instance of such storage being a *document*). His discussion falters, however, in not accounting for the possibility that some literary works are also works of visual art (which therefore must be acknowledged to have a material existence)[83] and in not sufficiently confronting the fact that versions and drafts need not coincide with the texts of surviving documents. He states that a version "is represented more or less well or completely by a single text as found in a manuscript, a proof, a book, or some other written or printed form" (p. 36) and that drafts "are represented more or less well by the manuscripts containing them" (p. 38). The phrase "more or less" alludes specifically to the fact that texts can incorporate slips or errors not intended by the author to be part of a version or its drafts;[84] it does not seem also

---

conception" [p. 289]) should "be denied final authority," thus "preserving the historicity of the earlier version" (p. 277). Despite the repeated emphasis on "final authority," his work appears to recognize that both the original and the revised versions are of independent value as satiric works.

82. Even a *text*, which is "the actual order of words and punctuation as contained in any one physical form," is immaterial because the text "can exist simultaneously in the memory, in more than one copy or in more than one form" (p. 38). Shillingsburg's point is correct, if awkwardly stated—for if a single text can exist in more than one form (as it can), then it should not be defined as being "contained in any one physical form." A text is simply one particular sequence of words and punctuation (which may or may not accurately represent a version or a draft). James McLaverty has also recently explored the ontological status of literary works—with more sophistication than Shillingsburg—in "The Mode of Existence of Literary Works of Art" (see note 30 above), an essay that helpfully summarizes the debate over whether printed texts of literary works are scores (notational systems) or instances of the work. In his essay on intention (see note 81 above), he makes use of the idea that the printed text is a score (p. 127).

83. I think he is unwise, here and elsewhere, to contrast literary art with pottery, suggesting that a vase does not undergo revision in the process of its creation. ("There is a pleasing simplicity in the notion that texts grow or develop or are shaped toward a final form— rather like a potter shaping a vase on a wheel. But the analogy is misleading. A book does not come in final shape directly from the artist's hands like a vase" [p. 36]). All created works, however, are subject to revision during their creation. The reason we sometimes have versions and drafts of literary works is that the physical forms in which they are recorded are separate from the work itself, whereas the earlier versions of a vase are necessarily destroyed in the process of shaping the final version. If earlier versions are part of the total work, then in many cases the full work cannot survive, and the extent of what does survive is fortuitous. Some versions of literary works never existed on paper but only in the minds of their creators; and often writers who use word processors destroy all trace of earlier versions or drafts as they create new ones. The total work, inclusive of all versions and drafts, is probably never fully recoverable; but in the case of literary works (and other works of which versions are recorded on paper) there is the chance that some of the documents containing versions and drafts have survived. This point has not been adequately dealt with by those who hold that variants are integral parts of works.

84. As Shillingsburg concisely puts it, "Texts may contain non-authorial parts; versions do not" (p. 39).

to refer to the fact that versions and drafts (in the abstract and, I think, appropriate sense employed by Shillingsburg) cannot be tied to the texts of physical documents.[85] Another chapter[86] enumerates the basic approaches to editing (or "orientations") as the "historical," the "aesthetic," the "authorial," and the "sociological." Much of what is said about them, as one would expect, is sensible; but the categories, as set out, are not entirely satisfactory. The "historical" approach includes texts with editorial emendations as well as diplomatic editions and facsimiles; how, then, does this approach differ from the "authorial" and the "sociological," both of which are critical and historical?[87] The "aesthetic" seems similarly to be blurred in conception, for it encompasses the activity of "Commercial editors, literary agents and other merchandizers of literary works"[88] as well as that of scholarly editors who limit

85. A single set of revisions, for instance, could be spread over two documents, with the result that the text of neither document would reflect the entirety of a particular version or draft. When Shillingsburg describes an eclectic text as one that "mixes material from two or more versions" (p. 40), one wonders whether he is rejecting the usual definition of "eclectic" as referring to the mixing of material from two or more documentary texts or whether he is equating versions with the (sometimes defective) texts of individual documents. A further hint of this problem occurs in his inaccurate description of the "historical orientation," when he speaks of "points in creation when the text reaches stasis in a document" (p. 61). The stasis conferred by a physical document does not necessarily represent a point of stasis in the development of a work. (I call the description inaccurate because the value of reproducing the text of a document does not depend on whether a "documentary form is a complete record of the work at some stage in its development"; no justification is needed other than the fact that the document survives and is therefore a piece of historical evidence.) In his "Key Issues" article (see note 90 below), Shillingsburg deals more incisively with this matter, making clear that he does indeed wish to define "eclectic" as referring to the mixing of versions, not merely of documentary texts. But in doing so he is moving beyond what scholarly editing normally encompasses and into "creative" or "aesthetic" editing: "Eclecticism," he writes, "does not attempt to conform to a single ascertainable version ever existing at one time even in the author's intention (or conception)" (pp. 7–8). If the term "eclectic" is to be applied to scholarly editing at all, it must refer to the mixing of documentary texts to produce a postulated version. Shillingsburg does recognize in his article that the integrity of a version—being an abstraction—is not tied to an individual documentary text; but that recognition should also have caused him to see that an editor who mixes readings from different texts in an effort to produce a text conforming to the author's intentions at a given time (and not to produce simply what the editor likes better) is not mixing versions but rather is reconstructing one.

86. It is rather puzzlingly called "Forms." The opening of the chapter suggests that forms are "details of presentation" as opposed to "substance" (p. 13). But the subject matter treated is certainly not limited to "accidentals."

87. Shillingsburg admits that "all violations of documentary historical forms (including Bowers' and McGann's) are supported by appeals to one or more competing formal orientation which is seen to take priority over the historical, even if only in some limited way" (p. 15). In that case, if the "orientations" are meant to represent the basic positions that are often mixed in practice, why not define the "historical" approach as simply the diplomatic (or noncritical) reproduction of documentary texts?

88. Despite the fact that Shillingsburg says in his introduction that he is dropping "from further consideration" what he calls "commercial editing and copy-editing" (p. 4).

themselves to readings "already existing in historical documents" (p. 16). But does not a distinction need to be made between those who improve a work according to their own aesthetic judgments and those who use aesthetic judgments in the historical task of reconstructing authors' or publishers' intentions?[89] Such shortcomings in Shillingsburg's discussion do not prevent its offering some enlightenment and do not lessen the persuasiveness of its tolerance for differing approaches.[90]

It may seem that nothing new has been said by these various writers, and in many ways that is true. The basic issues that confront textual critics and scholarly editors are unchanging, and the attitudes that may be taken toward those issues, though occasionally appearing in altered guises, remain the same. There will be no end to debates over these issues, because they are genuinely debatable; and the process of debate is the way in which each generation of editors thinks through the questions for itself. Some recent editors have claimed that the field is at present in a state of crisis. But the fact that different people hold different opinions about basic issues is not a sign of crisis; it points to the perennial situation in any challenging and lively field. The repeated advocacy of particular viewpoints is not wasteful, except when the advocates do not mend the internal flaws of their predecessors' arguments. Advocates of differing positions need not give up their positions if sound arguments can be made for them; but we do have reason to be discouraged when the arguments continue to suffer from the same defects. There is a prima facie case for the legitimacy of more than one approach to the editorial treatment of historical evidence: editors can produce diplomatic or facsimile editions of individual documentary texts; or they can through emendation create new texts that attempt to be historically faithful either to authors' or to publishers' intentions at particular times. Acceptance of this multiplicity does not, and should not, end debate, for one still has to decide which approach is to be followed in a given situation, and many factors bearing on that decision can usefully be discussed. But the debate thereby moves to a different, and

89. Shillingsburg says that "an editorial concern for the 'best' text is always an appeal to an aesthetic orientation" (p. 16) and at another point refers to "readings from several versions selected on the basis of the editor's aesthetic values in his attempt to present the author's 'best' text" (p. 10). But these statements are not helpful because they do not make clear that the best text for each of various historical purposes requires the editor's aesthetic judgment to be put to the service of deciding what someone in the past would have preferred.

90. Because Shillingsburg's book represents a fuller working out of the ideas he had earlier set forth in "Key Issues in Editorial Theory," *Analytical & Enumerative Bibliography*, 6 (1982), 3–16, it is not necessary here to discuss that generally less satisfactory essay. Some passages in it, however, are clearer than corresponding ones in the book (see note 85 above).

more productive, level. Advocacy of one position then occurs in the context of valid alternative positions; and criticism leveled at a given argument springs not from a belief that only one approach is correct but from the detection of logical flaws in the argument. Enlightened editors who understand this point have always existed; but there is also room, in the field of editing as in any other, for the further spread of enlightenment. Recent writings on editorial theory, like those in times past, provide the basis both for exasperation and for hope. If the acceptance of multiple approaches, as well as the insistence on rigorous argument in support of each, can become more widespread, the quality of the debate will improve, even as the points debated remain (as they must) the same. The recognition that all approaches to the past are partial and complementary helps one to appreciate the full complexity of the issues editors struggle with. Viewed in this way, scholarly editing appears, with more justice than ever, as one of the most demanding and rewarding forms of the critical study of history.